PC Troubleshooting Pocket Guide

Fifth Edition

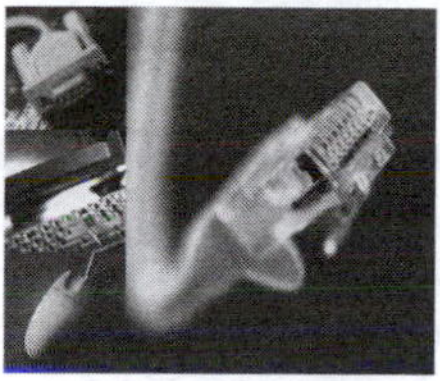

Jean Andrews

THOMSON
COURSE TECHNOLOGY

Australia • Canada • Mexico • Singapore • Spain • United Kingdom • United States

PC Troubleshooting Pocket Guide, Fifth Edition

By Jean Andrews

Executive Editor:	Steve Helba
Managing Editor:	Larry Main
Acquisitions Editor:	Nick Lombardi
Product Manager:	Michelle Cannistraci
Production Editors:	Matt Hutchinson, GEX Publishing Services
Editorial Assistant:	Claire Jeffers
Marketing Manager:	Guy Baskaran
Text Designer:	GEX Publishing Services
Compositor:	GEX Publishing Services
Cover Design:	Kun-Tee Chang

Disclaimer

BRIEF TABLE OF CONTENTS

TABLE OF CONTENTS

Section 4

Appendix E
Windows 2000/XP STOP Errors

Appendix F
CPUs and Chipsets

Appendix G
IRQs and I/O Addresses

Appendix H
Important URLs

Appendix I
Recordkeeping

PREFACE

The *PC Repair Troubleshooting Pocket Guide, Fifth Edition* is the best troubleshooting tool you'll find to solve PC problems. This book is written for the typical troubleshooter. You may be facing a PC problem, but have no idea what is causing it. Or you may already know which of your PC's subsystems is in trouble, but you are not sure how to remedy the situation.

Either way, this book will quickly point you to a series of step-by-step instructions and flowcharts to follow. You will discover the source of your problem and learn how to solve the problem, whatever it may be. This book is designed to be used with the *A+ Guide to Managing and Maintaining Your PC, Sixth Edition* (ISBN 0-619-21758-8) the *A+ Guide to Hardware: Managing, Maintaining, and Troubleshooting, Fourth Edition* (ISBN 0-619-21762-6), and the *A+ Guide to Software: Managing, Maintaining, and Troubleshooting, Fourth Edition* (ISBN 0-619-21760-X) by Jean Andrews, also published by Course Technology.

The *PC Repair Troubleshooting Pocket Guide, Fifth Edition* includes the following set of tools:

How to Use This Book to Solve Your PC Problems   Start here to acquaint yourself with this book and learn how to use it to solve computer problems. This brief section provides the fundamentals of using the Pocket Guide as a tool.

Troubleshooting Roadmap: Finding the Solution by Symptom or System   The Roadmap (which is a comprehensive annotated Table of Contents) is the key to the Pocket Guide. When faced with a troubleshooting problem, go first to the Roadmap to look up your machine's symptoms or the system that is having problems. The Roadmap will point you to the pages in the Troubleshooting Tool section with the appropriate checklists and flowcharts. Follow them to solve your problem.

The Troubleshooting Tool   This is the section with the step-by-step instructions you use to solve your troubleshooting problems. It is a series of **checklists** and **flowcharts** designed to guide you through identifying your problem and fixing it. These pages highlight both **systems** and **symptoms**, so you can easily find your way to a solution, regardless of your starting point. The flowcharts can be used to quickly locate the source of your problem and point you to the page in the book with the appropriate checklists.

For more in-depth information and support, look for these features, which reference additional material:

 TO LEARN MORE This feature points you to more in-depth explanations of concepts or procedures found in any of the core texts: the *A+ Guide to Managing and Maintaining Your PC, Sixth Edition* (ISBN 0-619-21758-8), the *A+ Guide to Hardware: Managing, Maintaining, and Troubleshooting, Fourth Edition* (ISBN 0-619-21762-6), and the *A+ Guide to Software: Managing, Maintaining, and Troubleshooting, Fourth Edition* (ISBN 0-619-21760-X).

 GO TO This feature provides additional page references within the Pocket Guide where you can go for additional information.

Technical Resources Useful tables of technical data, including error messages, what they mean, and what to do about them, are included in the Troubleshooting Tool and the appendices. The Troubleshooting Tool also includes exhaustive lists of URLs to further help you research any problem. The Roadmap, the step-by-step instructions, and the flowcharts all point you to the appropriate technical resources.

If You Are Troubleshooting for the First Time The Pocket Guide includes some extra support for those new to the challenges of troubleshooting. *Before You Begin: Protect and Prepare* describes how to protect you and your equipment from damage as you work. *Professional Fundamentals* discusses how to handle customers, and reviews the fundamental rules of problem-solving. If you are new to the troubleshooting process, turn to these sections before you start. If you are experienced, you may want to read the material to remind you about what you should be doing.

The key to the *PC Troubleshooting Pocket Guide* is its remarkable flexibility. This troubleshooting tool is written so you can quickly and easily find solutions to your PC problems.

ACKNOWLEDGMENTS

Thank you, Janet Weinrib, for the idea and the vision for this book. Many thanks to all those at Delmar and Course Technology who are committed to its success, especially Michelle Ruelos Cannistraci and Nick Lombardi. Thank you, Joy Dark, for your assistance and support here at home. This book is dedicated to the covenant of God with man on earth.

Jean Andrews, Ph.D.

How to Use This Book to Solve PC Problems

Y ou are about to solve a PC problem. This section of your *PC Troubleshooting Pocket Guide* explains how to use this book and guides you through the following processes:

☐ Facing a PC problem
☐ Identifying what the PC problem is
☐ Solving the PC problem
☐ Documenting your solution

Begin troubleshooting by interviewing the user. From this interview, you need to determine as much as the user can tell you about the problem and how to reproduce it. You also need to find out if data is present that is not backed up and if the system is under warranty. Ask the user about passwords that are needed to examine CMOS setup and access Windows. Section 2, *Before You Begin: Protect and Prepare*, gives you tips on how to relate to the user, safety precautions, how to back up data, and how to document what you did.

After you have interviewed the user, start troubleshooting by looking in the Roadmap in Section 3 for symptoms and systems you might be facing. Then turn to the appropriate pages for checklists, flowcharts, tables, and other technical data that will lead you to solve your problem. Use the Roadmap this way:

If You Know which PC Subsystem Has a Problem:

☐ Turn to the Roadmap on page 9.
☐ Look up the PC subsystem that has a problem (electrical, hard drive, video, and so on).
☐ Find the specific problem listed under the PC subsystem.
☐ Turn to the referenced flowchart, if there is one, or turn to the designated page and follow the problem-solving checklist.

If You Know Only the Symptom of the PC Problem:

☐ Turn to the Roadmap on page 9.
☐ Look up the symptom you are facing; these symptoms are highlighted in the Roadmap with a shaded background.
☐ Turn to the referenced flowchart (if there is one) or turn to the designated page and follow the problem-solving checklist.

☐ You will find the *Quick Reference: The Top 10 PC Problems* at the end of this section (page 3). You might want to look there first.

If You Need Some Technical Data:

☐ Turn to the Roadmap on page 9.
☐ Read through the information included in the appendices.
☐ Use the comprehensive index at the end of the Pocket Guide to help locate information.

If You Are New to Troubleshooting:

☐ Turn to *Before You Begin: Protect and Prepare* on page 5.
☐ Read about how to interview the user, protect the hardware and yourself, protect the data, and document what you did.
☐ Read about the basic philosophy behind troubleshooting (you will see this philosophy applied again and again in the book).
☐ Turn to the Roadmap on page 9.
☐ Look up the symptom or subsystem with which you are dealing.
☐ Turn to the referenced flowchart (if there is one) or turn to the designated page and follow the problem-solving checklist.

If You Want More Information:

☐ Turn to Appendix L, *Where to Go for More Help: Hardware Resources* (page L-1), or Appendix M, *Where to Go for More Help: Software Resources* (page M-1).

HOW THE POCKET GUIDE WORKS

The Pocket Guide is a troubleshooting tool that is organized to help you easily and quickly find what you need to solve a PC problem. Start solving the problem by turning to Section 3, *Troubleshooting Roadmap: Finding the Solution by System or Symptom*. This is a comprehensive list of symptoms and systems you might be facing during troubleshooting. Scan the Roadmap to easily locate the page references and begin troubleshooting.

Most of the references direct you to Section 4, *The Troubleshooting Tool: Checklists and Flowcharts*. In that section, you'll find checklists of things to check and try as well as flowcharts and tables of error messages. The flowcharts in Section 4 are intended to help you isolate problems and quickly get to the right checklist in the guide. The checklists point you to appropriate technical data in the appendices.

This troubleshooting tool also includes two features that refer you to more information that can be useful:

The GOTO feature points you to other troubleshooting support within the Pocket Guide.

The TO LEARN MORE feature points you to additional useful information in *A+ Guide to Managing and Maintaining Your PC*, *A+ Guide to Hardware*, and *A+ Guide to Software*.

The glossary at the back of the book helps you to learn technical terminology.

QUICK REFERENCE: THE TOP 13 PC PROBLEMS

Check out the list of the Top 13 PC problems listed in Table 1-1 to get a jump-start on some common problems.

Table 1-1 The Top 13 PC Problems

Problem	What to Do
Dead system	A system is often assumed to be a "dead" system when the problem is really with the monitor. • Verify that the monitor is plugged in, turned on, and adjusted correctly. • Listen for a spinning drive or fan and look for lights on the front panel of the PC case to verify the system has power. • Check power outlets, ON/OFF switches, cable connections, and fuses. • For more information, see *Troubleshooting the Boot Process* (page 31).
Forgotten password	For a power-on password, clear CMOS RAM; this action restores default settings. • To clear CMOS, short the two pins on the system board, which restores CMOS to default settings. • For more information, see Appendix B. For Windows passwords: • Ask your system administrator to reset your password. • Use your forgotten password floppy disk, if you have one. • Try logging onto the system with another user account, hopefully one with Administrative privileges, and then reset your forgotten password.
Series of beeps during booting	An error has occurred during POST before BIOS is able to use video to display an error message. • Identify the message encoded in the beeps. See Appendix A for codes. • For more information, see *Troubleshooting the Boot Process* (page 31).
Error message during booting: "Invalid configuration—Please run Setup" "CMOS checksum error"	These messages indicate that settings stored in CMOS don't match the hardware configuration detected during booting. • Enter setup and restore CMOS settings. Use the default settings if you have not saved previous settings. Reboot. • Suspect a bad or weak battery. • Go to *Troubleshooting the Boot Process* for more information (page 31).
Error message during booting before Windows starts to load: "Invalid drive specification"	"Invalid drive specification" most likely means that the file system on the hard drive is corrupted. • Boot from a CD or floppy disk and examine the hard drive for corruption. • Go to *Troubleshooting the Hard Drive File System* for more information (page 53).

(continued)

Table 1-1 The Top 13 PC Problems (continued)

Problem	What to Do
"Non-system disk"	"Non-system disk" may have two sources: • There is a CD or floppy disk in the drive during booting. Remove the disc or floppy to boot from the hard drive. • There is a problem with the hard drive file system and system files. Boot from a CD or floppy, and examine the hard drive for corruption. • Go to *Troubleshooting the Boot Process* (page 31).
Screen is blank	This problem may be caused by a dead system, or there may be a problem with the video subsystem. Go to Flowchart 4-1 (page 30).
A peripheral device in the system is not working	The Troubleshooting Tool covers problems with hard drives, CD and DVD drives, floppy drives, sound cards, keyboards, monitors, modems, and printers. Go to the Troubleshooting Roadmap, and find the subsystem. Within the subsystem, search for the symptom. If you can't find the symptom, begin with the Troubleshooting Tool for that subsystem.
Windows error message displays during booting	Go to *Troubleshooting Loading Windows 2000/XP* (page 64) or *Troubleshooting Loading Windows 9x* (page 87).
Cannot print	• Go to *Troubleshooting Printers* (page 116).
Windows is slow or gives errors; applications are slow or won't work	All these errors can be caused by a variety of problems. Check the following: • Check that the hard drive has enough free space. • Defrag the hard drive and check it for errors. • Clean up unwanted programs launched during startup. • Scan for viruses and worms. Go to *Removing Malware from Windows 2000/XP* (page 103). • Update Windows. • Go to *Speeding Up Windows 2000/XP* (page 101).
Network or Internet connection won't work or Internet Explorer gives errors	Go to *Troubleshooting Wired Networks* (page 132), *Troubleshooting Wireless Networks* (page 133), *Troubleshooting Connections to the Internet* (page 137), or *Troubleshooting Internet Explorer* (page 144).
Windows errors, application errors, a slow system, a failed Internet connection, or strange browser pop-up ads	All these symptoms can indicate the system is infected with malicious software. Do the following: • Run up-to-date antivirus software. If malware is found, scan the system a second time. • Run an anti-adware product. What AV software doesn't find, anti-adware might find. • Go to *Removing Malware from Windows 2000/XP* (page 103).

BEFORE YOU BEGIN: PROTECT AND PREPARE

Before you attempt to solve a PC problem, keep in mind professional fundamentals that will make your work more productive and satisfy your customer. Get whatever information you can from the user, take the necessary steps to protect yourself and the equipment from damage while you work, and, if you can, back up any important data that is not already backed up. Then ask yourself some vital questions that can simplify troubleshooting. These fundamentals are addressed next.

PROFESSIONAL FUNDAMENTALS

Professional PC technicians are good communicators, understand their customers' needs, and are willing to do their best to meet those needs. They are good communicators; they know technology, and they are good problem solvers. They are self-learners; they assume responsibility for staying abreast of new technology, and they are good investigators and researchers. Professional PC technicians also know their limitations and are willing to ask for help from a more qualified source when necessary.

What the Customer Expects from a PC Technician

Customers expect you to:

- ☐ Have technical proficiency and express a quiet confidence.
- ☐ Have a positive and helpful attitude and a friendly disposition and give them your respect.
- ☐ Own the problem so that the customer knows you can be counted on.
- ☐ Apologize when you or your company has made a mistake.
- ☐ Be dependable; do what you say you'll do and when you say you'll do it.
- ☐ Put their needs above your own, and, when you're working on their problem, devote your complete, undivided attention to the issue.
- ☐ Be honest. Your credibility is one of your most valuable assets.
- ☐ Admit when a problem is beyond your expertise, and use alternative resources as necessary.
- ☐ Be professional at all times, and dress and act appropriately. Be courteous, but keep a professional distance.

Fundamental Rules of Problem Solving

Use the following tips to help guide you as you solve a computer problem:

- ☐ **Interview the user before you face the computer.** The most important thing to the user might be to protect the data rather than fix the problem.
- ☐ **Check the simple things first.** Don't overlook the obvious. Most computer problems are simple and easy to solve.

☐ **Make no assumptions.** Check things firsthand. Do your own investigating. Verify everything.

☐ **Approach the problem systematically.** Start at the beginning, and walk your way through a problem-solving task one step at a time.

☐ **Isolate the source of the problem.** Decide if you think the problem is software or hardware related. Eliminate the unnecessary. For example, to isolate many problems, the best first step is to perform a clean boot and disconnect devices that are not essential. When trying to identify a bad device, either substitute a known good device for a suspected bad one or install a suspected bad device in a working system.

☐ **Be a researcher.** Use books, online help, the Internet, documentation, co-workers, friends, help desks, and technical support.

☐ **Know your starting point.** Verify what is working before you tackle what's not working.

☐ **Write things down.** Keeping organized notes helps you to think clearly and not repeat or miss a step. After you're done, these notes will help you with the next problem.

☐ **Know when to give up.** You won't be able to solve every computer problem. Sometimes the right thing to do is turn the problem over to someone with more experience or more resources.

☐ **Keep your cool.** Don't panic when you think you've made a mistake. Don't assume the worst. Catch your breath, think things through, and take your time.

☐ **When you've solved the problem, reboot one more time and check everything.** Ask the user to verify the fix is done to his or her satisfaction. Then complete the paperwork.

INTERVIEW THE USER

Troubleshooting a PC problem begins by first interviewing the user. From the interview, you want to accomplish these six goals:

☐ Demonstrate to the user that you are interested, listening, and attentive to his or her needs.

☐ Know what might have happened just before the problem appeared that could have contributed to the problem.

☐ Get a thorough description of the problem and its implications (for example, is valuable data at risk?)

☐ Know what you must do to recreate the problem.

☐ Know if a computer is under warranty, and what you can do without voiding that warranty.

☐ To effectively communicate with the user, know his or her level of technical proficiency.

Here are some questions that you can ask to help you accomplish these goals:

☐ When did the problem start?

☐ Can you describe the problem in detail?

☐ Were there any error messages or unusual displays on the screen?

☐ What programs or software were you using?

☐ Did you move your computer system recently?

☐ Has there been a recent thunderstorm or electrical problem?

☐ Have you made any hardware changes?

☐ Did you recently install any new software?

☐ Did you recently change any software configuration setups?
☐ Have there been any other recent changes to the system?
☐ Has someone else used your computer recently?
☐ Do you scan for viruses regularly?
☐ Is there some important or secure data on the hard drive that I should be aware of?
☐ Do you have the documentation for the hardware or software available?
☐ Is the computer system still under warranty? If so, what are the restrictions of that warranty?
☐ If the user will not be present while you work on the PC, ask for the passwords to view and change CMOS setup and log onto Windows as an administrator. Also suggest to the user that he change these passwords when you are finished with the work.
☐ What should I do to recreate the problem?

As you speak with the user, take notes, which might help later when you're searching for missing clues. Begin the paperwork. Get the customer's name, address, and phone number, and write down a brief description of the problem on the service call form.

For some sample service call forms, see Appendix I, *Record Keeping* (page I-1).

SAFETY PRECAUTIONS

After the interview, you are ready to start problem solving. As you work, don't forget to follow precautions to protect yourself and the equipment, especially against electrostatic discharge.

Protect against ESD

To protect the computer against electrostatic discharge (ESD), ground yourself and the computer parts, using one or more of the following static-control devices or methods:

☐ Ground bracelet
☐ Ground mat
☐ Static-shielding bags

Don't work inside a PC without a ground bracelet. Ground the bracelet to the PC by connecting it to a grounded surface such as the metal frame of the PC case. When passing a chip to another person, ground yourself. Leave components inside their protective bags until ready to use. Work on hard floors, not

CAUTION

When working inside a power supply, monitor, or laser printer, you don't want to be grounded, as you would provide a conduit for the voltage to discharge through your body. Capacitors inside these devices retain a powerful charge even when they are unplugged. In this situation, be careful not to ground yourself. Never open a monitor case or power supply unless you have been trained to work inside one.

carpet, or use antistatic spray on the carpets. Generally, don't work on a computer if you or the computer has just come inside from the cold.

 TO LEARN MORE about ESD and grounding, see pages 101-106 of Chapter 3 in *A+ Guide to Managing and Maintaining Your PC*, or pages 49-54 of Chapter 2 in *A+ Guide to Hardware*.

Protect Discs and Other Hardware

Take care to protect discs, the hard drive, expansion cards, and other hardware as you work:

- ☐ Don't touch chips or edge connectors on boards unless absolutely necessary.
- ☐ Don't stack boards.
- ☐ Don't touch chips with a magnetized screwdriver.
- ☐ Always turn the PC OFF before moving it (for even a few inches) to protect the hard drive.
- ☐ When unpacking hardware or software, remove the cellophane from the work area as soon as possible.
- ☐ Don't place a PC on the floor where it might get kicked.
- ☐ Keep optical discs away from heat, sunlight, and extreme cold. To keep discs from getting scratched, don't touch the shiny sides, and always store them in protective cases.
- ☐ Keep floppy disks away from magnetic fields, heat, and extreme cold.

CRITICAL THINGS TO VERIFY BEFORE YOU BEGIN

After you have interviewed the user, you should have a fairly clear picture as to the nature of the problem. Before you begin investigating for yourself, ask yourself these critical questions:

- ☐ Is the computer system still under warranty? If so, know the restrictions of that warranty so as not to invalidate it. It might be simpler for the user to take the PC to the vendor that services the warranty.
- ☐ Is valuable data not backed up? If so, try to back up the data before you tackle the problem.

 TO LEARN MORE about making backups, see pages 667-673 of Chapter 13 in *A+ Guide to Managing and Maintaining Your PC*, or page 227-233 of Chapter 4 of *A+ Guide to Software*.

- ☐ If the hard drive won't boot, most likely you'll use a setup CD or recovery CD to boot the system. If at all possible, be sure to use a CD that contains the same operating system as that installed on the hard drive. If you are booting from a floppy disk, make sure the disk is free of viruses; you don't want to spread a virus to this computer.
- ☐ You'll need to keep notes as you work and then, when you're finished, document the final outcome. Good support technicians have learned to use a method of documentation that works well for them and their organization. Appendix I

TROUBLESHOOTING ROADMAP: FINDING THE SOLUTION BY SYSTEM OR SYMPTOM

> *How to Use the Troubleshooting Roadmap:* To solve a PC troubleshooting challenge, scan this Roadmap's comprehensive list of symptoms and systems, find the one you are facing, and turn to the page references for checklists, flowcharts, and tables in the *PC Troubleshooting Pocket Guide* that will lead you to a solution.

TROUBLESHOOTING LOADING WINDOWS 9x

RECOVERY CONSOLE   D-1

LAUNCHING THE RECOVERY CONSOLE   D-1

RECOVERY CONSOLE COMMANDS   D-2

THE TROUBLESHOOTING TOOL: CHECKLISTS AND FLOWCHARTS

This Pocket Guide is designed to help you solve troubleshooting problems. It contains:

☐ Lists of highlighted systems and symptoms with step-by-step directions on how to solve PC problems.

☐ Flowcharts serving as high-level guides to help you quickly find the right place in the material to focus.

☐ Tables listing error messages, what they mean, and what to do about them.

☐ The GO TO feature points you to other troubleshooting support within the Pocket Guide.

☐ 🔲 The TO LEARN MORE feature points you to additional useful information in the *Comprehensive A+ Guide to Managing and Maintaining Your PC*, the *A+ Guide to Hardware*, and the *A+ Guide to Software*.

> 📖 **TO LEARN MORE** about general troubleshooting approaches, see page 124 of Chapter 3 in *A+ Guide to Managing and Maintaining Your PC* or page 72 of Chapter 2 in *A+ Guide to Hardware*.

Remember to start troubleshooting by turning to Section 3, *Troubleshooting Roadmap: Finding the Solution by System or Symptom*, which is a comprehensive list of symptoms and systems you might be facing, with page references where you can find checklists, flowcharts, and tables to help you solve your problem. Scan the Roadmap to quickly locate the information you need in this section and the appendices.

ISOLATING A BOOT PROBLEM

Begin by interviewing the user and asking questions such as the following:

☐ Please describe the problem. What error messages, unusual displays, or failures did you see?

☐ Is there important data on the hard drive that is not backed up?

☐ When did the problem start?

☐ What was the situation when the problem occurred?

☐ What programs or software were you using?

☐ Did you move your computer system recently?

☐ Has there been a recent thunderstorm or electrical problem?

☐ Have you made any hardware, software, or configuration changes?

☐ Has someone else been using your computer recently?

☐ Does the computer have a history of similar problems?

☐ Can you show me how to reproduce the problem?

After you have interviewed the user, take the first step toward isolating the problem by reproducing the problem or error. Determine whether the problem occurs during or after the boot. Then use Troubleshooting Flowchart 4-1 to serve as a guide to the rest of this section.

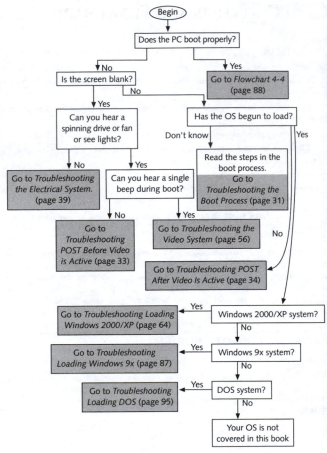

Flowchart 4-1   Troubleshooting the boot process

As you read Flowchart 4-1, remember these points:

☐ If the screen is blank, and you don't see lights on the front panel of the computer case or hear a spinning drive or fan, then you are dealing with a "dead system."

 Go to *Troubleshooting the Electrical System* (page 39).

☐ When POST completes successfully, it sounds a single beep that all is well, regardless of whether or not the monitor is working or even present. If you hear that single beep but the screen is blank, then the problem is with the monitor, and the next step is to troubleshoot it.

 Go to *Troubleshooting the Video System* (page 33).

☐ If you don't hear the single beep, you hear more than one beep, or you hear a voice message, then POST encountered an error. In that case, the problem is with the power subsystem, the video subsystem, or the motherboard. Begin with Flowchart 4-1 to isolate the problem.

☐ If you see an error on the screen but are not sure if the error was encountered during POST or while the OS was loaded, then the next step is to review the boot process to determine at what point the process failed. (If the error message scrolls by so quickly that you cannot read it, press the Pause/Break key.) Proceed to the next section.

TROUBLESHOOTING THE BOOT PROCESS

You have gotten to this point in the Troubleshooting Tool if the following is true:

☐ The PC does not boot properly.
☐ Video is working.
☐ You are not sure at what point during the boot process the problem occurred.

Review the following steps in the boot process, looking for clues on the screen that will tell you at what point the problem occurred. After you have identified the point of failure, go back to Flowchart 4-1, and pick up at that point.

 If you are still not sure where the boot process failed, then proceed to *Troubleshooting POST Before Video Is Active* (page 33).

Steps in the Boot Process

When you turn ON the power to a PC, the CPU begins the boot process by initializing itself. It then turns to the ROM BIOS for instructions that perform POST, find an OS, and begin loading it. The OS then completes the process. Listed below are the key steps in the entire process.

 For a list of error messages that can display during the boot process and what to do about them, see Table 4-2 (page 35).

☐ The power supply begins to generate power. When power is sufficient to run the computer, it raises the Power Good signal on the P1 connection of an ATX or BTX motherboard or the P8 connection of an AT motherboard.

☐ When the power is good, the system clock begins to generate clock pulses.

☐ The CPU begins working and initializes itself, resetting its internal values.

☐ The CPU turns to memory address FFFF0h, which is the memory address always assigned to the first instruction in the ROM BIOS startup program.

☐ This instruction directs the CPU to run the POST tests. Until video is checked, errors encountered by POST will be communicated by beep codes and/or voice messages. (Which method is used depends on system BIOS features and how they are configured. Some systems can also record the error message in an event log text file.) Errors are also placed on I/O addresses 80h, 84h, 280h, or 284h. Error messages placed on the I/O addresses can be read by POST diagnostic cards to give more information than that communicated just by beep codes or voice messages.

> A POST diagnostic card, also called a checkpoint card, displays numbers during the boot to indicate an error. To understand the meanings of these numbers, see the POST card documentation or the BIOS documentation on the BIOS manufacturer Web site.

> For more information about POST diagnostic cards, go to Table L-1 in Appendix L (page L-2).

☐ POST first checks the BIOS program operating it and then tests CMOS RAM.

☐ A test is done to determine that there has not been a battery failure.

☐ Hardware interrupts are disabled (thus pressing a key on the keyboard or using another input device at this point will not affect anything).

☐ Tests are run on the CPU, and the CPU is further initialized.

☐ A check is done to determine whether or not this process is a cold boot. If so, then the first 16 KB of RAM is tested.

☐ Hardware devices installed on the computer are inventoried and compared with configuration information.

☐ The BIOS looks for the video BIOS program on the video card and executes this program. This program initializes the video card and displays a message on the screen about the video. It is most likely the first thing you see on the screen during the boot process.

☐ If startup BIOS finds the video program, then video passes POST and error messages are displayed on the screen from this point forward instead of using beep codes or voice.

☐ The BIOS looks for more ROM BIOS programs on devices and executes these programs as they are found.

☐ The BIOS identifies itself by displaying a message on the screen.

☐ Memory is tested and a running count of memory is displayed. (If CMOS setup has been configured for a quick boot, this step and other diagnostic steps are skipped.)

☐ Memory, keyboard, floppy disk drives, hard drives, ports (COM and LPT assignments are made), and other hardware devices are tested and configured, including IRQ, I/O addresses, and DMA assignments. Legacy devices are configured.

☐ Plug and Play devices are configured. A PnP OS will later complete this process.

☐ Some devices are set up to go into "sleep mode" to conserve electricity.

☐ The DMA controller is checked.

☐ Interrupt vectors are moved into the interrupt vector table.

☐ The interrupt controller is checked.

☐ A summary screen showing the major system components and the configuration of devices is displayed as a table or list. During a quick boot, this display might not show.

☐ CMOS setup is run if requested.

> For more information about making changes to CMOS setup, see Appendix B (page B-1).

☐ BIOS begins its search for an OS, searching drives in the order specified in CMOS (most likely, first the hard drive and then the optical drive or floppy drive).

☐ For a hard drive, BIOS executes the master boot program stored at the very beginning of the hard drive.

☐ This program looks to the partition table for the location of the logical drive that is designated as the boot device (most likely drive C).

TO LEARN MORE about the hard drive partition table, the OS boot record, and how they are used in the boot process, see Chapter 2, beginning with page 48, and Chapter 11, beginning with page 505, of *A+ Guide to Managing and Maintaining Your PC* or Chapter 1, beginning with page 14, and Chapter 2, beginning with page 65, of *A+ Guide to Software*.

☐ The program executes the OS boot record at the beginning of the boot drive (usually drive C) that loads the first part of the operating system. Windows NT/2000/XP uses Ntldr and DOS and Windows 9x use IO.SYS.

For the steps in loading each OS, see the sections *Troubleshooting Loading Windows 2000/XP* (page 64), *Troubleshooting Loading Windows 9x* (page 87), and *Troubleshooting Loading DOS* (page 95) later in this section.

Troubleshooting POST Before Video Is Active

You have gotten to this point in the Troubleshooting Tool if the following is true:

☐ The PC does not boot properly.
☐ The screen is blank.
☐ You can hear a spinning drive or fan and see lights (electrical system is working).
☐ You did not hear a single beep indicating that POST completed successfully.

Use the following list as your troubleshooting tool at this point. It describes what can go wrong when startup BIOS is performing POST and what to do about it.

Symptom: Beeps or voice messages occur during POST.

Before the video is checked, during POST, the ROM BIOS communicates error messages with a series of beeps or a voice message. For example, a voice message might be "Video card error." However, these messages might be difficult to understand and you might have to reboot a couple of times to catch the message.

Each BIOS manufacturer has its own beep codes. Table 4-1 lists some sample beep codes typical of many BIOS codes. For specific beep codes for your BIOS, first look in the motherboard documentation or on top of the BIOS chip for the brand and version number of the BIOS.

For AMI, Phoenix, and Award BIOSes, go to Appendix A; for all other BIOSes, look on the Web site of the BIOS manufacturer. URLs for BIOS manufacturers are listed in Appendix H (page H-1).

Table 4-1 Common beep codes

Beep Code	Description
1-3, 1-4, or 1-5 beeps	Motherboard problems, possibly with DMA, CMOS setup chip, timer, or system bus
2 beeps	POST numeric code is displayed on the monitor
2-3, 2-4, or 2-5 beeps	First 64K of RAM has errors
3-3, 3-4, or 3-5 beeps	Keyboard controller failed or video controller failed
4-2, 4-3, or 4-4 beeps	Serial or parallel ports, system timer, or time of day
Continuous beeps	Power supply

Symptom: **You cannot identify the beep code, or you can't hear beeps.**

☐ If you hear beeps but the beep code cannot be identified, try rebooting into CMOS setup. If you can load the setup utility, look for a way to enable the POST voice messages or error logging. If the quick boot feature is turned ON, turn it OFF so that startup BIOS will perform a more thorough diagnostic.

☐ Search the Web site of the motherboard manufacturer for explanations of the beep codes.

☐ Try a diagnostic card, which can read POST codes that BIOS places on the ISA or PCI bus.

 Go to Appendix L (page L-1) for a listing of some diagnostic cards and an explanation of how to use them.

☐ Sometimes a dead computer can be fixed by simply disassembling it and reseating cables, adapter cards, socketed chips, and memory modules. Bad connections and corrosion are common problems.

☐ Check jumpers and DIP switches on the motherboard, especially those that control the CPU, memory bus, and cache memory.

☐ Troubleshoot the video subsystem.

 Go to *Troubleshooting the Video System* (page 56).

☐ Check the drive light on the floppy drive or hard drive. If the light stays on, suspect that the data cable connected to the drive is oriented incorrectly. Check that the edge color of the cable is connected to Pin 1.

☐ Exchange the motherboard, but before you do that, if possible, measure the output voltage of the power supply in case it is producing too much power and has damaged the board.

Troubleshooting POST After Video Is Active

You have gotten to this point in the Troubleshooting Tool if the following is true:

☐ The PC does not boot properly.
☐ Video is working.
☐ The OS has not started to load, or you are still not sure at what point during the boot process the problem occurred.

Symptom: **An error message is displayed during POST.**

If you see an error message on the screen, then use Table 4-2 as your troubleshooting tool at this point. The table lists errors that can occur during POST after video is active, including when POST first begins the search for an OS.

Table 4-2 Error messages during POST after video is active

Error	Meaning of Error Message and What to Do
Configuration/ CMOS error	• BIOS detected a problem with CMOS RAM, or setup information does not agree with the actual hardware that the computer found during the boot process. • Check setup for errors, and suspect a bad battery.
Fixed disk configuration error	• The drive type set in CMOS setup is not supported by the BIOS, or the drive setup information does not match the hard drive type. • Enter CMOS setup and correct the drive configuration. Use Auto Detection if that is available.
Fixed disk controller failure	• The hard drive controller has failed. • Check the drive, data cable, adapter card, and power cord.
No boot sector on fixed disk	• The hard drive partition table is missing or corrupted. • For Windows 2000/XP, boot from the Windows setup CD and launch the Recovery Console. Use Diskpart to examine the hard drive partitions • For Windows 9x or DOS, boot from a floppy disk, and use FDISK to examine the partition table.
No timer tick interrupt	• The interrupt controller has failed. • Contact a service center to service the motherboard.
Time of day not set	• Run CMOS setup, and set the system time. • Suspect a weak or bad CMOS battery.
Keyboard stuck key failure	• A key is jammed or something is lying on the keyboard • Fix the key, or replace the keyboard.
Numeric POST code is displayed on the screen	Troubleshoot the subsystem identified by the POST code. For a list of additional POST codes, see Appendix A (page A-1).
Code in the 100 range	• Configuration errors in setup
Code in the 200 range	• RAM errors
Code in the 300 range	• Keyboard errors
Code in the 600 range	• Floppy drive errors
Code in the 900 range	• Parallel port errors

(continued)

Table 4-2 Error messages during POST after video is active
(continued)

Error	Meaning of Error Message and What to Do
Code in the 1100-1200 range	• Motherboard errors; Async communications adapter errors
Code in the 1300 range	• Game controller or joystick errors
Code in the 1700 range	• Hard drive errors
Code in the 6000 range	• SCSI device or network card errors
Code in the 7300 range	• Floppy drive errors
POST did not count up all of memory	• Reseat DIMMs, RIMMs, or SIMMs. • Move a DIMM to a different slot. • For more help, go to *Troubleshooting the Motherboard and CPU* (page 44).
Fixed disk error Hard drive not found No boot device available	• The PC cannot locate the hard drive or the controller card is not responding. • Boot from a CD or removable drive, and then go to *Troubleshooting the Hard Drive* (page 47).
"Bad sector" errors	• Bad sectors on the hard drive are encountered when trying to load the OS. • Boot from a Windows 2000/XP setup CD, load the Recovery Console, and run `Chkdsk C: /R`. • For a Windows 9x system, boot from a floppy and run ScanDisk or third-party diagnostic software such as SpinRite.
Invalid drive specification	• The PC is unable to find a hard drive or a floppy drive that setup tells it to expect. The hard drive might have a corrupted partition table. • Boot from a setup CD or floppy disk and go to *Troubleshooting the Hard Drive* (page 47).
Invalid or missing COMMAND.COM	• This is a DOS or Windows 9x problem; it might be caused by a nonbooting disk in drive A, or COMMAND.COM on drive C might have been erased. • Remove the floppy, and boot from the hard drive. Verify Command.com is on the drive.
Non-system disk or disk error or "Missing operating system"	• System files necessary to load an OS are missing from the hard drive or floppy disk. • Remove the floppy disk and boot from the hard drive. • If this error occurs when booting from the hard drive, load the Recovery Console and examine the hard drive for errors.
Not ready reading drive A: Abort, Retry, Fail?	• The disk in drive A is missing, is not formatted, or is corrupted. • Try another disk, or remove the disk and boot from the hard drive.

Symptom: POST does not complete correctly but no error message displays during POST, or the error message cannot be identified.

The problem might be caused by a damaged motherboard or its components, incorrect CMOS settings, or problems with the hard drive or floppy drive. Try these things.

 If the problem is still not solved, go to *Troubleshooting the Motherboard and CPU* (page 44).

□ If a problem arises during a soft boot, try a hard boot. A soft boot might not work because TSRs are not always "kicked out" of RAM with a soft boot, or an ISA bus might not be initialized correctly.
□ Check CMOS settings.

 See Appendix B (page B-1) for information about CMOS settings.

□ If new hardware has just been installed, disconnect it. If this step solves the problem, troubleshoot the new device.
□ For Windows 2000/XP or Windows 9x, try to boot into Safe Mode.
□ For Windows 2000/XP, boot from the setup CD, load the Recovery Console, and use the Diskpart command to examine the hard drive. If the system will not boot from the CD, go into CMOS setup, and change the boot sequence to first boot from the CD drive. While you're there, turn off the quick boot feature so that startup BIOS will give more thorough diagnostics.
□ For Windows 9x, boot from a floppy disk. You should boot to an A prompt. If you are successful, the problem is in the hard drive subsystem and/or the software on the drive.
□ Try to access the hard drive from the Windows 2000/XP Recovery Console or the DOS A prompt. Use the command DIR C:.
□ If you can access the hard drive, then the problem is in the software that is used on the hard drive to boot the system such as the partition table, master boot record (MBR), operating system hidden files, or command interface files.

 Go to *Troubleshooting the Hard Drive* (page 47).

□ Open the case, check all connections, and reseat all boards.
□ Remove all unnecessary devices and cards (modem, network, sound, printer, scanner, and so on) from computer and reboot.
□ Replace the mouse and keyboard with a known good mouse and keyboard.
□ Verify that DIMMs, RIMMs, or SIMMs are properly seated. Move DIMMs to different slots.
□ Reseat the CPU.
□ Look for bent pins or chips installed the wrong way on cache memory, BIOS, and other socketed chips.
□ Place your fingers on the individual chips. Sometimes a bad chip will be noticeably hotter than the other chips.

☐ Reduce the system to essentials. Remove any unnecessary hardware, and then try to boot again. Follow this procedure:

- The only components essential for a PC to boot are the power supply, the motherboard with CPU and memory installed, and the video card. Disconnect both the data cable and the power cable on all other components. Disconnect all drives, and remove all expansion cards except the video card. Connect the monitor to the video card, and connect the keyboard.
- Boot the PC. Enter CMOS setup, and make sure that the quick boot feature is turned off. Exit CMOS setup. You should see POST count up memory on the screen and then give an error message about missing devices. Memory should count up correctly, and there should not be a keyboard error.
- Turn off the PC, reconnect the floppy drive, and reboot with a bootable floppy disk. You should boot to the A prompt.
- Turn off the PC, reconnect the hard drive, and reboot. The OS on the hard drive should boot.
- Add each device back into the system until you identify the problem and then troubleshoot that device.

 If you still have not identified the problem, then go to *Troubleshooting the Motherboard and CPU* (page 44).

Symptom: Forgotten power-on password.

☐ If the power-on password has been forgotten, clear CMOS, which restores CMOS to the default values. Most systems have a supervisor password (with permission to make changes to CMOS setup) and user password (with permission to view CMOS setup).

☐ Most motherboards have two jumper pins that, when closed, clear CMOS. See the motherboard documentation to locate these pins. They are sometimes called clear real-time clock (CLRTC).

☐ Unplug the PC, and close the pins by placing a jumper cover over them. Remove the jumper cover and reboot. An error message appears on the screen, and default settings are restored.

☐ When you reboot, enter CMOS setup, and reenter user preferences.

 For more information on clearing CMOS, see Appendix B (page B-1).

Symptom: When you first turn on a system, the computer continually reboots.

This is most likely a hardware problem. Could be the CPU, motherboard, RAM, or overheating. Do the following:

☐ Disconnect or remove all nonessential devices such as USB or FireWire devices.
☐ Inside the case, check all connections.
☐ Reseat RAM. Check for fans that are not working.
☐ Press F8 during the boot to launch the Windows 2000/XP Advanced Options Menu, and select Disable automatic restart on system failure. Reboot.
☐ On the next reboot, on the Advanced Options Menu, select Enable Boot Logging. Reboot and check the log file for errors. The file is in the Windows installation folder, most likely at C:\Windows\Ntbtlog.txt.

☐ Enter CMOS setup, and check the CPU temperature. If the temperature is too high, allow the system to cool and reboot. Is the CPU cooler installed and working correctly? Has thermal compound been installed correctly? Is the room excessively hot? Check all fans inside the case, and tie cables up and out of the way of airflow. Are case air vents unobstructed?

 Intel documentation gives the maximum temperature for each processor. Many processor temperatures should not exceed 185°F (85°C).

TROUBLESHOOTING THE ELECTRICAL SYSTEM

You have gotten to this point in the Troubleshooting Tool if the following is true:

☐ The PC does not boot properly.
☐ The screen is blank.
☐ You cannot hear a spinning drive or fan or see lights (electrical system is not working).
☐ The system appears to be "dead."

Use the following list as your troubleshooting tool at this point. It lists possible problems that can prevent the electrical system from functioning and explains what to do about them.

☐ Verify that the system is not in doze or sleep mode. Press any key to cause the system to resume.
☐ Check that the PC is plugged in and that all power cord connections to the PC, the monitor, and the power source are solid.
☐ Check that all switches are turned ON, including the computer (both front and back of case), monitor, surge protector, and/or uninterruptible power supply. When you press the power-on button on the front of the monitor, you should see a yellow or green light that indicates power.
☐ Verify that the wall outlet and/or surge protector is good. (You can use a circuit tester to do so or simply plug in a lamp and turn it on.)
☐ Verify that the circuit breaker does not need resetting.
☐ Look for a voltage switch on the back of the computer case, and verify that it is set to 115 V rather than 220 V.
☐ If the fan is not running, turn the computer OFF, open the case, and check that the connections to the power supply are secure and that all cards are securely seated.
☐ If you notice any burnt parts or odors, try to find the source of the odors, and replace any burnt parts.
☐ Check for loose parts inside the case or on the motherboard.
☐ Check all cable and power cord connections. Reseat expansion cards.
☐ For an ATX or BTX motherboard, there is a wire that runs from the power switch on the front of the case to the motherboard. This wire must be connected properly, and the switch turned on before the power comes up. This wire and its motherboard connection might be labeled "REMOTE SW," "PWR SW," or something similar. Also, for most ATX and BTX cases, the front panel of the case must be in place before the power will come on.
☐ Remove memory modules, and reseat them. For a DIMM, try a different memory slot.

☐ Sometimes a dead computer can be fixed by simply disassembling it and reseating cables, adapter cards, socketed chips, and memory modules. Bad connections and corrosion are common problems.

☐ Check jumpers and DIP switches on the motherboard, especially those that control the CPU, the memory bus, and cache memory.

☐ Check the voltage output from the power supply at a female power supply connector. Acceptable voltage ranges for the AT power supply are listed in Table 4–3.

Table 4-3 Twelve leads to the AT motherboard from the AT power supply

Connection	Lead	Description	Acceptable range
P8	1	Power good	
	2	Not used or +5 V	+4.4 to +5.2 V
	3	+12 V	+10.8 to +13.2 V
	4	−12 V	−10.8 to −13.2 V
	5	Black ground	
	6	Black ground	
P9	7	Black ground	
	8	Black ground	
	9	−5 V	−4.5 to −5.5 V
	10	+5 V	+4.5 to +5.5 V
	11	+5 V	+4.5 to +5.5 V
	12	+5 V	+4.5 to +5.5 volts

☐ Table 4–4 lists the acceptable ranges for the 20-pin ATX power supply, and Table 4–5 lists the acceptable ranges for the 24-pin enhanced ATX power supply. Figure 4–1 shows the 20-pin power connection on an ATX motherboard, and Figure 4–2 shows the power connector for a 24-pin P1 connector.

Table 4-4 Twenty leads to the ATX motherboard from the ATX power supply

Unnotched side			Notched side		
Lead	Description	Acceptable range (volts)	Lead	Description	Acceptable range (volts)
1	+3.3 V	+3.1 to +3.5 V	11	+3.3 V	+3.1 to +3.5 V
2	+3.3 V	+3.1 to +3.5 V	12	−12 V	−10.8 to −13.2 V
3	Black ground		13	Black ground	
4	+5 V	+4.5 to +5.5 V	14	Power supply ON	
5	Black ground		15	Black ground	
6	+5 V	+4.5 to +5.5 V	16	Black ground	
7	Black ground		17	Black ground	
8	Power good		18	−5 V	−4.5 to −5.5 V
9	+5 V standby	+4.5 to +5.5 V	19	+5 V	+4.5 to +5.5 V
10	+12 V	+10.8 to +13.2 V	20	+5 V	+4.5 to +5.5 V

Table 4-5 Twenty-four leads to the enhanced ATX or BTX motherboard from the 24-pin ATX power supply

Unnotched side			Notched side		
Lead	Description	Acceptable range (volts)	Lead	Description	Acceptable range (volts)
1	+3.3 V	+3.2 to +3.5 V	13	+3.3 V	+3.2 to +3.5 V
2	+3.3 V	+3.2 to +3.5 V	14	-12 V	-10.8 to -13.2V
3	Communication		15	Communication	
4	+5 V	+4.75 to +5.25 V	16	PS on	Power supply is good
5	Communication		17	Communication	
6	+5 V	+4.75 to +5.25 V	18	Communication	
7	Communication		19	Communication	
8	Power good	All voltages are within range	20	NC	
9	+5 V standby	Always on	21	+5 V	+4.75 to +5.25V
10	+12 V	+11.4 to +12.6 V	22	+5 V	+4.75 to +5.25V
11	+12 V	+11.4 to +12.6 V	23	+5 V	+4.75 to +5.25V
12	+3.3 V	+3.2 to +3.5V	24	Communication	

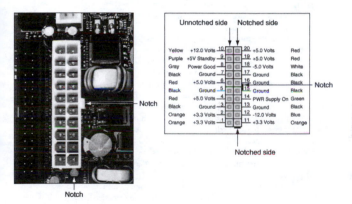

Figure 4-1 ATX 20-pin power connector on the motherboard

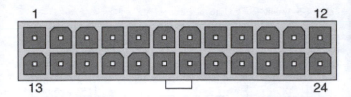

Figure 4-2   ATX and BTX 24-pin power connector on the motherboard

 TO LEARN MORE about how to measure voltage output of a power supply, see page 1220 of Appendix B in *A+ Guide to Managing and Maintaining Your PC* or page 648 of Appendix B of *A+ Guide to Hardware*.

☐ Dell ATX power supplies might not use the standard P1 pinouts, although the connectors look the same. Use a Dell power supply with a Dell motherboard, or you can buy a pinout converter such as the one made by End PC Noise (*www.endpcnoise.com*).

☐ The BTX motherboard and power supply are designed so that the power supply monitors the range of voltages provided by the motherboard and halts the motherboard if voltages are inadequate. Therefore, measuring voltage for a BTX system isn't usually necessary. The voltages pin outs are the same as for the 24-pin ATX power supply.

☐ Measure the temperature inside the case. It might be that there are too many cards or the CPU is overclocked, causing the computer to overheat. The temperature inside the case should not exceed 113°F.

☐ To prevent overheating, make sure that all fans are running. Remove the dust from the power supply's fan vent by either blowing it out or vacuuming it out. Excessive dust causes overheating. Tie ribbon cables up and out of the way of airflow. Make sure the case vents are not obstructed.

☐ For serious overheating problems, you can exchange the CPU fan and heat sink cooling unit for a peltier cooler, which cools with refrigeration.

☐ Remove all nonessential expansion cards (modem, sound card, mouse) one at a time. Verify that they are not drawing too much power and pulling the system down. It is possible that the expansion cards are all good, but the power supply is not capable of supplying enough current for all of the add-on boards.

☐ Trade the power supply for one you know is good. For AT motherboards, be certain to follow the black-to-black rule when attaching the power cords to the motherboard.

☐ Check for strong magnetic or electrical interference. Sometimes an old monitor will emit too much static and electromagnetic interference (EMI) and bring an entire system down.

 TO LEARN MORE about how to check for EMI, see page 159 of Chapter 4 in *A+ Guide to Managing and Maintaining Your PC* or page 107 of Chapter 3 of *A+ Guide to Hardware*.

☐ If the fan is running, reseat or trade the CPU, BIOS, or RAM. A POST code diagnostic card is a great help at this point.

TO LEARN MORE about Energy Star (green) systems, see page 163 of Chapter 4 in *A+ Guide to Managing and Maintaining Your PC* or page 111 of Chapter 3 of *A+ Guide to Hardware*.

☐ Exchange the motherboard, but before you do that, measure the output voltage of the power supply in case it is producing too much power and has damaged the board.

Power Supply Problems

Symptoms: Any one of the following might indicate a problem with the power supply or the house current to the PC.

☐ The computer stops or hangs for no reason. Sometimes it might even reboot itself.
☐ The system is dead, and the fan is not working.
☐ During booting, the system might hang, but after several tries, it boots successfully.
☐ During booting, beep codes occur, but the errors come and go.
☐ Memory errors appear occasionally, including intermittent parity check errors.
☐ Data is written incorrectly to the hard drive.
☐ The keyboard stops working at odd times.
☐ The motherboard fails or is damaged.
☐ The power supply overheats and becomes hot to the touch, or the fan is not working.

Try these things:

☐ Check for too many devices using the same house circuit. Remove a copy machine, laser printer, or other heavy equipment from the same circuit.
☐ Measure the voltage output of the power supply, or exchange it for one that you know is good.
☐ The problem might be overheating. In CMOS setup, check the temperature of the CPU and case. Clean out dust, and tie cables up and out of the way. Make sure that all fans are working and that the case is properly vented.
☐ Install an electrical conditioner to monitor and condition the voltage to the PC.
☐ If the system halts at strange times, the problem might be the OS, memory, CPU, motherboard, hard drive, or power supply. Check Event Viewer for errors. Troubleshoot the OS before you exchange hardware. Check CMOS setup for an error-logging feature, and turn it on. If the problem persists, first try exchanging the least expensive device or the device for which you have a spare part on hand.

Symptom: The fan on the power supply stops working.

Usually just before a fan stops working, it hums or whines. If this event has just happened, replace the fan or the entire power supply. If you replace the power supply or fan and the fan still does not work, the problem might not be the fan or power supply. It might be caused by a short, somewhere else in the system, that is drawing too much power. Some fans are thermostatically controlled. Check your motherboard manual to see if your power supply uses this type of fan. This section is about troubleshooting a short somewhere else in the system.

☐ Don't operate the PC if the fan is not working. Computers without cooling fans can quickly overheat and damage chips.

☐ Turn the power OFF and remove all power cord connections to all components, including power to the motherboard, and all power cords to drives. Turn the power back ON. If the fan comes on, the problem is probably with one of the systems you disconnected, not with the power supply.

☐ Turn the power OFF, and reconnect the power cords to the drives one at a time. If the fan comes on, you can eliminate the drives as the problem. If the fan does not come on, try another drive until you identify the drive with the short.

☐ If the drives are not the problem, suspect the motherboard subsystem. With the power OFF, reconnect all power cords to the drives.

☐ Turn the power OFF, and remove the power to the motherboard by disconnecting P1 or P8 and P9. Turn the power back ON.

☐ If the fan comes back on, the problem is probably not the power supply but a short in one of the components powered by the power cords to the motherboard. The power to the motherboard also powers expansion cards.

☐ Remove all expansion cards, and reconnect the power to the motherboard.

☐ If the fan still works, the problem is with one of the expansion cards. If the fan does not work, the problem is with the motherboard or something still connected to it.

☐ Check for missing standoffs that might be allowing a motherboard component to improperly ground to the computer case.

☐ Look for damage on the bottom side of the motherboard that might be causing shorted circuits on the board.

☐ Frayed wires on data cables can also cause shorts. Disconnect hard drive cables connected directly to the motherboard. Power up with power to the motherboard connected but all cables disconnected from the motherboard. If the fan comes on, the problem is with one of the systems you disconnected.

☐ Inexpensive power supplies might not work or can even be damaged if they are turned ON without a full power load applied. For these power supplies, leave the hard drive power cable connected.

☐ Never replace a damaged motherboard with a good one without first testing or replacing the power supply. You don't want to subject another good board to possible damage.

TROUBLESHOOTING THE MOTHERBOARD AND CPU

You have gotten to this point in the Troubleshooting Tool if the following is true:

☐ The PC might or might not boot properly.
☐ Video is working.
☐ The OS might or might not load properly from the hard drive.
☐ If there is a problem with booting, you are following the troubleshooting steps outlined in Flowchart 4–1, which have already eliminated several possible sources of errors and then brought you to this point.

Problems with the motherboard can cause the PC to not boot properly or can cause the system to be unstable, producing intermittent errors or causing the system to hang. Problems with other devices or with software can cause these same symptoms, so troubleshooting the motherboard is only one of several things to do to locate the source of a problem.

Use the following lists as your troubleshooting tools to identify and solve problems with a motherboard.

Is the Motherboard Newly Installed?

If this motherboard is newly installed, then check the installation to verify the following:

☐ Jumpers are set correctly on the board. Reread the motherboard documentation and verify that the CPU, bus clock speed, and cache memory jumper settings are correct.

☐ Verify that the CPU is supported by the motherboard.

☐ Verify that the motherboard is securely mounted. Check these things:
  - The board cannot move in the case. You should not be able to move the board when you lightly push on it.
  - The board can't touch the bottom of the case. Spacers should be located along all sides of the board, and no bare wires should touch the board.

☐ There are no loose screws anywhere inside the case.

☐ Check for loose wires or cables in the way of the CPU fan.

☐ For ATX and BTX motherboards, check the power wire from the front of the case to the motherboard. Verify that it is not frayed, bent at sharp angles, or loosely connected to the board. Verify that the wire is connected to the correct pins on the board.

☐ Reseat the main power connector on the motherboard.

☐ Verify that all wires to the motherboard are connected to the correct pins.

☐ For AT motherboards, verify that P8 and P9 are correctly connected using the black-to-black rule. (Black wires on P8 and P9 connections are side by side.)

 If memory does not count up correctly during POST, go to *Troubleshooting Memory on the Motherboard* (page 47).

☐ Remove the motherboard from the case, and look for frayed, scratched, or damaged places on the board. A trace on the motherboard might be bad.

☐ Verify that the memory modules are the correct type and that the voltage is set correctly.

☐ Reseat and then replace memory modules.

☐ Examine all the capacitors on the motherboard. A normal capacitor should be perfectly flat along the top and should not leak fluid.

☐ Verify that the CPU is aligned correctly and the voltage is set correctly.

☐ Flash BIOS.

 TO LEARN MORE about how to flash BIOS, see page 251 of Chapter 6 in *A+ Guide to Managing and Maintaining Your PC* or page 199 of Chapter 5 in *A+ Guide to Hardware*.

☐ Reseat the CPU. If that doesn't work, then replace the CPU.

☐ Replace the motherboard.

Symptom: The system is generally unstable.

☐ Troubleshoot the electrical system (power supply) to eliminate an electrical problem before you continue here.

☐ Verify that the CPU fan is running and that the system is not overheating.

☐ Verify CMOS settings. A low battery could cause correct CMOS settings to be lost.

☐ First back up CMOS settings and then restore them to default settings.

TO LEARN MORE about how to back up CMOS, see page 250 of Chapter 6 in *A+ Guide to Managing and Maintaining Your PC* or page 198 of Chapter 5 in *A+ Guide to Hardware*.

☐ Check that the power connections are secure.
☐ Examine all the capacitors on the motherboard. A normal capacitor should be perfectly flat along the top and should not leak fluid.
☐ Check that the CPU is seated securely and that the fan is attached firmly.
☐ Was thermal paste required between the CPU and the heat sink and was not applied when the CPU was installed?
☐ Remove the motherboard from the case and look for frayed, scratched, or damaged places on the board. A trace on the motherboard might be bad.

The problem might be with memory. Go to *Troubleshooting Memory on the Motherboard* (page 47).

☐ Replace memory modules.
☐ Replace the CPU. If this step solves the problem, try the old CPU again. The old CPU might not have been seated properly.
☐ If the motherboard has a diagnostic CD that came from the motherboard manufacturer, run the diagnostic program.
☐ Check the motherboard manufacturer's Web site for suggestions and things to try.
☐ Suspect a virus that has damaged BIOS. Flash BIOS.
☐ Check the Web site of the BIOS manufacturer for suggestions and things to try.

See Appendix H for URLs of BIOS manufacturers (page H-1).

☐ Replace the motherboard. If this step solves the problem, check jumper and CMOS settings on the old motherboard, which might be the problem.

Symptom: The PC does not boot after upgrading the BIOS.

☐ If you have physically replaced the BIOS chip, check the chip for proper orientation. Check that all pins are inserted in the socket and that no pins are bent.
☐ Try replacing the chip with the original BIOS chip. If that works, verify that you have upgraded with the correct new BIOS chip.
☐ Suspect a bad BIOS chip.
☐ If you have flashed BIOS, you might have used the wrong upgrade version. If you made a backup of the old BIOS to floppy disk, try restoring BIOS from the floppy. (When flashing BIOS, always create a backup of the old BIOS to floppy disk before you perform the upgrade. Follow the manufacturer's directions to create the backup.)
☐ If you still cannot boot, your only recourse is to replace the BIOS chip. Contact the motherboard manufacturer for a replacement.
☐ If you accidentally powered down the PC while you were trying to flash BIOS, your BIOS might be corrupted. Restore the BIOS from the floppy disk backup or replace the BIOS chip.

Symptom: The system does not work properly after flashing BIOS.

You likely have used the wrong BIOS upgrade version.

☐ If you made a backup of the previous BIOS, attempt to restore the BIOS from backup, and then repeat the upgrade using the correct version.
☐ Replace the BIOS chip.

Symptom: After upgrading BIOS, you get the error message "Incompatible BIOS translation detected. Unable to load disk overlay."

This is caused by upgrading BIOS to support LBA mode, but the system is already using hard drive overlay software to compensate for not having LBA mode.

☐ Either disable LBA mode in CMOS setup or uninstall the overlay software. Most likely, you will want to use LBA mode rather than the overlay software.

Troubleshooting the CPU

Symptom: The system does not boot after upgrading the CPU.

☐ Check the motherboard documentation to verify that you have used the correct CPU for your motherboard.
☐ Consider that the documentation that came with your motherboard might not be the correct documentation for that board. Look for the motherboard model number embedded on the board, and check the motherboard manufacturer's Web site for compatible CPUs.
☐ Check that power cords from the CPU to the motherboard are connected.
☐ Check that the CPU is properly seated in the socket or slot. Is the thermal compound installed correctly and not spilled over onto CPU connectors?
☐ Reinstall the original CPU and flash BIOS. Then reinstall the new CPU.

Troubleshooting Memory on the Motherboard

☐ Reseat DIMMs, RIMMs, and SIMMs. Move DIMMs to a different slot.
☐ Make sure the DIMMs, RIMMs, or SIMMs have the correct or consistent part number. For example, if there are four installed SIMMs, they usually must be the same size (in megabytes), the same parity, and the same speed (in nanoseconds).
☐ Run diagnostic software bundled with your motherboard that can troubleshoot memory problems.
☐ Replace memory modules one at a time. For example, if the system recognizes only 256 out of 512 MB of RAM, swap the two DIMM modules. Did the amount of recognized RAM change?
☐ Use SIMM modules with the same part number.

 TO LEARN MORE about the details of selecting and matching DIMMs, SIMMs, and RIMMs for a motherboard, see Chapter 7, beginning with page 283 in *A+ Guide to Managing and Maintaining Your PC* or Chapter 6, beginning with page 231 of *A+ Guide to Hardware*.

☐ Use DocMemory (*www.docmemory.com*), Memtest (*www.memtest86.com*), or other diagnostic software to test the RAM on the motherboard.

TROUBLESHOOTING THE HARD DRIVE

You have gotten to this point in the Troubleshooting Tool if the following is true:

☐ The PC does not boot properly.
☐ Video is working.
☐ You see lights and hear a spinning drive or fan within the computer case, indicating that the electrical system is working.
☐ You cannot boot from the hard drive.

During POST, startup BIOS verifies that the hard drive subsystem is functioning and, if no errors are encountered, reports the presence of the hard drive. Later in the boot process, it normally turns to the hard drive to load the OS. Therefore, the two main categories of troubleshooting the hard drive are:

☐ Problems encountered during POST
☐ Problems encountered while trying to load the OS

The file system on the hard drive can be corrupted, and the hard drive will still pass the POST, but, when loading the OS, the file system must be intact. Use Flowchart 4-2 as your troubleshooting tool at this point to isolate the hard drive problem.

Symptom: S.M.A.R.T. reports a hard drive problem.

Self-Monitoring Analysis and Reporting Technology (S.M.A.R.T.) is a self-diagnostic feature on most newer drives that predicts hard drive failure. If a failure seems likely to occur in an IDE drive, S.M.A.R.T. reports this to the BIOS (if the BIOS is S.M.A.R.T. compatible) or the driver software, which then sends a message to your OS. (In a SCSI drive, S.M.A.R.T. only reports a good or failure state.) In CMOS setup, make sure that monitoring S.M.A.R.T is enabled. If you get a S.M.A.R.T. error message, do the following:

☐ Don't focus on fixing the boot problem if there is valuable data on the drive. Before the drive totally fails, focus on saving the data.
☐ Immediately back up your data and then replace the drive. If the drive won't boot, save your data using the Recovery Console.
☐ Use another media to back up your data, and be sure to not overwrite any previous good backups in case the drive fails during the backup process.

Symptom: During POST, startup BIOS reports a problem with the hard drive.

Refer to Table 4–6 for a list of hard drive errors during POST, what they mean, and what to do about them.

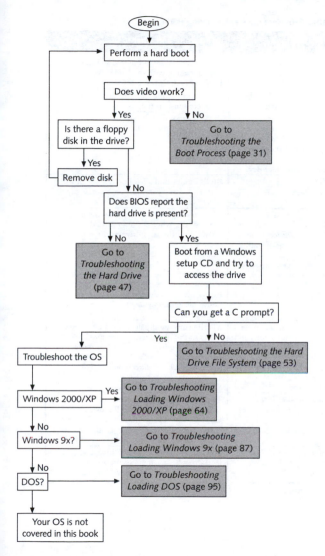

Flowchart 4-2 Troubleshooting the hard drive

Table 4-6 Hard drive errors during POST

Error message	Its meaning and what to do
Configuration/ CMOS error	The hard drive setup information in CMOS does not agree with the hard drive that POST found. Check CMOS setup for errors.
Numeric POST codes in the 1700 range	POST cannot find the hard drive or the hard drive controller is not responding properly.
Fixed disk error Hard drive not found Disk boot failure, insert system disk and press Enter Inaccessible boot device	POST cannot find the hard drive. Suspect a problem with the hard drive subsystem hardware.
No boot device available	BIOS cannot find a hard drive or floppy disk with an OS installed. Suspect a corrupted file system on the hard drive.
Invalid boot disk Inaccessible boot device Invalid partition table Error loading operating system Missing operating system No operating system found	These messages are displayed by the program in the MBR when it cannot find the active partition on the hard drive or the boot sector on that partition. Load the Recovery Console and use Diskpart to check the hard drive partition table for errors. Sometimes Fixmbr or Fixboot might solve the problem. Third-party recovery software such as PartitionMagic might help. Try running diagnostic software provided by the hard drive manufacturer.
An error displays in text against a blue screen and then the system halts. These Windows NT/ 2000/XP errors are called stop errors or blue screens.	STOP errors are usually caused by viruses, errors in the file system, a corrupted hard drive, or a hardware problem. For more information, search the Microsoft support site (*www.support.microsoft.com*) on the 10-character value that identifies the STOP error.
Stop 0x00000024 or NTFS_File_System	The NTFS file system is corrupted. Immediately boot into the Recovery Console, and copy important data files that have not been backed up to another media before attempting to recover the system.
Stop 0x00000077 or Kernel_Stack_Inpage_ Error	Bad sectors are on the hard drive, there is a hard drive hardware problem, or RAM is defective. Try running Chkdsk or Scandisk.

(continued)

Table 4-6 Hard drive errors during POST (continued)

Error message	Its meaning and what to do
Stop 0x0000007A or Kernel_Data_Inpage_ Error	There is a bad sector on the hard drive where the paging file is stored; there is a virus or defective RAM. Try running Chkdsk from the Recovery Console.
Stop 0x0000007B or Inaccessible_Boot_ Device	There is a boot sector virus or failing hardware. Try Fixmbr and Fixboot from the Recovery Console.

 For a more comprehensive list of Windows 2000/XP STOP errors and what to do about them, go to Appendix E, *Windows 2000/XP STOP Errors* (page 1).

If one of the errors listed in Table 4-6 appears, proceed as follows:

☐ Try a cold boot.

☐ A virus might have attacked the MBR. Boot from a Windows setup CD into the Recovery Console. Use the Diskpart command to examine the partition table. Try using the Fixmbr and Fixboot commands.

☐ Check CMOS, and verify that the drive is recognized. If CMOS supports Auto Detection and BIOS recognizes the drive, the drive should be listed. Verify that the hard drive settings in CMOS are correct. If you have previously saved CMOS settings to disk, restore CMOS from this backup.

 For more information on CMOS settings, see Appendix B (page B-1). If the set- tings are not correct, suspect a failing CMOS battery.

☐ Verify that the drive is spinning during POST. Remove the case cover, and turn on the PC. Listen for the spinning drive, or carefully place your hand on top of the drive housing to feel the vibrations. Be careful to not touch anything else inside the case while the power is on, including any circuitry on the drive housing.

☐ If you hear a grinding noise from the drive, the drive has probably crashed and might not be repairable. There are companies that specialize in recovering data from a crashed drive. Look for these data-recovery services on the Internet.

☐ If the drive is not spinning, check the power cord connection. Try a different power cord. Test the voltage of the power connection with a multimeter. Readings should be:
- Pin 1: +12V (acceptable range is +10.8 to +13.2V)
- Pin 2: Ground
- Pin 3: Ground
- Pin 4: +5V (acceptable range is +4.5 to +5.5V)

☐ If power is good and the drive still does not spin, then try powering down the system and removing the drive from the bay. Hold the drive firmly in both hands and give the drive a quick and sudden twist in one direction to force the platters to turn. Reinstall the drive and try again. If this step works, then imme- diately back up the data and replace the drive. You might have to try this action several times for it to work.

☐ If the drive refuses to spin, then replace the drive.

☐ If the drive is spinning, check the data cable connections, and verify that Pin 1 is oriented correctly at both ends of the cable.

☐ Check the master/slave jumper settings on an IDE drive.

☐ For a SCSI drive, check termination, and reseat the host adapter card.
☐ If the drive is still not recognized by POST, try performing the following procedures in order:

- Reconnect or swap the drive data cable.
- Clean the edge connectors on an adapter card if one is present.
- If the drive uses an adapter card, reseat or exchange it. Move it to a
  different slot.
- Exchange the hard drive with one you know is in working condition.
- If the known good drive does not work, then suspect the motherboard
  including the BIOS, the IDE connector, and the chipset.
- For SCSI drives, exchange the host adapter.

☐ If the problem is solved by exchanging one of the above modules, try reinstalling
the old module to verify that the problem was not caused by a bad connection.
☐ Check the Web site of the drive manufacturer for suggestions and tools. Most
hard drive manufacturers offer diagnostic software for their drives.

 Go to Appendix H (page H-1) for URLs of hard drive manufacturers.

Symptom: The hard drive passes POST, but errors occur when loading the OS.

Refer to Table 4-7 for a list of error messages that are displayed when loading
the OS and indicate a problem with the hard drive and its file system.

Table 4-7 Error messages while loading the OS from a hard drive

Error message	Its meaning and what to do
Invalid drive specification	BIOS did not find the boot volume. Suspect a corrupted partition table.
Non-system disk or disk error	• OS system files are missing. For DOS and Windows 9x, these files are IO.SYS, MSDOS.SYS, and COMMAND.COM. It's possible there is damage to the file system. • A floppy disk is in the drive. Remove the disk.
"Bad sector" errors, Sector not found, Track 0 not found	Suspect a corrupted file system, corrupted boot sector, or fading track and sector markings on the drive. Go to *Troubleshooting the Hard Drive File System* (page 53).
Invalid or missing COMMAND.COM Invalid system disk Command file not found	DOS or Windows 9x system files are missing. Replace the files in the root directory of the boot volume using the COPY or SYS command.
Non-DOS disk Unable to read from drive C Invalid media type Missing operating system Error loading operating system	These errors indicate a corrupted or missing OS boot record or a translation problem on large drives (more than 1024 cylinders). Go to *Troubleshooting the Hard Drive File System* (page 53).

When you are not able to boot the OS from the hard drive, try these things:

☐ Perform a cold boot.
☐ Is there a non-bootable floppy disk in the floppy disk drive? If so, remove it and try again.
☐ For Windows 2000/XP, boot from a Windows setup CD and launch the Recovery Console. Try the Diskpart command to examine the hard drive partition table. Then try the Dir C: command to access drive C. You should get a C prompt.
☐ For Windows 9x, boot from a startup disk. You should get an A: prompt. Enter the command Dir C: to access drive C. You should get a C prompt. If you can't get a C prompt, try the Fdisk /mbr command.
☐ If you get a C prompt, then the problem is related to the OS on the hard drive. Go to the troubleshooting sections for loading each OS.
☐ Reboot and look for the message that POST found the hard drive as it was configured in CMOS setup. If POST reported an error, then go back to *Troubleshooting the Hard Drive* (page 47). If POST found the drive, then the problem is probably with the file system on the drive. Continue to the next section.

Troubleshooting the Hard Drive File System

Before you begin troubleshooting the hard drive file system, first find out if there is important data on the hard drive. If so, evaluate the situation carefully and take appropriate action to protect the data. If the data is backed up, don't assume the backup is good until that has been verified. Don't do anything that might damage the data (such as formatting the drive) without first discussing the situation with the user of the data. Recovering corrupted data is covered later in this section. To find references to specific data recovery topics, see the Troubleshooting Roadmap.

☐ Check CMOS setup to confirm that BIOS recognizes the drive and that CMOS settings are correct for the hard drive.

> **GO TO** For more information about CMOS hard drive settings, see Appendix B (page B-1).

☐ For Windows 2000/XP, load the Recovery Console and run the Diskpart command to verify the partitions. Use Fixmbr to restore the master boot record program.

> **TO LEARN MORE** For a listing of the Recovery Console commands for Windows 2000/XP, see Appendix D, *Recovery Console*.

☐ For Windows 9x, boot from a startup disk, and run FDISK. From the FDISK menu, display the partition information. If FDISK says that the partition table is missing or corrupted, then restore the master boot record program with the command Fdisk /mbr and try to boot from the hard drive again.
☐ If this command solves the problem, then immediately run a current version of antivirus software to check for a virus. If the problem is not a virus, then sectors on the hard drive are probably fading. Plan to replace the drive soon, and immediately back up important data.
☐ Try to view the partition table information again. If you still cannot do this and you have a backup copy of the partition table, restore it now.

☐ Try to boot from SpinRite, Partition Magic, or Norton Utilities rescue disks, and use the rescue programs on these disks to attempt to repair the file system structure on the drive.

☐ If the partition table is corrupted and you don't have a backup, you most likely have lost the hard drive contents. Rebuild the drive: For Windows 2000/XP, for a second hard drive, use Disk Management to partition and format the drive. If Windows 2000/XP is installed on the drive, boot from the Windows 2000/XP setup CD and reinstall Windows, which will also partition and format the drive. For Windows 9x, run FDISK and reinstall Windows 9x. Then reinstall the software and restore the data from backups.

☐ If you get errors when attempting to rebuild the drive, consider a low-level format. Only use a low-level format program provided by or recommended by the hard drive manufacturer. Check the manufacturer's Web site. If you get errors when attempting a low-level format, replace the drive.

☐ If you have an identical hard drive that is partitioned identically to the one you are repairing, you can try to save the partition table on the good hard drive to floppy disk. Use this DOS 5.0 command: MIRROR /PARTN. "Restore" the partition table to the bad hard drive using this command: UNFORMAT /PARTN. Sometimes this strategy works.

☐ If Diskpart in the Windows 2000/XP Recovery Console or FDISK in Windows 9x displays the partition information correctly, then the partition table is good. The OS boot record on the boot volume is the next suspected source of the problem.

☐ Error messages that indicate a damaged OS boot record are:
  ■ Non-DOS disk
  ■ Unable to read from drive C
  ■ Invalid media type

☐ For Windows 2000/XP, load the Recovery Console, and use the Fixboot command to write a new boot sector to the system partition. Then run this command: Chkdsk C: /R.

☐ Try SpinRite, Norton Disk Doctor, or Norton Utilities rescue disk, any of which might repair the OS boot record.

☐ Once you are able to access the drive, immediately run a current version of an antivirus program to check for a virus, and run Chkdsk to check for file system errors. For Windows 9x, run ScanDisk. For Windows 2000/XP, under the Tools tab of the drive Properties window, perform error-checking.

☐ For Windows 9x, the problem with the file system might be caused by a corrupted FAT16 or FAT32. Boot from a floppy disk, and run ScanDisk. For FAT32 drives, it's important to use a Windows 98 version of ScanDisk that can handle FAT32 and long filenames.

☐ Once you can access the drive, immediately run a current version of antivirus software, and run Defragmenter to optimize the drive.

☐ If you gain access to the drive, but discover that data is seriously corrupted, as a last resort rebuild the drive: For Windows 2000/XP, for a second hard drive, use Disk Management to partition and format the drive. If Windows 2000/XP is installed on the drive, boot from the Windows 2000/XP setup CD and reinstall Windows, which will also partition and format the drive. Then reinstall the software and restore the data from backups. For Windows 9x, run FDISK and reinstall Windows 9x.

Symptom: The file system on the hard drive is damaged, and the drive contains important data.

If the hard drive gives errors indicating a damaged file system (for example, "Invalid drive specification"), but it holds important data, before you rebuild the drive, you might be able to recover important data. Try these things.

☐ Try recovery software such as Norton Disk Doctor or Ontrack. See *www.symantec.com* or *www.ontrack.com*.

 TO LEARN MORE about data recovery techniques, see page 676 of Chapter 13 in *A+ Guide to Managing and Maintaining Your PC* or page 236 of Chapter 4 of *A+ Guide to Software.*

☐ See the Web site of the hard drive manufacturer for suggestions and tools. Hard drive manufacturers offer diagnostic software to test their drives.

 Go to Appendix H (page H-1) for URLs of hard drive manufacturers.

☐ Here's a trick that might work: Using an identical hard drive that is partitioned identically to the damaged one, lay the good hard drive on top of the computer chassis, and plug in the data cable and power cord to the good drive. Plug a second power cord in the bad drive. Turn on the PC and get to a C prompt on the good drive. *Very carefully* move the data cable from the good drive to the bad drive. If the file system, directories, and data are intact, you should be able to immediately copy data from the bad drive to another media. *Be very careful to not touch anything else in the computer case as you move the data cable.*

☐ Consider contacting a professional data-recovery service. Using any Internet search engine, search on "data recovery" to locate a recovery service. Before you use a service, which is most likely very expensive, consider its guarantees and, if possible, check a reference.

Symptom: The hard drive was accidentally formatted.

Note that if the hard drive has been formatted, the data is most likely lost.

☐ If the data is very important, try using a data-recovery service.
☐ To recover from an accidental format, run Norton Utilities UNFORMAT program.

Symptom: Computer will not recognize a newly installed hard disk.

Consider the following if the disk is brand new or has no information you want to keep on it:

☐ IDE drives are already low-level formatted, but really old drives require the user to perform this routine. Verify that, for these very old drives, the low-level format is performed.
☐ For Windows 2000/XP, for a second hard drive, run Disk Management to examine and partition the drive.
☐ If the hard drive is the single drive intended for a Windows 2000/XP installation, you can boot to the Recovery Console and use Diskpart to examine the partition table on the drive.
☐ For Windows 9x, run FDISK, and choose Display Partition Information from the FDISK menu to verify the status of the partition table. Be sure that you have an active partition. Verify that FORMAT C:/S has been done.
☐ Verify that CMOS setup has been configured correctly.

TO LEARN MORE about how to configure CMOS setup for your hard drive, begin with page 340 of Chapter 8 in *A+ Guide to Managing and Maintaining Your PC* or page 288 of Chapter 7 of *A+ Guide to Hardware*.

☐ Make sure BIOS can see the drive. If BIOS cannot see the drive, then, as far as the PC is concerned, the drive does not exist.
☐ Verify that the drive spins when power is turned ON.
☐ Check DIP switches or jumpers on the drive for master/slave selections. You can't have two masters on the same cable.
☐ Verify that the colored edge of the data cable is connected to Pin 1 on the edge connectors of both the card and the cable.
☐ Check to see if the power cord is connected.
☐ Try a different power cord.
☐ Try disabling Power Management features in CMOS setup.
☐ Check the Web site of the drive manufacturer for suggestions in troubleshooting. Call the drive vendor if the above steps are not productive.

Symptom: The hard drive LED on the computer case front panel stays lit continuously or does not work at all.

This light indicates hard drive activity. Try these things:

☐ If the hard drive is working properly, check the orientation of the wire coming from the light to the motherboard pins. Try reversing the wire on these pins.

 If the hard drive is not working, then go to *Troubleshooting the Hard Drive* (page 47).

☐ If using an IDE controller card, replace the card.

TROUBLESHOOTING THE VIDEO SYSTEM

You have gotten to this point in the Troubleshooting Tool if the following is true:

☐ The PC does not boot properly.
☐ Video is not working.
☐ You see lights and hear a spinning drive or fan within the computer case, indicating that the electrical system is working.

One of the first things you see displayed on the monitor screen during POST is the video card BIOS identifying itself after POST executes this BIOS on the card. If you don't see this message about the system video and the screen is blank, but you do hear beeps indicating that POST is functioning, then suspect a problem with the video system.

Symptom: The system has power, but video does not work.

Use this list as your troubleshooting tool:

☐ Check the video cable connections and power cable connections to the monitor. Verify that the power outlet to the monitor is working.
☐ If the monitor has an ON/OFF switch on the back of the monitor, verify that it is ON.
☐ Verify the monitor is turned ON by checking that the light on the monitor is green.
☐ When you first turn on the monitor, if you hear a click and the light changes color within a couple of seconds, have it serviced by a qualified service technician.

☐ If the monitor has a voltage selection switch, verify that it is set to 110 V.

☐ Use the buttons on the front of the monitor to verify that the brightness/contrast settings on the monitor are set correctly. Try each extreme on these settings, and then return them to somewhere in the middle.

☐ If the monitor has a fuse accessible from the rear of the monitor, verify that it is good.

☐ Smell the monitor over its air vents. If it smells funny, like something electrical is fried, turn it OFF. Is it still under warranty?

☐ Try a different monitor.

☐ Examine the monitor connector that plugs into the video card. Look for broken pins. A normal connector should be missing one pin.

☐ Remove all unnecessary devices and cards (modem, network, sound, printer, scanner, etc.) from the computer and reboot.

☐ Reseat the video card. Move it to a different slot. Clean the card's edge connectors using a contact cleaner or a white eraser. Be certain to prevent crumbs from the eraser from falling into the expansion slot.

☐ Remove the card, and check that each socketed chip on the card is seated securely. Use a screwdriver to press down on all four corners of all socketed chips on the card.

☐ If you have just installed a new hardware device, suspect a resource conflict. If the video card is a PCI card, the problem might arise from the PCI slot using a conflicting IRQ. Try these things:

■ Move the video card to another PCI slot.

■ Disconnect the new device. If the problem goes away, go into CMOS setup and reserve the IRQ that the video card's PCI slot is using for PCI only.

GO TO
Go to *Resolving Resource Conflicts Using Legacy Devices* (page 114).

☐ If you are using a PCI video card and the motherboard has a video slot (PCI Express or AGP), then disable the unused video slot in CMOS setup. Figures 4-3 and 4-4 can help you identify PCI Express and AGP slots.

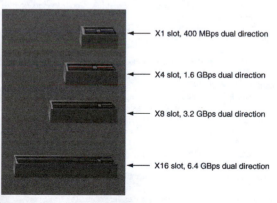

← X1 slot, 400 MBps dual direction

← X4 slot, 1.6 GBps dual direction

← X8 slot, 3.2 GBps dual direction

← X16 slot, 6.4 GBps dual direction

Figure 4-3 Current PCI Express slots

Front of
motherboard

Rear of motherboard
(bracket side of slots)

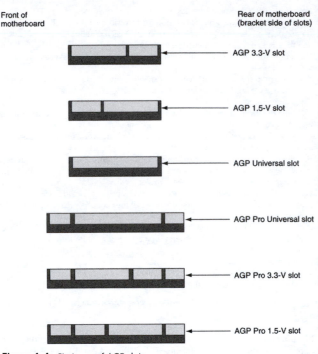

AGP 3.3-V slot

AGP 1.5-V slot

AGP Universal slot

AGP Pro Universal slot

AGP Pro 3.3-V slot

AGP Pro 1.5-V slot

Figure 4-4 Six types of AGP slots

- ☐ If you are using a video card with a motherboard that has onboard video, go into CMOS setup and disable onboard video.
- ☐ Confirm that the proper system configuration has been set up. Some older motherboards have a jumper or DIP switch that can be used to select the monitor type.
- ☐ Try a known good video card. If this step works, try the old card again. The old card might have been loose in the slot. (Alternately, you can install the suspected-bad video card in a working PC.)
- ☐ For an AGP or PCI Express video card, try using a PCI video card instead and disable the AGP or PCI Express slot. The first slot might be damaged.
- ☐ If you have just installed video RAM on the card, remove the RAM. If the problem goes away, then verify that the RAM is the correct type for this card.
- ☐ Exchange video RAM.
- ☐ Check that socketed chips on the card are seated. Firmly press down on the corner of each chip with a screwdriver.
- ☐ If the video card has some socketed chips that appear dirty or corroded, consider removing them and trying to clean the pins. You can use a clean pencil eraser to do so. Normally, however, if the problem is a bad video card, the most cost-effective measure is to replace the card.
- ☐ Trade the motherboard for one you know is good. Sometimes, albeit rarely, a peripheral chip on the motherboard of the computer causes the problem.

Monitor Problems

Poor cable connections or bad contrast/brightness adjustments cause many monitor problems. Check the warranty on the monitor. Don't void the warranty by taking the monitor to an unauthorized service center. Don't open the monitor case unless you are trained to work inside one.

Symptom: Power light (LED) does not go on, and there is no video display.

☐ Verify that the monitor is plugged in and turned ON and that the wall outlet works by plugging in a lamp, radio, or other electrical appliance.

☐ If the monitor power cord is plugged into a power strip or surge protector, verify that the power strip is turned ON.

☐ If the monitor power cord is plugged into the back of the computer, verify that the connection is tight, and that the computer is turned ON.

☐ Check for a fuse in the monitor. If one is present, it should be visible from the back of the monitor. Look for a black knob that you can remove (no need to go inside the monitor cover). Check the fuse for a broken wire indicating a bad fuse.

☐ Check that air vents are clear of dust or other obstructions.

☐ Check for a switch on the back of the monitor for choosing between 110 V and 220 V. Check that the switch is in the correct position.

☐ If none of these steps work, take the monitor to a service center.

Symptom: Power LED light is on, but no picture on power up.

☐ Check the contrast adjustment. If there's no change, then leave it at a middle setting.

☐ Check the brightness adjustment. If there's no change, then leave it at a middle setting.

☐ Check that the cable is connected securely to the computer.

☐ For an LCD monitor, check for a switch set incorrectly to use either the DVI port or VGA analog port.I

☐ If the monitor-to-computer cable detaches from the monitor, exchange it for a cable you know is good or check the cable for continuity.

 TO LEARN MORE about how to use a multimeter to check for continuity, begin with page 1220 of Appendix B in A+ *Guide to Managing and Maintaining Your PC* or page 648 of Appendix B in A+ *Guide to Hardware.*

☐ If this step solves the problem, reattach the old cable to verify that the problem was not simply a bad connection.

☐ Test the monitor that isn't working on a computer that works with another monitor.

☐ Test a monitor you know is good on the computer you suspect to be bad. If you think the monitor is bad, make sure that it also fails to work on a good computer.

☐ Suspect the video card.

 Go to *Troubleshooting the Video System* (page 56).

Symptom: Power is ON, but the monitor displays the wrong characters.

☐ Boot into CMOS setup. If the CMOS setup screen is correct, then the problem is most likely a Windows problem. The system might have a virus. Run current antivirus software.

□ If the problem is not isolated to Windows, consider it a hardware problem. Wrong characters are usually not the result of a bad monitor but rather a problem with the video card. Trade the video card for one you know is good.

□ If the new video card doesn't work, exchange the motherboard. Sometimes a bad chip, ROM or RAM, on the motherboard will display the wrong characters on the monitor.

Symptom: Monitor flickers and/or has wavy lines.

□ Check the cable. Monitor flicker can be caused by poor cable connections.

□ If the monitor has a degauss button to eliminate accumulated or stray magnetic fields, press it.

□ Check whether or not something in the office is providing a high amount of electrical noise. For example, you might be able to stop a flicker by moving the office fan to a different outlet. Bad fluorescent lights, large speakers, or two monitors placed close to each other might cause interference. Try moving the monitor to a new location or to an altogether different circuit.

□ If the vertical scan frequency (the refresh rate at which the screen is drawn) is below 60Hz, a screen flicker might appear in the normal course of operation.

□ Try using a different refresh rate if your monitor supports it. (In Windows, right-click the desktop, and select Properties on the menu.) Set the refresh rate to the highest value supported by your monitor.

□ Try a different monitor set in the same location. Does the same problem happen on the alternate monitor? If so, suspect interference.

□ Check Control Panel, Display, Settings to see if a high resolution (greater than 800 × 600 with more than 256 colors) is selected. Consider these issues:

- The video card might not support this resolution/color setting.
- The monitor might not support this resolution or refresh rate.

□ Check the software configuration on the computer. Boot into Safe Mode, which forces the OS to use a generic video driver and low resolution. If this step works, then change the driver and resolution.

 For information about Windows 2000/XP Safe Mode, see *Using Safe Mode to Troubleshoot Windows 2000/XP* (page 72).

 For information about Windows 9x Safe Mode, see *Using Safe Mode to Troubleshoot Windows 9x* (page 90).

□ There might not be enough video RAM; 4 MB or more might be required.

□ The added (socketed) video RAM might be of a different speed than the soldered memory.

□ Go into setup and disable the shadowing of video ROM.

Symptom: No graphics display, or the screen goes blank when loading certain programs.

□ A special graphics or video accelerator card is defective or not present.

□ Software is not configured to do graphics, or the software does not recognize the installed graphics card.

□ The video card might not support this resolution and/or color setting.

□ For Windows 2000/XP, press F8 during the boot process, and choose Enable VGA Mode from the Advanced options menu. This will load the OS with a 640 × 480 resolution. Once loaded, increase the resolution if needed.

TO LEARN MORE about the Windows 2000/XP Advanced Options menu, see page 698 of Chapter 14 in *A+ Guide to Managing and Maintaining Your PC* or page 258 of Chapter 5 in *A+ Guide to Software*.

☐ Download and install the latest video drivers for your operating system and video card from the video card manufacturer. Make sure the driver has been digitally signed (required on Windows 2000/XP). Contact your computer manufacturer to obtain the newest set of video card drivers, if necessary.

☐ There might not be enough video RAM; 4 MB or more might be required.

☐ The added (socketed) video RAM might be of a different speed than the soldered memory.

☐ The wrong adapter/display type might be selected. Start Windows from Safe Mode to reset display.

☐ Using Windows, remove and reinstall the video drivers.

☐ Consider you have downloaded the wrong video drivers. Verify the video card manufacturer and model, and double check the Web site.

Symptom: Screen goes blank 30 seconds or one minute after not touching the keyboard.

☐ A "green" motherboard (which follows energy-saving standards) used with an Energy Star monitor can be configured to go into a standby or doze mode after a period of inactivity. The monitor LED light changes from green to orange to indicate doze mode.

 TO LEARN MORE about power-saving features for video, see page 164 of Chapter 4 in *A+ Guide to Managing and Maintaining Your PC* or page 112 of Chapter 3 in *A+ Guide to Hardware*.

☐ Try to change the doze features in CMOS, using a menu option such as Power Management, or, in Windows, using Control Panel, Display, Screen Saver.

☐ Try disabling the power-management features in CMOS and using only those in Windows.

☐ If the monitor has a Power Save switch on the back of the monitor, check that it is set correctly.

Symptom: Poor-quality color display.

☐ Use the color-adjusting buttons on the outside of the monitor to fine-tune the color. (See the monitor documentation for instructions.)

☐ In Windows, remove and reinstall the video drivers.

☐ Exchange video cards.

☐ If the monitor is inexpensive, try a higher-quality monitor to determine whether or not the image is affected.

☐ Add more video RAM; check the video card documentation for recommendations.

☐ Check whether or not a fan or large speaker (which has large magnets) or another monitor nearby might be causing interference.

☐ Less-expensive monitors and video cards don't use quality components, which can cause poor quality display. Try a quality monitor to determine if the image is affected.

Symptom: Picture out of focus or out of adjustment.

☐ Check the adjustment knobs on the control panel on the outside of the monitor.

☐ Change the refresh rate. Sometimes this step can make the picture appear more in focus.

□ Adjustments can be made inside the monitor that might solve the problem. If you have not been trained to work inside the monitor, take the monitor to a service center for adjustments.

Symptom: Crackling sound.

An accumulation of dirt or dust inside the unit might be the cause. Clean the monitor vents using a vacuum on the outside of the monitor. Make sure the vents are not obstructed. Someone trained to work on the inside of the monitor can vacuum the inside.

Symptom: Whining sound.

This noise is a common occurrence with some monitors, especially less expensive ones.

□ Try moving the monitor to a new location.
□ Try a different refresh rate.
□ Vacuum the monitor vents, and check for good airflow around the vents.
□ Take the monitor to a service center for adjustments.
□ Replace the monitor if you can't ignore the whine.

TO LEARN MORE about how to change monitor settings and video drivers in Windows, begin with page 421 of Chapter 9 in *A+ Guide to Managing and Maintaining Your PC* or page 369 of Chapter 8 in *A+ Guide to Hardware*.

TROUBLESHOOTING THE KEYBOARD

Because of the low cost of keyboards, most often if a keyboard does not work, the best solution is to replace it. However, there are a few simple things you can do to repair a keyboard that is not working.

Symptom: A cordless keyboard is not working.

□ Cordless keyboards have a transceiver plugged into the keyboard port, and the keyboard contains a compatible transceiver. They use either IR (infrared) or RF (radio frequency) signals for communication. IR only works with line of sight, so make certain the keyboard is aimed at the receiver and that nothing is interfering with the signal.
□ Replace the batteries in the keyboard.

Symptom: A few keys don't work.

□ Remove the cap on the bad key with a flat head screwdriver. Spray contact cleaner into the key well. Repeatedly depress the contact to clear it out. Don't use rubbing alcohol to clean the key well, as it can add a residue to the contact.
□ If this method of cleaning solves the problem, then clean the adjacent keys as well.
□ Turn the keyboard upside down and tap the keyboard lightly to dislodge debris.
□ Use compressed air to blow out debris.

Symptom: The keyboard does not work at all.

□ Check that the cable is securely plugged in.
□ Exchange the keyboard for a known good one.
□ For a USB keyboard, try a different USB port.
□ If the problem is in the keyboard, if possible, swap the existing cable with a cable known to be good—perhaps from an old, discarded keyboard. Accomplish this task by removing the few screws that hold the keyboard case together and then unplugging the cable. Be careful as you work; don't allow the key caps to fall out!

☐ For a keyboard proven to be bad, if the problem is not the cable, discard the keyboard.

☐ If the problem is with the computer, consider the following: on the mother-board, the two chips that affect the keyboard functions are the keyboard chip and the ROM BIOS chip. You might choose to swap each of these chips on the motherboard. Otherwise, the entire motherboard might have to be replaced.

☐ If the motherboard keyboard port is not working, rather than repairing or replacing the motherboard, use a USB keyboard. You might have to go into CMOS setup and disable the keyboard port.

Symptom: Key continues to repeat after being released.

☐ The problem might be a dirty contact. Some debris has conductive properties and can therefore short the gap between the contacts, causing the key to repeat. Try cleaning the key switch with contact cleaner.

☐ Very high humidity and excess moisture might short key switch contacts and cause keys to repeat. The problem will usually resolve itself once the humidity level returns to normal. You can hasten the drying process by using a fan (not a hot hair dryer) to blow air at the keyboard.

Symptom: Keys produce the wrong characters.

☐ Is the NumLock switch set correctly? For some laptops, the Fn key is used with a Function key to toggle the keypad and character keys.

☐ This problem is usually caused by a bad chip on the keyboard. Try swapping the keyboard for one you know is good. If the problem goes away, replace the original keyboard with a new one.

Symptom: A major spill on the keyboard.

For major spills on the keyboard, thoroughly rinse the keyboard in running water. Allow the keyboard to dry thoroughly. You can speed up the process if you set it out in the sun or in front of a fan. In the meantime, use a different keyboard.

TROUBLESHOOTING THE MOUSE

Symptom: The cursor on the screen is difficult to move with the mouse.

The problem is probably dirty rollers inside the mouse. Do the following:

☐ For a mechanical mouse, remove the cover to the mouse ball from the bottom of the mouse. The cover usually comes off with a simple press and shift motion.

☐ Clean the rollers with a cotton swab dipped in a very small amount of liquid soap or contact cleaner. If necessary, use a flat head screwdriver to lightly scrape off any material that remains. Be sure to also clean the mouse pad and check the ball for debris. It can be washed with soapy water or alcohol.

☐ For an optical mouse, use a mouse pad that is a solid color. Don't use an optical mouse on a glass surface. Make sure no hair or dust is obstructing the optical sensor.

☐ For a wireless mouse, replace the mouse battery or recharge the mouse.

Symptom: The mouse does not work at all, or the cursor is not visible on the screen.

☐ Check the mouse cable connection to the PC. If you find it loose, connect it and reboot the PC.

☐ For a serial mouse, verify that the serial port is enabled in CMOS setup and that there are no resource conflicts.

☐ For a USB mouse, verify that USB is enabled in CMOS setup, and use Device Manager to verify that USB is enabled and there are no conflicts.
☐ For a wireless mouse, check the batteries in the mouse receiver.

 If you suspect a resource conflict, go to *Resolving Resource Conflicts Using Legacy Devices* (page 114).

☐ Reboot the PC.
☐ Try a known good mouse.
☐ Using Device Manager, update the mouse drivers.
☐ When using Windows 9x, try using a real-mode driver loaded in CONFIG.SYS. If this step solves the problem, then try restoring Windows system files.

 TO LEARN MORE about installing a real-mode mouse driver in CONFIG.SYS, see Chapter 15 in *A+ Guide to Managing and Maintaining Your PC*, beginning on page 748, or see Chapter 6 in *A+ Guide to Software*, beginning on page 308.

☐ If using a motherboard mouse, try using a serial mouse or a USB mouse.

TROUBLESHOOTING LOADING WINDOWS 2000/XP

You have gotten to this point in the Troubleshooting Tool if the following is true:

☐ Windows 2000/XP has started to load but loads slowly, gives errors, does not load, or the Windows 2000/XP PC keeps rebooting or freezing.
☐ Video is working.

Note that Windows 2000 and Windows XP use about the same troubleshooting approaches and tools, so they are both included in this section. Where differences exist, they are noted.

Use Flowchart 4-3 as your troubleshooting tool at this point. One step in the flowchart is to use the Windows 2000/XP Advanced Options Menu. Items on the menu are listed and described in Table 4-8.

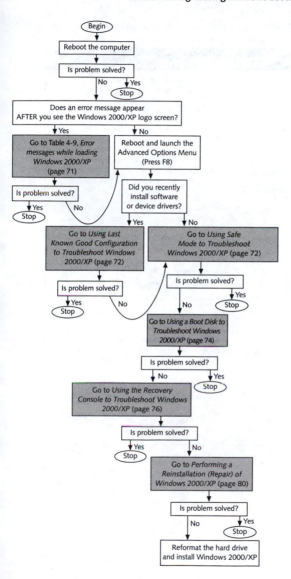

Flowchart 4-3 Troubleshooting loading Windows 2000/XP

Table 4-8 Windows 2000/XP Advanced Options menu
(press F8 during boot)

Advanced options menu	What it means and when to use it
Safe Mode	This is usually the first option to try if you have not installed any new device drivers or software and Windows 2000/XP has failed to start successfully. Safe Mode will load the minimum number of device drivers and services that are required to start Windows 2000/XP. Once Windows 2000/XP has loaded, you can review the Event Viewer logs, modify the registry, roll back device drivers, modify startup items via msconfig.exe (Windows XP only), modify advanced system properties, or perform a virus scan.
	If you have just made a hardware or software change, first try using the Last Known Good Configuration on the Advanced Options Menu before you use Safe Mode.
	If you are unable to load 2000/XP via Safe Mode, then your next option is the Recovery Console. Once inside the Recovery Console, you might be able to repair Windows 2000/XP. If not, you might be able to at least restore the ability to logon via Safe Mode.
Safe Mode with Networking	This option behaves exactly like Safe Mode. In addition, support for networking devices is provided so that the local network or Internet can be accessed. This option provides an ideal testing environment for troubleshooting networking issues because third-party software, devices, and services are not loaded.
	The Internet can be used for obtaining device driver updates, definition updates for antivirus software, or researching the problem further through a search engine *(www.google.com)* or the Microsoft Knowledge Base *(search.microsoft.com/advanced_search.asp)*.
Safe Mode with Command Prompt	This option behaves similarly to Safe Mode except that the normal Windows shell (Explorer.exe) is not loaded. Instead, a non-graphical shell (CMD.exe) is loaded, which provides the same 32-bit environment as the standard Windows shell. This option can be selected if you prefer a DOS-type user interface over the normal Windows graphical user interface.

(continued)

Table 4-8 Windows 2000/XP Advanced Options menu
(press F8 during boot) (continued)

Advanced options menu	What it means and when to use it
Enable boot logging	This option creates a log file that describes the boot process and can be used along with other Advanced Options Menu items listed in this table except for Last Known Good Configuration. The log file that is generated is named Ntbtlog.txt and is saved in the Windows 2000/XP installation folder, (most likely C:\Windows).
	TIP If you can't figure out how to solve the problem in Safe Mode, then choose this option and examine Ntbtlog.txt. It may help pinpoint problems with drivers and services that you can investigate the next time you boot into Safe Mode (after the log is created).
Enable VGA Mode	Starts Windows 2000/XP using the default Microsoft VGA driver (Vga.sys) at a resolution of 640 × 480 and 16 colors instead of the current video card drives. This option is useful when troubleshooting issues between video adapter settings and the monitor. For example, the monitor might not support the resolution of the video adapter, which might stop Windows 2000/XP from loading properly.
	TIP If display settings have been changed so that video is unreadable, reboot using Enable VGA Mode, and then fix the problem.
Last Known Good Configuration	This option is most effective if used after installing new device drivers or software that has caused Windows 2000/XP to not load properly. Data from your last successful log on is restored over faulty data in the registry.
	TIP If choosing LKGC fails to solve the problem, then the next option to try is Safe Mode.
Directory Services Restore Mode (Windows domain controllers only)	This mode should only be used on domain controllers. Therefore, it is not designed to solve normal Windows 2000/XP problems. This mode can be used to help restore the system state, SYSVOL directory, and Active Directory on a Windows 20003, Windows 2000, or .NET domain controller.

(continued)

Table 4-8 Windows 2000/XP Advanced Options menu
(press F8 during boot) (continued)

Advanced options menu	What it means and when to use it
Debugging Mode	This option forces Windows 2000/XP to enter into a debug mode when loading. Information collected from booting a computer in this mode can be redirected along a serial cable (uses COM 2) to a second computer that is running debugging software. Debugging software can be used to analyze and troubleshoot problems with applications, services, drivers, and the Windows kernel.
	TIP You can download "Debugging Tools for Windows" software for free from Microsoft at *www.microsoft.com/ddk/debugging/*.
Start Windows Normally	This option ignores any attempt at solving the problem and tries to load Windows 2000/XP normally. If Windows 2000/XP does not load properly, then the computer might have to be manually shut down and rebooted into another mode on the Advanced Options menu.
Reboot	Reboots the computer.
Return to OS Choices Menu	Selecting this option will display the boot menu if you have more than one OS installed or if you have installed the Recovery Console from the Windows 2000/XP setup CD. For example, if you have installed the Recovery Console, then selecting this option will display a list of choices such as "Microsoft Windows XP Professional," (or "Microsoft Windows XP Home Edition" if installed,) and the "Microsoft Windows Recovery Console."
	TIP The boot option on the OS Choices Menu is collected from the Boot.ini file located on the root of your system drive, most likely drive C:.

Symptom: Windows 2000/XP starts slowly.

Do the following steps to perform a general cleanup of startup processes:

☐ To get a general idea of processes running in the background that might be tying up system resources, reboot the PC, and check the Applications tab and the Processes tab in Task Manager for unwanted or malicious processes. To help you identify Windows processes, Figure 4-5 shows processes running after a fresh installation of Windows XP.

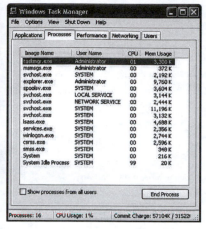

Figure 4-5 Processes showing under Task Manager for a fresh installation of Windows XP

☐ Investigate any unknown processes, searching the Internet for information. Web sites with trustworthy information are:
  - Answers That Work at *www.answersthatwork.com*
  - Jim Foley, The Elder Geek at *www.theeldergeek.com*
  - Process Library by Jelsoft Enterprises, Ltd. at *www.processlibrary.com*
  - Uniblue at *www.liutilities.com*
  - All the antivirus software sites listed in Appendix H.

☐ If you find unwanted processes, use msconfig.exe to find out how a process is loaded at startup.

☐ To remove unwanted processes, do the following:
  - First back up important data.
  - If you suspect a virus, run a current version of antivirus software.
  - Use the Add or Remove Programs applet to uninstall software you don't want.

If software does not uninstall or uninstalls with errors, do the following to manually remove software:

☐ Delete the software folder in the C:\Program Files folder.

☐ Using the Registry Editor, export this key to the Windows desktop:

HKLM\Software\Microsoft\Windows\CurrentVersion\Uninstall

☐ Scroll through the entries in this key looking for all references to the software. Delete each reference, and be sure to search the entire list because there might be several entries.

☐ Reboot the PC, and check for errors. If you encounter errors, you can undo registry changes by double-clicking on the exported key.

Search these startup folders for unwanted startup processes:

☐ C:\Documents and Settings*username*\Start Menu\Programs\Startup
☐ C:\Documents and Settings\All Users\Start Menu\Programs\Startup
☐ C:\Windows\Profiles\All Users\Start Menu\Programs\Startup
☐ C:\Windows\Profiles*username*\Start Menu\Programs\Startup

Search these folders for startup processes put there by Group Policy:

☐ C:\WINDOWS\System32\GroupPolicy\Machine\Scripts\Startup
☐ C:\WINDOWS\System32\GroupPolicy\Machine\Scripts\Shutdown
☐ C:\WINDOWS\System32\GroupPolicy\User\Scripts\Logon
☐ C:\WINDOWS\System32\GroupPolicy\User\Scripts\Logoff

Search this folder for startup processes put there by as scheduled tasks:

☐ C:\Windows\Tasks

Do the following to clean up services, drivers, and the registry:

☐ Use the Services Console (services.msc) to look for unwanted services launched at startup.
☐ Use Device Manager to uninstall or disable unwanted devices.
☐ Using Appendix J as your reference, search the registry for other unwanted startup processes.

 For a complete list of registry keys and other entry points for startup processes, see Appendix J, *Entry Points for Startup Processes*.

If Windows 2000/XP still starts or runs slowly, do the following:

☐ Verify the hard drive has enough free space (at least 15%). Defrag the hard drive and use the Check Disk process to clean up the drive.
☐ If you don't have enough free hard drive space, consider adding a second drive. Purchase the fastest drive the motherboard can support.
☐ Use System Information to verify you have enough RAM (at least 512 MB, but more is better). Consider upgrading RAM.

Symptom: An error message appears while loading Windows 2000/XP.

Use Table 4-9 as your troubleshooting tool at this point, which contains the most common STOP errors.

Table 4-9 Error messages while loading Windows 2000/XP

Error message	What it means and what to do
Hard drive not found Fixed disk error Disk boot failure, insert system disk and press enter. No boot device available	Startup BIOS cannot find the hard drive. Proceed to *Troubleshooting the Hard Drive* (page 47).
Invalid boot disk Inaccessible boot device Invalid partition table Error loading operating system Missing operating system No operating system found	These messages are displayed by the program in the MBR when it cannot find the active partition on the hard drive or the boot sector on that partition. Load the Recovery Console and use Diskpart to check the hard drive partition table for errors. Sometimes Fixmbr or Fixboot will solve the problem. Third-party recovery software such as PartitionMagic might help. Try running diagnostic software provided by the hard drive manufacturer.
A disk read error occurred NTLDR is missing NTLDR is compressed	These errors occur if Ntldr has been moved, renamed, or deleted, or is corrupted, if the boot sector on the active partition is corrupted or if you have just tried to install an older version of Windows such as Windows 98 on the hard drive. First, boot from a Windows 2000/XP boot disk. If the OS loads properly, then replace Ntldr. Then check Boot.ini settings.
An error displays in text against a blue screen and then the system halts. These Windows NT/2000/XP errors are called stop errors or blue screens.	STOP errors are usually caused by viruses, errors in the file system, a corrupted hard drive, or a hardware problem. For more information, search the Microsoft support site (*support.microsoft.com*) on the 10-character value that identifies the STOP error.
Stop 0x00000024 or NTFS_File_System	The NTFS file system is corrupted. Immediately boot into the Recovery Console, and copy important data files that have not been backed up to another media before attempting to recover the system.
Stop 0x00000050 or Page_Fault_in_Nonpaged_Area	Most likely, RAM is defective.
Stop 0x00000077 or Kernel_Stack_Inpage_Error	Bad sectors are on the hard drive, there is a hard drive hardware problem, or RAM is defective. Try running Chkdsk or Scandisk.

(continued)

Table 4-9 Error messages while loading Windows 2000/XP
(continued)

Error Message	What It Means and What To Do
Stop 0x0000007A or Kernel_ Data_Inpage_Error	There is a bad sector on the hard drive where the paging file is stored; there is a virus or defective RAM. Try running Chkdsk from the Recovery Console.
Stop 0x0000007B or Inaccessible_Boot_Device	There is a boot sector virus or failing hardware. Try Fixmbr and Fixboot from the Recovery Console.
Stop: 0xc000026C or Stop: 0xc0000221 or Unable to Load Device Driver *drivername*	Use the Recovery Console to replace the specified driver file with one from the Windows setup CD.

For a more comprehensive list of Windows 2000/XP STOP errors and what to do about them, go to Appendix E, *Windows 2000/XP STOP Errors* (page E-1).

Using Last Known Good Configuration to Troubleshoot Windows 2000/XP

This option is most effective if used after installing new device drivers or software that have caused Windows 2000/XP to not load successfully. Selecting Last Known Good Configuration (LKGC) is similar to performing an "undo." Windows 2000/XP will load with the most recent settings that worked (settings in place during your last successful logon). During a LKGC recovery, data in the registry key HKEY_LOCAL_MACHINE\System\CurrentControlSet is restored from a known good backup that was tucked away in the registry. The restored data includes information on how Windows manages hardware, services, and other critical system settings.

Please note that if you've somehow managed to logon to the computer after the problem occurs and before attempting a LKGC, then performing a LKGC recovery will be useless. The LKGC data that had been backed-up in the registry was overwritten with flawed data when you logged in.

☐ If choosing LKGC doesn't work, then try Safe Mode.

TO LEARN MORE about the Windows 2000/XP Last Known Good Configuration, see page 702 of Chapter 14 in *A+ Guide to Managing and Maintaining Your PC* or page 262 of Chapter 5 in *A+ Guide to Software.*

Using Safe Mode to Troubleshoot Windows 2000/XP

When Windows 2000/XP has failed to load successfully and you have not just installed any new device drivers or software, try Safe Mode. Safe Mode loads the minimum number of device drivers and services that are required to start Windows 2000/XP. Please note that startup programs and network support will not run in Safe Mode. Safe Mode loads the default Microsoft VGA driver (vga.sys) with a screen resolution of 640 × 480 at 16 colors. Serial devices (COM ports) are not supported in Safe Mode.

For Windows XP, when Safe Mode is first loaded, if it detects a problem, it will give you the opportunity to go directly into System Restore to restore the system to a previous restore point. Follow the instructions on screen to select the most recent restore point.

Symptom: You have just loaded new device drivers or software, and using the Last Known Good Configuration has failed.

It is possible that the Last Known Good Configuration data is corrupt. Do the following:

☐ Boot into Safe Mode.
☐ Use Windows XP System Restore to restore the system to a previous state, before the problem occurred.
☐ Reboot the computer.

If the problem remains, return to Safe Mode and do the following:

☐ Run Device Manager, and manually roll back the drivers for the new device to their previous state.
☐ If you installed new software, run Add/Remove Programs and uninstall it.
☐ Reboot your computer.

Symptom: Windows 2000/XP fails to boot normally but will boot into Safe Mode.

Do the following and reboot after each change:

☐ Update virus definitions (if the PC can access the Internet) and perform a full virus scan. To access the Internet, choose Safe Mode with Networking on the Advanced Options Menu.
☐ Use Device Manager to uninstall or disable a device with problems or to roll back a driver.
☐ If you suspect a software program you have just installed, use the Add or Remove Programs applet to uninstall it.
☐ Review the Event Viewer logs. Focus on the most recent alerts.
☐ Download and apply the latest Windows updates.
☐ For Windows XP, if you suspect a recent configuration change is causing the problem, then run System Restore, and restore Windows XP to a previous state. If the latest restore point doesn't solve the problem, try a previous restore point, but know that all configuration changes made since the restore point was created will be lost.

TO LEARN MORE about using System Restore, see page 583 of Chapter 12 in *A+ Guide to Managing and Maintaining Your PC* or page 143 of Chapter 3 of *A+ Guide to Software.*

When applying a Windows XP restore point, you might inadvertently remove a user account that was added after the restore point was created. In this case, know that the user's My Documents folder has not been deleted. Back up the user's data, and recreate the user account.

☐ Run a Check Disk on your hard drive and check the two options to "Automatically fix file system errors" and "Scan for and attempt recovery of bad sectors." Reboot your computer. Check Disk should automatically run.
☐ Verify the hard drive has enough free space to run Windows. 15% free space is adequate.
☐ Defrag your hard drive. Depending on the amount of data on your hard drive, the process could take an hour or more.

☐ To verify Windows system files, run System File Checker (sfc.exe).
☐ The problem might be associated with a faulty application that is set to load when you start Windows 2000/XP. Run MSConfig.exe, and disable all programs that are set to run when Windows 2000/XP loads. Reboot to see if the problem disappears. If it does, then run MSConfig.exe again and re-enable one application at a time (reboot after enabling an application) until the error occurs again. This process will help track down the offending application. Uninstall the offending application, and find a newer version that is compatible with Windows 2000/XP.
☐ Check the event log file, ntbtlog.txt, for error messages.
☐ If you have a recent backup of the System State, restore the system from this backup.
☐ The problem might be associated with a component failure. Remove all unneeded devices and expansion cards from your computer. This includes printers, scanners, modems, sound cards, network cards, Zip drives, and CD-ROM drives. Reboot your computer.
☐ You might have a bad sector, master boot record (MBR), or Ntldr file, or your computer might be infected with a boot virus. Alternately, you might have a low-level component failure such as a faulty hard drive, power supply, hard drive controller, or motherboard. Proceed to *Using a Boot Disk to Troubleshoot XP.*
☐ If you suspect a hardware problem, replace your keyboard and mouse and then reboot. If you're using a USB keyboard and mouse, try replacing them with a standard keyboard and mouse.
☐ Replace your video adapter with a known good video adapter, preferably the same make and model.
☐ Have you modified your BIOS settings or flashed BIOS? If so, undo the BIOS changes you made or downgrade your BIOS to its previous version.

TO LEARN MORE about flashing BIOS, see page 251 of Chapter 6 in *A+ Guide to Managing and Maintaining Your PC* or page 199 of Chapter 5 in *A+ Guide to Hardware.*

☐ Check all IDE data cables for cuts or frays. Replace if necessary.

Using a Boot Disk to Troubleshoot Windows 2000/XP

You have gotten to this point in the Troubleshooting Tool if the following is true:

☐ Windows 2000/XP has started to load but gives errors or does not load, or the computer keeps rebooting or freezing.
☐ Video is working.
☐ You have already tried to solve the problem using Last Known Good Configuration and booting into Safe Mode.

Using the procedures in this section, you will create a Windows 2000/XP boot disk and use it to attempt to boot to the Windows 2000/XP desktop. If Windows 2000/XP loads successfully after booting from the boot disk, then the problem is associated with a missing or damaged boot sector, master boot record, Ntldr file, ntdetect.com file, ntbootdd.sys (if it exists), boot.ini file, or a virus infection. However, a boot disk cannot be used to troubleshoot problems associated with unstable device drivers or problems that occur after the Windows 2000 or Windows XP logo screen is displayed.

You will first create the boot disk by formatting the disk using a working Windows 2000/XP computer and then copying files to the disk. These files can be copied from (1) a Windows 2000/XP setup CD or (2) a Windows 2000/XP computer that is using the same version of Windows 2000 or Windows XP as the problem PC. Do the following to create the disk:

☐ Obtain a floppy disk, and format it on a Windows 2000/XP computer.
☐ Using Explorer, copy Ntldr and ntdetect.com from the \i386 folder on the Windows 2000 or Windows XP setup CD or a Windows 2000/XP computer to the root of the floppy disk.
☐ If your computer boots from a SCSI hard drive, then obtain a device driver (*.sys) for your SCSI hard drive, rename it ntbootdd.sys, and copy it to the root of the floppy disk. (If you used an incorrect device driver, then you will receive an error after booting from the floppy disk. The error will mention a "computer disk hardware configuration problem" and that it "could not read from the selected boot disk." If this occurs, contact your computer manufacturer for the correct version of the SCSI hard drive device driver for your computer.)
☐ After viewing Boot.ini on the problem computer, obtain an identical copy from another known good computer (or create your own) and copy it to the root of the floppy disk.

If the problem computer is booting from an IDE hard drive then its Boot.ini should be similar to:

```
[boot loader]
timeout=30
default=multi(0)disk(0)rdisk(0)partition(1)\WINDOWS
[operating systems]
multi(0)disk(0)rdisk(0)partition(1)\WINDOWS="Microsoft
 Windows XP Professional" /fastdetect
```

Please note that there is a carriage return after the /fastdetect switch.

☐ Write-protect the floppy disk so it cannot become infected with a virus.

TO LEARN MORE This section uses a Windows XP boot disk for troubleshooting. To learn more about this boot disk, see the Microsoft Knowledge Base Articles 305595 and 314503 at the Microsoft site *support.microsoft.com*.

TO LEARN MORE This section uses a Windows 2000 boot disk for troubleshooting. To learn more about this boot disk, see the Microsoft Knowledge Base Articles 301680 at the Microsoft site *support.microsoft.com*.

You have now created the Windows 2000 or Windows XP boot disk. Use the following troubleshooting steps in order to determine the cause of the boot failure:

☐ Enter the BIOS setup, and make sure the first boot device is set to the floppy disk.
☐ Insert the boot disk, and reboot your computer.
☐ If you are able to enter Windows 2000/XP successfully, with error messages, then continue following the steps here.

If you did not enter Windows 2000/XP successfully by using the boot disk, then proceed to *Using the Recovery Console to Troubleshoot 2000/XP.*

☐ Once Windows 2000/XP has loaded, update your virus definitions (if your computer has Internet access) and run a full virus scan.

☐ Open the Disk Management console, and verify that your computer's partition(s) is correct.

☐ Open Windows Explorer, and make sure "Show hidden files and folders" is selected.

☐ Open %SystemDrive%\boot.ini (usually C:\boot.ini) in WordPad, and verify its configuration using the sample Boot.ini file above.

☐ Copy Ntldr, Ntdetect.com, and Boot.ini from your floppy disk to %SystemDrive%, the root of the hard drive).

☐ If you're using a SCSI hard drive, copy Ntbootdd.sys from your floppy disk to %SystemDrive%.

☐ Remove the floppy disk, and reboot the computer to see if the problem has been resolved.

☐ If the problem has not been resolved, then boot from the floppy disk again, and back up your data on the hard drive to another disk or backup tape.

If you still cannot boot Windows 2000/XP successfully, then proceed to *Using the Recovery Console to Troubleshoot Windows 2000/XP*.

Using the Recovery Console to Troubleshoot Windows 2000/XP

You have reached this point in the Troubleshooting Tool if the following is true:

☐ Windows 2000/XP has started to load but gives errors or does not load, or the computer keeps rebooting or freezing.

☐ Video is working.

☐ You have already tried to solve the problem using Last Known Good Configuration, booting into Safe Mode, and booting from a Windows 2000 or Windows XP boot disk.

The Recovery Console is the next tool to use in attempting to solve the Windows 2000/XP boot problem. The Recovery Console is a DOS-like user interface that runs completely separate from Windows 2000/XP. In other words, it's like having a second operating system that you can use to repair the first one (Windows 2000/XP).

In general, here are some steps you can take when using the Recovery Console:

☐ Repair the MBR or repair the boot sector.

☐ Replace damaged system files and folders.

☐ Replace damaged or missing boot files.

☐ Enable and disable services that start when Windows 2000/XP loads.

☐ Copy important data files to another media.

☐ Create and format partitions.

For a complete listing of Recovery Console commands, see Recovery Console Commands in Appendix D (page D-1).

There are three ways to access the Recovery Console:

☐ **Boot from the Windows 2000 or Windows XP CD**. Change CMOS setup to boot from the CD-ROM drive. Insert the Windows 2000 or Windows XP

CD and reboot. When the Windows 2000/XP menu appears, select R to Repair Windows 2000/XP using the Recovery Console.

☐ **Select the Recovery Console boot option**. If you've installed the Recovery Console from inside Windows 2000/XP (by running ...\I386\Winnt32.exe / cmdcons from the Windows 2000 or Windows XP CD), you can select the boot option to load the Recovery Console from the Windows boot menu.

☐ **Boot from Windows 2000/XP Setup boot floppies**. For Windows 2000, boot from the setup floppy disks. For Windows XP, you can create a set of six boot floppy disks that allow you to access the Recovery Console.

 TO LEARN MORE about the six Windows XP boot disks and to obtain the executable file needed to create them, see the Microsoft Knowledge Base Article 310994 at the Microsoft Web site *support.microsoft.com*.

Do the following to load, log on, and use the Recovery Console:

☐ Using one of the methods above, load the Recovery Console.
☐ When the Recovery Console loads without errors, you are prompted to select the Windows 2000 or Windows XP installation folder. Select the folder.
☐ You'll then be prompted to enter the local administrator password. Enter the password.
☐ If the Recovery Console loads with errors, it will not require you to select an installation folder or enter the administrator password. Here are the errors it might encounter when it loads:

  ■ If the Recovery Console cannot find a hard drive, it displays the message, "Setup did not find any hard disks drives installed in your computer."

 GO TO If the Recovery Consider cannot find a hard drive, consider the problem a hardware problem and go to *Troubleshooting the Hard Drive* (page 47).

  ■ If the Recovery Console can find a hard drive but cannot read from it, it displays the message, "The path or file specified is not valid." A C prompt displays. Try the Diskpart command. The Fixmbr and Fixboot commands might help.
  ■ If the Recovery Console can read from the hard drive, but cannot find a Windows installation, a C prompt displays. Try the Dir command to see what files and folders are present. The Chkdsk command might help. If the Windows folder is seriously corrupted, you probably need to reinstall Windows rather than trying to repair it. Be sure to back up data before you leave the Recovery Console.

☐ If you are able to reach files and folders on the drive, take the time to back up any important data on the hard drive before proceeding to the next steps. Normally, the Recovery Console does not allow you to access folders other than the system folder, to copy data to another media, or to use wildcard characters. Use these Set commands to allow these actions:

```
Set allowallpaths = true
Set allowremovablemedia = true
Set allowwildcards = true
```

☐ Now use the Copy command to copy the data to another media. If you need to know the drive letter of a removable drive, use the Map command to display all drive letters and file system types.

After data is backed up, try the following steps to attempt to repair the Windows 2000/XP installation using the Recovery Console:

☐ Type CHKDSK C: /R to repair and recover from boot sector damage. If you receive an error message stating that Chkdsk cannot access your hard drive, then the problem is likely to be with the hard drive, hard drive controller, IDE data cable, or an incorrect hard drive jumper setting.

☐ When you run Chkdsk, if you receive an error message referring to a failure to fix all hardware problems, then the file system or Master Boot Record might be damaged (perhaps by a virus). Type Fixmbr to write a new Master Boot Record. For Windows 2000, you will receive the following message.

```
"This computer appears to have a non-standard or
invalid master boot record..."
```

This is an erroneous message that can be ignored, and is caused by a known flaw in the Fixmbr command.

 TO LEARN MORE about the problem with the Fixmbr command, see the Microsoft Knowledge Base Article 266745 at the Microsoft Web site *support.microsoft.com*.

If Fixmbr was successful, then you will receive the following message:

```
"Writing new master boot record on physical drive
\Device\Harddisk0\Partition0
The new master boot record has been successfully
written."
```

Continue with the following steps:

☐ Type Fixboot to write a new boot sector to the system partition.
☐ Reboot your computer to see if the problem has been resolved.
☐ If the problem has not been resolved, next try to disable services from running when Windows 2000/XP loads. A corrupted program file, newly installed software, or conflicting services might result in a service causing the boot to fail.

 For steps to use the Recovery Console to disable a service, see Appendix D, *Recovery Console Commands* (page D-1).

☐ Check for a corrupted registry. Typical error messages that indicate a corrupted registry might be, "Windows XP could not start because the following file is missing or corrupt: \WINDOWS\SYSTEM32\CONFIG\SYSTEM." Other corrupt files might be listed as: \WINDOWS\SYSTEM32\CONFIG\ SOFTWARE, \WINDOWS\SYSTEM32\CONFIG\SAM, \WINDOWS\ SYSTEM32\CONFIG\SECURITY, or \WINDOWS\SYSTEM32\ CONFIG\DEFAULT.

☐ If you suspect that the registry is corrupted, do the following to restore the registry from a previously saved state. You will first back up the corrupted registry files to the C:\Windows\Tmp folder, and then restore the registry from a special repair folder. In the steps below, we assume Windows is installed in C:\Windows. If your Windows is installed in a different folder (for example, C:\Winnt), substitute it in the command lines. Performing these steps will modify your program and user settings, so don't do this unless you're sure the registry is corrupted. Do the following:

- Load the Recovery Console and, when prompted, select the Windows 2000 or Windows XP installation folder, and enter the administrator password.
- Type the following commands, and press Enter after each command.

```
md tmp

copy c:\windows\system32\config\system
     c:\windows\tmp\system.bak
copy c:\windows\system32\config\software
     c:\windows\tmp\software.bak
copy c:\windows\system32\config\sam
     c:\windows\tmp\sam.bak
copy c:\windows\system32\config\security
     c:\windows\tmp\security.bak
copy c:\windows\system32\config\default
     c:\windows\tmp\default.bak
delete c:\windows\system32\config\system
delete c:\windows\system32\config\software
delete c:\windows\system32\config\sam
delete c:\windows\system32\config\security
delete c:\windows\system32\config\default
copy c:\windows\repair\system
     c:\windows\system32\config\system
copy c:\windows\repair\software
     c:\windows\system32\config\software
copy c:\windows\repair\sam c:\windows\system32\
     config\sam
copy c:\windows\repair\security
     c:\windows\system32\config\security
copy c:\windows\repair\default
     c:\windows\system32\config\default
```

☐ Type Exit to log out from the Recovery Console, and reboot your computer.

 TO LEARN MORE For Windows XP, if you use System Restore (turned on by default), you can use it to restore your user and program settings. For more information and additional instructions, see the Microsoft Knowledge Base Article 307545 at the Microsoft Web site *support.microsoft.com*.

Using the Recovery Console to Disable Services in Windows 2000/XP

You have gotten to this point in the Troubleshooting Tool if the following is true:

☐ Windows 2000/XP has started to load but gives errors or does not load, or the computer keeps rebooting or freezing.

☐ Video is working.

☐ You are using the Recovery Console to systematically eliminate services and other background tasks that might prevent Windows 2000/XP from loading.

A service that is set to automatically start when the operating system starts might be preventing Windows 2000/XP from loading properly. The service causing the problem might have been introduced from newly installed software, might be an existing service that has become corrupted, or might be conflicting with another service. The solution is to first identify the offending service and then disable it from within the Recovery Console. Do the following:

☐ Try once again to load Windows 2000/XP in Safe Mode, but this time, while the OS is attempting to load in Safe Mode, watch for information that can help you determine which service is causing the problem. You can also examine the C:\Windows\Ntbtlog.txt file after the Safe Mode desktop loads.

 Boot logging is automatically turned on when you boot into Safe Mode.

☐ If the computer hangs while entering Safe Mode, then the last line listed should be the offending service. For example, if the last line refers to Agp440.sys, then the operating system is hanging when it attempts to load the Agp440 service. (The Agp440 service might not load properly if problems exist with your video driver configuration.)

☐ If Safe Mode loads properly, then uninstall any software that was just installed. If you cannot load Safe Mode, proceed to the next step.

☐ Enter the Recovery Console and type "disable agp440" (without quotes). This stops the Agp440 service from automatically loading when Windows 2000/XP starts.

☐ Restart your computer. If the problem is solved, then it was caused by the Agp400 service. Then you might need to upgrade the video driver software on your computer.

☐ If the problem still exists, then enter the Recovery Console and type "listsvc" (without quotes). This command will display a list of all installed services and their current setting (for example, load automatically, load manually, disabled). Disable any services that are set to automatically start and might have been introduced from newly installed software.

 TO LEARN MORE For more information about disabling services when troubleshooting Windows 2000/XP, see the Knowledge Base Article 310602 at the Microsoft site *support.microsoft.com*.

 TO LEARN MORE For more information about problems with the Agp440 service, see the Knowledge Base Article 324764 at the Microsoft site *support.microsoft.com*.

Performing a Reinstallation (Repair) of Windows 2000/XP

You have reached this point in the Troubleshooting Tool if the following is true:

☐ Windows 2000/XP has started to load but gives errors or does not load, or the computer keeps rebooting or freezing.
☐ Video is working.
☐ You have already tried to solve the problem using Last Known Good Configuration, booting into Safe Mode, booting from a Windows 2000 or Windows XP boot disk, and using the Recovery Console.

Performing a reinstallation of Windows 2000/XP might be your last option for repairing a computer that will not load Windows 2000/XP successfully. If you perform the steps described in this section to reinstall Windows 2000/XP, you might lose data or program settings. You will also be required to reactivate

Windows XP after completing the successful reinstallation. Follow the steps listed below.

☐ Insert the correct version of the Windows 2000 or Windows XP CD (either Home or Professional) into your CD-ROM drive.

☐ Enter CMOS setup, and make sure that the first boot device is set to the CD-ROM drive. Also verify that write protection to the boot sector is disabled.

☐ Reboot your computer, and, when prompted, press any key to boot from the Windows 2000 or Windows XP CD.

☐ If your setup CD does not include Windows XP Service Pack 1 (SP1), then boot into the Recovery Console and delete %SystemRoot%\System32\ Undo_guimode.txt. Deleting this file fixes a bug that was patched in SP1 that caused data and program settings to be lost after reinstalling Windows XP.

☐ Press Enter to start the Windows 2000/XP setup process.

☐ Press F8 to accept the license agreement. The setup screen in Figure 4-6 appears.

☐ Verify that your original installation of Windows 2000 or Windows XP is selected, and press R to begin the repair process. During the installation, you'll be asked for the product key.

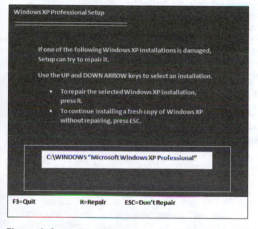

Figure 4-6 Windows XP Setup can repair the selected Windows installation

 The Windows XP product key is affixed to the back of the setup documentation booklet. Technicians sometimes paste the product key sticker on the side of a computer case or the bottom of a notebook.

☐ If the repair process gives problems or the original problem is still not solved, back up important data, and perform a clean installation of the OS.

Tricky Boot Problems, Solutions, and Tips

In order to diagnose Windows 2000/XP boot failures, it's important to understand how Windows 2000/XP is loaded. The following is a brief overview of the boot process.

> **TO LEARN MORE** For more detailed information on the Windows 2000/XP boot process, begin with page 686 in Chapter 14 of *A+ Guide to Managing and Maintaining Your PC* or page 246 of Chapter 5 in *A+ Guide to Software*.

- ☐ Turn ON the computer (cold boot).
- ☐ A power-on self-test (POST) is run.
- ☐ The operating system begins to load.
- ☐ The Windows 2000/XP logo screen appears, and the user enters a valid user account and password.
- ☐ The Windows 2000/XP desktop appears.

Here are some valuable computing practices that will help to prevent problems:

- ☐ Regularly run real-time antivirus software, and keep the virus definitions updated.
- ☐ Run a good software firewall. For Windows XP, turn on Windows Firewall.
- ☐ Regularly use the Microsoft Windows Update site (*windowsupdate.microsoft.com/*) to install patches and service packs as needed. For example, there is a known problem with the released version of Windows XP where the hard drive can become unreadable when caching is enabled. This problem causes the computer to boot to a blue screen with the error message "Unmountable_Boot_Volume" displayed. This error has been fixed in Service Pack 1.
- ☐ Perform monthly maintenance of your computer by running the error-checking (chkdsk.exe) and defragmentation (defrag.exe or dfrg.msc) utilities.
- ☐ Review the Event Viewer logs, and watch for problems and critical errors.

Symptom: The computer is frozen and will not shut down after pressing the power button.

- ☐ To shut the computer down, try pressing and holding the power button down for 10 seconds.
- ☐ Unplug the power cord from the back of the computer.

Symptom: Windows 2000/XP has started to load (or is currently running) and automatically reboots.

- ☐ By default, Windows 2000/XP is set to automatically reboot if it encounters a system failure.
- ☐ To change this setting after the problem is occurring, try booting into Safe Mode and then right-click My Computer, and select Properties from the short-cut menu. Then click the Advanced tab. Under the Startup and Recovery pane, click Settings. In the Startup and Recovery dialog box, uncheck Automatically Restart. The next time this error occurs, a screen will appear that describes the source of the error. These errors are called STOP errors.
- ☐ For Windows XP, if the system is continually restarting because of an error, press F8 to access the Advanced Options Menu, and select "Disable automatic restart on system failure."

GO TO For a comprehensive list of Windows 2000/XP STOP errors and what to do about them, see Appendix E, *Windows 2000/XP STOP Errors* (page E-1).

Symptom: From a cold boot, POST runs successfully, but Windows 2000/XP boots to a black screen after displaying the Windows 2000/XP logo screen.

- ☐ Make sure the video cable is securely connected to the computer.
- ☐ Make sure the video adapter drivers are compatible with Windows 2000/XP. If the drivers are not compatible, you are notified as the drivers are installed.

Contact the video adapter manufacturer to obtain the newest video drivers for Windows 2000/XP.

☐ Your current computer resolution might not be supported by the video adapter or might be set incorrectly. Press F8 during the boot to access the Advanced Option menu, and choose "Enable VGA Mode." After Windows 2000/XP loads, reset the resolution.

☐ Replace the video adapter with a known good adapter, preferably the same make and model.

☐ Replace the monitor with a known good monitor.

☐ Reseat memory modules.

☐ Remove all unneeded devices, ISA cards, and PCI cards from your computer. These include printers, scanners, modems, sound cards, network cards, Zip drives, and CD-ROM drives. Reboot your computer.

Symptom: POST runs successfully, but Windows 2000/XP boots to a black screen and does NOT display the Windows 2000/XP logo screen.

☐ This problem might be due to a damaged or missing Master Boot Record, partition table, boot sector, Ntldr file, ntdetect.com file, or incorrect ntbootdd.sys driver. Your computer might also be infected with a virus.

 Proceed to *Using Last Known Good Configuration to Troubleshoot Windows 2000/XP* (page 72).

Symptom: Windows 2000/XP has started to load but gives a blue-screen error message (a STOP error).

☐ See Table 4-9, Error messages while loading Windows 2000/XP. If the STOP error is not listed in the table, search the Microsoft Knowledge Base Web site for the error message.

 For more information about STOP errors, see Appendix E, *Windows 2000/XP STOP Errors*.

 TO LEARN MORE To identify a Windows stop error, type the 10-character error number or the error message in the search box of the Microsoft Knowledge Base Web site at *support.microsoft.com* to identify the Windows STOP error.

☐ Review the Event Viewer logs.

☐ By default, a small memory dump file (named memory.dmp) is generated whenever a STOP error occurs. This file is saved in the %SystemRoot%\Minidump folder. Rename memory.dmp after the computer restarts in order to prevent it from being overwritten, and then perform an analysis of the file using dumpchk.exe.

Symptom: Windows 2000/XP has started to load but gives an error message as soon as the logon window is displayed.

☐ If you've recently installed any software, uninstall it and reboot your computer.

☐ If the problem still exists, write down the error message and then run regedit.exe. Check the registry key HKEY_LOCAL_MACHINE\ SOFTWARE\Microsoft\Windows NT\CurrentVersion\Winlogon for a registry entry whose name matches the error. If found, delete the registry entry.

☐ Some versions of antivirus software are known to create this type of error if a failure has occurred during installation or uninstallation. Check the antivirus software Web site for more information.

☐ Use Msconfig to disable all startup processes and services. Reboot. If the problem has disappeared, enable one after another until you find the process causing the problem. Reboot after you have enabled each process or service.

Symptom: Windows XP has started to load, is stuck in a check disk (Chkdsk) loop, and does not load the user interface.

☐ This error can occur if you've run error checking (Chkdsk) and checked the options to "Automatically fix file system errors" and "Scan for and attempt recovery of bad sectors."

☐ To solve this problem, manually shut down your computer, and choose the "Last Known Good Configuration" option on the Advanced Options menu.

☐ This problem has been fixed in Service Pack 1. Download and apply Service Pack 2, which includes previous patches.

TO LEARN MORE about Windows Update and applying service packs, see page 534 of Chapter 11 in *A+ Guide to Managing and Maintaining Your PC* or page 94 of Chapter 2 in *A+ Guide to Software*.

Symptom: Windows XP displays a "System Has Recovered from a Serious Error" message after every restart.

☐ This problem can occur after a memory dump file is written. A Windows XP bug sets a flag on the paging file that tells Windows XP to write a memory dump file even though it has already been written.

☐ Uninstall any software that was recently installed to see if the error disappears. This error has been seen after installing some versions of Palm Pilot software.

☐ To correct the problem, apply the latest Windows XP service pack.

Symptom: Need to run Recovery Console and do not have a Windows XP CD.

☐ If you do not have access to the Windows XP CD, you might not be able to boot your computer into the Recovery Console.

☐ Your first option is to borrow a Windows XP CD.

☐ Your second option is to create a set of six boot disks that allows you to run Windows XP setup. After booting from the six disks, you should be able to log on to the Recovery Console. The boot disk set can be created from a single executable program, which can be downloaded from Microsoft.

TO LEARN MORE about the six Windows XP boot disks and to obtain the executable file needed to create them, see the Microsoft Knowledge Base Article 310994 at the Microsoft site *support.microsoft.com*.

Symptom: Once the Recovery Console has loaded, you are unable to log on successfully.

☐ When prompted for a password, be sure to type the administrator's password on the local computer.

Symptom: Once the Recovery Console has loaded, you are unable to log on successfully when using the local administrator password.

The following error message displays when using the correct local administrator password:

```
The password is not valid. Please retype the password.
Type the Administrator password:
```

This problem is caused by Sysprep (version 2.0), a Microsoft utility used by many computer manufacturers and network administrators to deploy Windows XP. Sysprep modifies how passwords are stored in the Windows XP registry, causing the Recovery Console to be unable to verify the local administrator's password. If you cannot load the Windows XP desktop, you might have to reinstall Windows XP.

Once you can load the Windows XP desktop, do one of the following to fix the logon problem when using the Recovery Console:

☐ Install Windows XP Service Pack 1.
☐ Configure the Recovery Console so you will not be prompted for a local administrator password. Do the following:
  ■ Open the Control Panel.
  ■ Click Administrative Tools, Local Security Policy.
  ■ Under Security Settings, click Local Policies, Security Options.
  ■ Scroll through the settings on the Policy pane until you find "Recovery console: Allow automatic administrative logon."
  ■ Double-click the Recovery Console setting, and set it to Enable.
  ■ Click OK, and close all windows.

Symptom: For Windows XP, the error message "Procedure Entry Point Not Found in Msvcrt.dll File" appears, and the boot fails.

Use the Recovery Console to replace the msvcrt.dll file. Do the following:

☐ Insert the Windows XP setup CD in the CD-ROM drive.
☐ Load the Recovery Console, and log in.
☐ Enter these commands:

```
cd system32
ren msvcrt.dll msvcrt.bak
D: (substitute the drive letter of your CD-ROM drive)
cd \i386
expand msvcrt.dl_ C:\windows\system32 (substitute a different
path to Windows as necessary)
exit
```

☐ Note that if you don't know the drive letter of the CD-ROM drive, use the Recovery Console Map command. In the resulting display, the CD-ROM drive letter is listed as \Device\Cdrom0.

TO LEARN MORE about this problem with msvcrt.dll, see the Microsoft Knowledge Base Article 324762 at *support.microsoft.com*.

Symptom: Windows XP continually reattempts to load, and the logon screen does not appear.

This problem is likely caused by a corrupted kernel32.dll file. Do the following to restore the file from the Windows XP setup CD:

☐ Insert the Windows XP setup CD in the CD-ROM drive.
☐ Load the Recovery Console and log in.

☐ Enter the following commands:

```
cd system32
ren kernel32.dll kernel32.bak
expand D:\i386\kernel32.dl_  (Substitute the drive letter of your
CD-ROM drive)
exit
```

☐ Note that if you don't know the drive letter of the CD-ROM drive, use the Recovery Console Map command. In the resulting display, the CD-ROM drive letter is listed as \Device\Cdrom0.

TO LEARN MORE about this problem with continuous restarts, see the Microsoft Knowledge Base Article 310396 at *support.microsoft.com*.

Symptom: The Windows XP error message "Windows Could Not Start Because of a Computer Disk Hardware Configuration Problem" appears, and the boot fails.

This problem is caused by an error in the Boot.ini file, a corrupt or missing Ntoskrnl.exe file, or a general hardware failure. Do the following:

☐ Load the Recovery Console, and log in.
☐ Use the following command:

```
bootcfg /rebuild
```

☐ During the resulting operation, you must answer several questions:
  ■ When the question "Add installation to boot list?" is asked, type "Y."
  ■ When asked "Enter Load Identifier," type "Windows XP Professional" or "Windows XP Home Edition."
  ■ When asked "Enter OS Load options," leave the field blank, and press Enter.
☐ Restart the computer. When you get to the Windows desktop, check the Boot.ini file for errors.
☐ If Windows XP fails to load, try using the Recovery Console to restore the Ntoskrnl.exe file from the Windows XP setup CD.

TO LEARN MORE about this problem with the Boot.ini file and other errors, see the Microsoft Knowledge Base Article 314477 at *support.microsoft.com*.

Symptom: How can I automatically install the Recovery Console on every computer in my organization from a login script?

☐ Undocumented tip! Run ...\I386\Winnt32.exe /cmdcons /unattend from the Windows 2000/XP CD setup files stored on your network server.

TROUBLESHOOTING LOADING WINDOWS 9X

You have gotten to this point in the Troubleshooting Tool if the following is true:

□ The PC does not boot properly.
□ There is confirmed power to both the PC and the monitor.
□ Windows 9x has started to load but gives errors.

Table 4-10 lists noteworthy function keys when loading Windows 9x. Use Troubleshooting Flowchart 4-4 as your troubleshooting tool at this point.

Table 4-10 Important function keys while loading Windows 9x

Function key	Purpose
F4	Load previous version of MS-DOS
F5	Start in Safe Mode
F8 or Ctrl	Display Startup menu
Shift-F8	Step-by-step confirmation

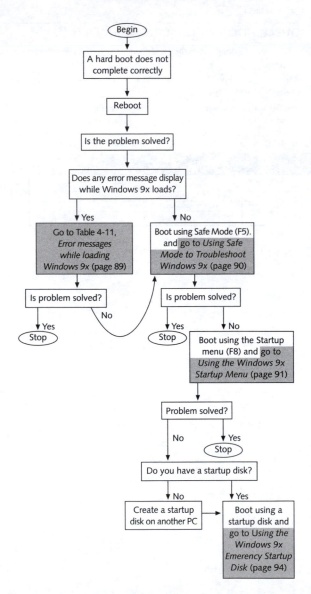

Flowchart 4-4 Troubleshooting loading Windows 9x

Symptom: An error message appears while loading Windows 9x.

Use Table 4–11 as your troubleshooting tool at this point.

Table 4-11 Error messages while loading Windows 9x

Error message	What to do
MS-DOS compatibility mode	• Windows is using real-mode drivers to access the hard disk rather than the preferred 32-bit drivers. Remove any references to real-mode drivers for the hard disk in CONFIG.SYS and system.ini. Back up these files first. • The problem might be with an outdated motherboard BIOS. Consider updating the BIOS.
Bad or missing file Real-mode driver missing or damaged	• Check the CONFIG.SYS, AUTOEXEC.BAT, or System.ini entries for errors. • Verify that the file is present and in the right location. • Verify the integrity of the file.
Windows gives an error message about BIOS being incompatible	• CMOS might be set so that Windows Setup cannot write to the boot sector so as to protect it from a virus. Disable the setting in CMOS.
Cannot open file *.INF	• This error is caused by not enough memory. Disable any TSRs running in AUTOEXEC.BAT. • Close any applications running.
Insufficient disk space	Run ScanDisk and Defragmenter. Check free space on the hard drive.

Invalid system disk	• Suspect a boot sector virus. Run a current version of antivirus software.
	• IO.SYS is missing or corrupted. Restore the file from a backup or an emergency startup disk. To restore all real-mode files needed to begin loading Windows 9x, do the following:
	  – Boot from a Windows 9x emergency startup disk.
	  – To restore IO.SYS, MSDOS.SYS, DRV-SPACE.BIN, and COMMAND.COM, execute the command SYS C:.
	  – Remove the floppy disk and reboot.
	• If this error occurs while installing Windows, disable boot sector protection in CMOS setup, and remove any antivirus software running as a TSR. The problem is caused by these programs not allowing Windows to write to the boot sector.
	• If this error occurs while installing Windows when disk management software (for example, DrivePro) is running, Windows might have damaged the hard drive MBR. To recover from the problem, see the documentation for the disk management software.

Invalid VxD dynamic link call from IFSMGR	This error is caused by a missing or corrupted MSDOS.SYS file. Restore the file from a backup or from an emergency startup disk.
Missing system files	Run the SYS C: command as described above.

(continued)

Table 4-11 Error messages while loading Windows 9x (continued)

Error message	What to do
System Registry file missing	Either SYSTEM.DAT or USER.DAT is corrupted or missing. For Windows 98/Me, restore using Scanreg. For Windows 95, restore using either SYSTEM.DA0 or USER.DA0. If these two files are also missing or corrupted, then restore the registry from a backup, or run Windows Setup.
VxD error returns to command prompt	• A VxD file might be missing or corrupted. Run Windows Setup, and choose to Verify installed components. • Right-click Network Neighborhood, and click Properties. Check to see if the network card is listed twice. If so, delete both listings and reboot.

TO LEARN MORE about MS-DOS compatibility mode, see page 803 of Chapter 16 in *A+ Guide to Managing and Maintaining Your PC* or page 363 in *A+ Guide to Software*.

Using Safe Mode to Troubleshoot Windows 9x

Press F5 while Windows 9x is loading to enter Safe Mode.

If the OS cannot load in Safe Mode, proceed to the next section, *Using the Windows 9x Startup Menu* (page 91).

Safe Mode starts Windows 9x with a minimum default configuration to give you an opportunity to correct an error in the configuration. Safe Mode does not execute entries in the registry, CONFIG.SYS, AUTOEXEC.BAT, and the [Boot] and [386Enh] sections of System.ini. Only the mouse, keyboard, and standard VGA drivers are loaded.

Once in Safe Mode, do the following:

☐ Use a current version of antivirus software to scan for a virus.
☐ Sometimes loading into Safe Mode is all that is needed. Try to reboot the PC in Normal mode.
☐ If the Safe Recovery dialog box appears, select the option Use Safe Recovery. Windows 9x will then attempt to recover from previous boot problems. Try to boot again.
☐ If you were having problems with a device installation before the Windows failure, disable the device in Device Manager. Reboot after disabling each device that you suspect.
☐ If you just installed new software or hardware, remove the hardware device or uninstall the software.
☐ If you had just made configuration changes, undo the changes and reboot.
☐ Remove all unnecessary devices and cards (modem, network, sound, printer, scanner, etc.) from computer and reboot.

☐ Look for real mode drivers or TSRs (programs loaded in either CONFIG.SYS, AUTOEXEC.BAT, or System.ini) that might be causing a problem and disable them by inserting a REM at the beginning of the command line.

☐ Try to boot again. If the problem is still not solved, restore the registry by running Scanreg. For Windows 95, overwrite SYSTEM.DAT with SYSTEM.DA0 and USER.DAT with USER.DA0. First make backup copies of the Registry files.

 TO LEARN MORE about recovering from a corrupted registry using the Windows 98 Scanreg utility, see page 817 of Chapter 16 in *A+ Guide to Managing and Maintaining Your PC* or page 377 of Chapter 7 in *A+ Guide to Software*.

☐ Run ScanDisk to repair errors on the hard drive and optimize the drive. (While in Safe Mode, select Start, Programs, Accessories, System Tools, and ScanDisk. Under Type of Test, select Thorough.)

☐ Run Defrag to optimize the drive.

☐ For Windows 98, run System File Checker to verify system files.

☐ For Windows 98, run Automatic Skip Driver Agent to skip loading any driver that is causing a problem. Reboot and examine the Asd.log file for recorded errors.

☐ For Windows 98, use System Configuration Utility (Msconfig.exe) to further reduce the system to essentials, and reboot. If the problem goes away, restore one item at a time until the problem returns so as to identify the item that is the source of the problem.

 TO LEARN MORE about the System Configuration Utility, see page 813 of Chapter 16 in *A+ Guide to Managing and Maintaining Your PC* or page 373 of Chapter 7 in *A+ Guide to Software*.

☐ Using Windows Explorer, search for files in system folders that have recently changed. To sort file and folder names by date last modified using Explorer, click Modified. To reverse the sort order, Ctrl-click Modified. If software or drivers have been installed recently, suspect them to be the source of the problem.

Using the Windows 9x Startup Menu

The Startup menu is useful in solving boot problems. Press Ctrl or F8 while the message "Starting Windows 98" displays during the boot process to display the following Startup menu:

```
1.   Normal
2.   Logged (\BOOTLOG.TXT)
3.   Safe Mode
4.   Safe Mode with network support
5.   Step-by-step confirmation
6.   Command prompt only
7.   Safe Mode command prompt only
8.   Previous version of MS-DOS
Enter a choice: 1
```

 If the Startup Menu does not load, then go to the section *Using the Windows 9x Emergency Startup Disk* (page 94).

The following text describes what to expect when you select each option on the menu.

Option 1: Normal

In MSDOS.SYS, if BootGUI=1, then this option starts Windows 9x. If BootGUI=0, then this option will boot to the DOS 7.0 or DOS 7.1 prompt. Either way, the commands in AUTOEXEC.BAT and CONFIG.SYS are executed.

Option 2: Logged (\BOOTLOG.TXT)

This option is the same as choosing Normal, except that Windows 9x tracks the load and startup activities and logs them to this file. Check the file content for clues for problem solving.

Option 3: Safe Mode

Windows loads with a minimum configuration.

 For more information, see the previous section, *Using Safe Mode to Troubleshoot Windows 9x* (page 90).

Option 4: Safe Mode with Network Support

Network drivers are loaded when booting into Safe Mode. This option is useful if Windows 9x is stored on a network server and you need to download changes to your PC in Safe Mode. This option applies only to Windows 95; Windows 98 automatically includes network support with Safe Mode.

To eliminate the network connection as a source of the problem, first boot in Safe Mode without network support, and then boot in Safe Mode with network support. If the boot without network support is successful, but the boot with network support gives errors, then suspect the network drivers to be the source of the problem.

Option 5: Step-by-Step Confirmation

The option asks for confirmation before executing each command in IO.SYS, CONFIG.SYS, and AUTOEXEC.BAT. You can accomplish the same thing by pressing Shift-F8 when the message "Starting Windows 95/98" is displayed. This step is extremely useful in determining the exact point of failure during the Windows 9x boot process.

Option 6: Command Prompt Only

This option executes the contents of AUTOEXEC.BAT and CONFIG.SYS but doesn't start Windows 9x. You will be given a DOS prompt. Type WIN to load Windows 9x.

Option 7: Safe Mode Command Prompt Only

This option does not execute the commands in AUTOEXEC.BAT or CONFIG.SYS. You will be given a DOS prompt. Type WIN to load Windows 9x.

Option 8: Previous Version of MS-DOS

This option loads a previous version of DOS if one is present. You can get the same results by pressing F4 when the message "Starting Windows 95/98" is displayed. This option is not available with Windows 98SE or Windows Me.

Troubleshooting with the Windows 9x Startup Menu

Use the following list as your troubleshooting tool at this point.

- ☐ Try a hard boot. A soft boot might not do the trick, because TSRs are not always "kicked out" of RAM with a soft boot.
- ☐ If you have not already done so, try Safe Mode next.

 Go to *Using Safe Mode to Troubleshoot Windows 9x* earlier in this section (page 90).

- ☐ Try the option Step-by-Step Confirmation next. Look for error messages caused by a missing or bad driver file. Try not allowing real-mode drivers to load. Once the problem command is identified, you can eliminate the command or troubleshoot it.
- ☐ Use the Logged option next, and examine the BOOTLOG.TXT file created. Perhaps the log will identify the problem.
- ☐ Try booting using the Command Prompt Only option.
- ☐ From the command prompt, run the real-mode version of ScanDisk to scan the hard drive for errors. Use one of these two methods:
  - From a command prompt, enter this command:

    `C:\Windows\Command\Scandisk`

    If the Scandisk.exe program on the hard drive is corrupted, use the one on the emergency rescue disk.
  - If you are working from a command prompt and are using a compressed drive, add this parameter to the Scandisk command:

For DriveSpace 3: `C:\Windows\Command\Scandisk drvspace.nnn`

For DoubleSpace: `C:\Windows\Command\Scandisk dblspace.nnn`

  - In the command line, substitute the file extension for the compressed volume file on the host drive—for example, Drvspace.000 or Dblspace.000.

- ☐ For Windows 98, from the command prompt, type Scanreg/Fix and try to reboot.
- ☐ For Windows 98, from the command prompt, next type Scanreg/Restore, and select the latest known good backup of the Windows 9x registry. Try to reboot.
- ☐ From the command prompt, you can use the WIN command with switches to try loading Windows. Try the following switches:

`WIN /D:F`	Turns off 32-bit disk access. Use this option if there appears to be a problem with hard drive access.
`WIN /D:S`	Instructs Windows to not use memory address F000:0 as a break point.
`WIN /D:V`	Instructs Windows that system BIOS should be used to access the hard drive.
`WIN /D:X`	Excludes all upper memory addresses from real-mode drivers.

- [ ] If one of these commands solves the problem, look for real-mode drivers that might be in conflict, eliminating those that you can. Examine the BOOTLOG.TXT file for errors. Try booting in Safe Mode again.
- [ ] Try booting with Safe Mode Command Prompt Only. When in Safe Mode, the registry is not executed. If you suspect a corrupted registry, restore it to its last saved version: For Windows 98/Me, use the Scanreg command. For Windows 95, copy SYSTEM.DA0 to SYSTEM.DAT and USER.DA0 to USER.DAT. Next try the WIN command to execute Windows normally. If that step doesn't work, try the WIN command using the same switches listed above.

If you still are unable to boot, proceed to the next section, *Using the Windows 9x Emergency Startup Disk*.

Using the Windows 9x Emergency Startup Disk

You have gotten to this point if the following is true:

- [ ] Power to the computer and the monitor is confirmed working.
- [ ] You are unable to boot from the hard drive using Safe Mode or any of the options under the Windows 9x Startup menu.

Use the following list as your troubleshooting tool at this point:

- [ ] Try booting from the emergency startup disk (ESD). You should get an A prompt. If not, verify that your floppy disk is bootable by trying it on another machine. (Be careful not to spread a virus in doing so.)

TO LEARN MORE about the Windows 9x emergency startup disk, including how to create one, begin with page 766 of Chapter 15 in *A+ Guide to Managing and Maintaining Your PC* or begin with page 326 of Chapter 6 in *A+ Guide to Software*.

- [ ] Try to access the hard drive from the A prompt using the command DIR C:. If this step works, then the problem lies in the software that is used on the hard drive to boot, including the partition table, master boot record, OS hidden files, and command interface files. If you cannot access the hard drive, the problem is with the hard drive subsystem. In either case, you need to examine the hard drive for errors.
- [ ] One of the first things you will do when troubleshooting the hard drive is to check for a virus. If you find one, consider the ESD you just used to be contaminated and destroy it.

Go to *Troubleshooting the Hard Drive* (page 47).

- [ ] After you have completed troubleshooting the hard drive, eliminating physical problems with the hard drive subsystem, CMOS, and the partition table, then the next step is to run the Windows 9x Setup program. When given the opportunity, select Verify installed components. Setup will then restore damaged or missing system files.

Symptom: Windows 9x stalls during the first restart after installation.

- [ ] This is likely because legacy hardware was configured incorrectly. Comment out all references to the hardware in CONFIG.SYS and AUTOEXEC.BAT.
- [ ] Check that all SCSI devices are terminated correctly.

☐ Disable the ISA enumerator. To do that remove this line from the [386Enh] section of System.ini: device = ISAPNP.386.

☐ If you get a "Bad or missing file" message, check the syntax of the command line entry in CONFIG.SYS or AUTOEXEC.BAT. Check that the file is in the right location. Restore the file.

☐ If you get an error message about the computer's BIOS, disable the Boot Sector protection feature in CMOS setup, and then reinstall Windows.

☐ If you get an error message about a missing or damaged VxD file, run Windows Setup, and select Verify to replace the missing VxD.

Symptom: After an upgrade from Windows 95 to Windows 98, the startup screen still says Windows 95.

This problem can have two possible causes:

☐ The IO.SYS file has not been updated. Replace IO.SYS by running the SYS C: command.

☐ The file Logo.sys is in the root directory, which overrides the logo screen embedded in IO.SYS. Delete or replace the file.

TROUBLESHOOTING LOADING DOS

You have gotten to this point in the Troubleshooting Tool if the following is true:

☐ The PC does not boot properly.
☐ Video is working.
☐ DOS has started to load but gives errors.

Once startup BIOS turns to the hard drive to load DOS, the components/files on the drive needed to load DOS successfully are the MBR, the partition table, the DOS boot record on the active partition, IO.SYS (or IBMBIO.COM), MSDOS.SYS (or IBMDOS.COM), and COMMAND.COM. CONFIG.SYS and AUTOEXEC.BAT are optional.

 TO LEARN MORE about the details of the DOS boot process, see page 742 of Chapter 15 in A+ Guide to Managing and Maintaining Your PC or page 302 of Chapter 6 of A+ Guide to Software.

Symptom: An error message is displayed while loading DOS.

Table 4–12 lists error messages that display while loading DOS and what to do about them.

Table 4-12 Error messages while loading DOS

Error	Meaning of error message and what to do
"Bad sector" errors	• Bad sectors on the hard drive are encountered when trying to load the OS. • Boot from a floppy, and run ScanDisk.
Incorrect DOS version	• You are attempting to use a DOS command such as FORMAT. When DOS looks at the FORMAT.COM program file, it finds that the file belongs to a different version of DOS than the one that is now running. • Use the DOS software from the same version that you are running.
Invalid drive specification	• The PC is unable to find a hard drive or a floppy drive that setup tells it to expect. The hard drive might have a corrupted partition table. • Boot from a floppy disk, and go to *Troubleshooting the Hard Drive* (page 47).
Invalid or missing COMMAND.COM	• This error might be caused by a nonbooting disk in drive A, or COMMAND.COM on drive C might have been erased. • Remove the disk, and boot from the hard drive. • After booting from the hard drive, if you still get the error, restore COMMAND.COM to the root directory. Look for a backup copy of the file in the \DOS directory.
Non-system disk or disk error	• COMMAND.COM or one of two DOS hidden files is missing from the disk or the hard drive. • Remove the disk and boot from the hard drive. • After booting from the hard drive, if you still get the error, then system files are missing from the hard drive. Boot from a floppy disk and restore system files using the SYS C: command.
Not ready reading drive A: Abort, Retry, Fail?	• The disk in drive A is missing, is not formatted, or is corrupted. • Try another disk.

Symptom: The system hangs, or an unidentified error message is displayed while loading DOS.

Use the list below as your troubleshooting tool at this point:

☐ Press Shift-F8 while DOS is loading. For some PCs, this option allows you to step through the boot process as commands in CONFIG.SYS and AUTOEXEC.BAT are executed. If you encounter an error in either file, then troubleshoot that command line. If Shift-F8 does not work on your PC, you can bypass individual lines in these two files by putting REM in front of the line. Restore first one line and then the other until you identify the problem line. Work at first getting a C prompt before you attempt to load Windows 3.x by commenting out the command WIN in AUTOEXEC.BAT to load Windows.

☐ Rename CONFIG.SYS and AUTOEXEC.BAT, and reboot to bypass both files entirely. If you get a C prompt, then the problem is with one of these files. First return CONFIG.SYS to its original name, and reboot to eliminate it as the problem. Then rename AUTOEXEC.BAT to its original name to eliminate it. The idea is to isolate the problem to the file and the command within the file.

☐ Boot from a floppy disk using the same version of DOS as on the hard drive. It's important that the versions be the same because you might need to restore DOS files on the hard drive from the floppy. You should get an A prompt. (Note: Later if you discover a virus on the hard drive, destroy this disk.)

☐ Attempt to access the hard drive using the command DIR C:.

If you can't access the hard drive, then go to *Troubleshooting the Hard Drive* (page 47).

☐ If you can access the hard disk, run a current version of antivirus software to check for a virus.

☐ The problem might be the system files on the hard disk. Execute the command SYS C: to restore these files, and reboot.

☐ Check CONFIG.SYS and AUTOEXEC.BAT for TSRs that can be eliminated to create the cleanest boot possible.

TROUBLESHOOTING PROBLEMS AFTER THE PC BOOTS

To solve a PC problem after the PC boots, after interviewing the user, if important data on the hard drive is not backed up, first try to save it to another media. Then begin troubleshooting by recreating the problem. Next, decide if the problem is caused by software or hardware. Then isolate the problem by eliminating the unnecessary, including hardware and software as appropriate, trading suspected bad for known good, or installing a suspected bad component in a working system. (See Flowchart 4-5 for guidance on how to isolate the problem.) Once you have identified the source of the problem, see the general instructions in the next section to help you solve the problem, consult the Troubleshooting Roadmap, where you can find the symptom or problem you are facing, and consult the referenced sections of the Pocket Guide. The section below provides checklists of other steps to try for Windows and several hardware devices.

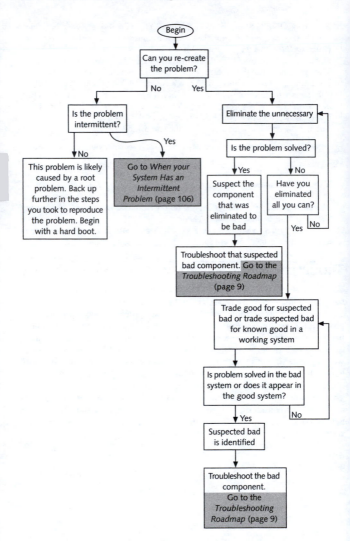

Flowchart 4-5   Steps to solving a PC problem after a successful boot

General Instructions for Problems with Software

☐ If you get a STOP error, search the Microsoft Web site (*support.microsoft.com*) to identify the error. Using a search engine, search the Internet for additional information. Look for the exact error message with an explanation of its cause.

- [ ] If you don't find the error message, search the *support.microsoft.com* Web site for other errors associated with this application.
- [ ] Reboot the PC. If you suspect Windows configuration changes, when you reboot, go to the Advanced Options menu and use the Last Known Good Configuration.
- [ ] Run a current version of antivirus software.
- [ ] Make sure Windows updates are current.
- [ ] Windows system files might be corrupted. Run the System File Checker (sfc.exe).
- [ ] You might be low on system resources. Check Task Manager for any unnecessary processes that are running. The Performance tab shows CPU and memory use.
- [ ] Download updates and patches for the application.
- [ ] Uninstall and reinstall the application.
- [ ] For Windows 2000/XP, try running the application under a different user account. Try using an account with administrative privileges.
- [ ] Install the application under a different user account. Use an account with administrative privileges.
- [ ] Consider data corruption. Try a new data file or a different data file with the application.
- [ ] Eliminate the hard disk as the source of the problem by running Chkdsk and Defragmenter. For Windows 9x, run ScanDisk.
- [ ] Try restoring default settings within the application.
- [ ] For Windows XP, use System Restore, and for Windows 2000, restore the system state.
- [ ] For Windows 9x, the problem might be associated with a DLL file that has been downgraded by newly installed software. Uninstall any newly installed software, and run System File Checker.
- [ ] For Windows 9x, validate and restore the registry using Registry Checker.

 TO LEARN MORE about System Restore in Windows XP, see page 583 of Chapter 12 in *A+ Guide to Managing and Maintaining Your PC* or page 143 of Chapter 3 in *A+ Guide to Software*.

 TO LEARN MORE about restoring the system state in Windows 2000/XP, see page 699 of Chapter 14 in *A+ Guide to Managing and Maintaining Your PC* or page 259 of Chapter 5 in *A+ Guide to Software*.

- [ ] For general protection fault errors, first try to reproduce the error to determine if it is consistent or intermittent.
- [ ] Use the Dr. Watson debugging tool to diagnose the problem. Turn on Dr. Watson, and reproduce the problem. Click Details on the application fault message box. Look in the Diagnosis dialog box to determine the source of the problem. Use this information to search the Microsoft Web site at *support.microsoft.com* for the cause and solution of the problem.

 TO LEARN MORE about Dr. Watson in Windows 200/XP, see page 568 of Chapter 12 in *A+ Guide to Managing and Maintaining Your PC* or page 128 of Chapter 3 in *A+ Guide to Software*. Dr. Watson in Windows 9x is covered on page 814 of Chapter 16 in *A+ Guide to Managing and Maintaining Your PC* or on page 374 of Chapter 7 in *A+ Guide to Software*.

- [ ] If the PC is old and the OS has been installed for some time, reinstall the OS.

GO TO For where to go for more help when solving software problems, see Appendix M, *Where to Go for More Help: Software Resources*.

General Instructions for Problems with Windows 2000/XP

Use these general troubleshooting tips when problems arise after the Windows 2000/XP desktop has loaded:

☐ Begin with any error messages displayed. Search the Web for the error message text. Search the Microsoft Web site (*support.microsoft.com*) or the Web site of the application or device that is causing the error.

☐ Talk with technical support within your own company or organization. They might have encountered the same problem.

☐ Check Event Viewer for error messages that occurred just before the problem arose, which can give clues as to the source of the problem.

☐ Is the hard drive full? Are too many applications loaded bringing the system down? What applets are loaded in the system tray that can be closed? Check Task Manager for unneeded running processes. Use Msconfig.exe to reduce startup processes to essentials.

☐ If new hardware has just been added, remove it. Reseat expansion cards and check all cable connections inside and outside the case.

☐ If you have just installed an OS or application service pack, uninstall it. Try booting into Safe Mode.

☐ Scan the entire hard drive for a virus using the latest updated version of antivirus software.

☐ If new software has just been installed, verify the software is Windows 2000/XP compatible. If it is not compatible, look for a patch on the software manufacturer's Web site or uninstall the software.

☐ Make sure Windows updates are current.

☐ Use System File Checker (sfc.exe) to verify system files.

☐ Flash BIOS.

☐ Suspect faulty RAM. Run memory-testing software such as DocMemory (*www.docmemory.com*) or Memtest (*www.memtest86.com*).

☐ Suspect overheating. Check the internal temperature of the system, and install additional coolers or fans and take other measures to control overheating.

TO LEARN MORE For more information about overheating and what to do about it, see page 170 of Chapter 4 of *A+ Guide to Managing and Maintaining Your PC* or page 118 of Chapter 3 in *A+ Guide to Hardware*.

Symptom: When using the Add or Remove Programs applet, software does not uninstall or uninstalls with errors.

Do the following to manually remove the software:

☐ Delete the software folder in the C:\Program Files folder.

☐ Using the Registry Editor, back up the following key by exporting it to the Windows desktop:

HKLM\Software\Microsoft\Windows\CurrentVersion\Uninstall

☐ In the registry, scroll through the entries in this key looking for all references to the software. Delete each reference; be sure to search the entire list, because there might be several entries.

☐ Reboot the PC, and check for errors. If you encounter errors, you can undo registry changes by double-clicking on the exported key.

☐ If the software is uninstalled without errors, delete the exported key from your desktop.

Speeding Up Windows 2000/XP

Symptom: Windows 2000/XP starts up slowly or runs slowly.

If Windows 2000/XP starts or runs slowly, do the following to perform a general cleanup of startup processes:

☐ To get a general idea of processes running in the background that might be tying up system resources, reboot the PC and check the Applications tab and the Processes tab in Task Manager for unwanted or malicious processes. To help you identify Windows processes, Figure 4–7 shows processes running after a fresh installation of Windows XP.

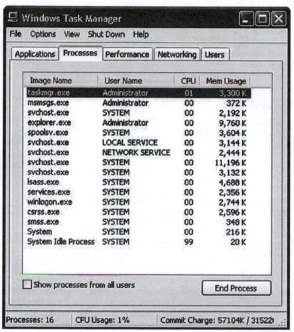

Figure 4-7 Processes showing under Task Manager after a fresh installation of Windows XP

☐ Investigate any unknown processes, searching the Internet for information. Web sites with trustworthy information are:
- Answers That Work at *www.answersthatwork.com*
- Jim Foley, The Elder Geek at *www.theeldergeek.com*
- Process Library by Jelsoft Enterprises, Ltd. at *www.processlibrary.com*
- Uniblue at *www.liutilities.com*
- All the antivirus software sites listed in Appendix H.

☐ If you find unwanted processes, use Msconfig.exe to find out how a process is loaded at startup.
☐ To remove unwanted processes, do the following:
  ■ First back up important data.
  ■ If you suspect a virus, run a current version of antivirus software. Also run one or more anti-adware utilities.
  ■ Use the Add or Remove Programs applet to uninstall software you don't want.

If software does not uninstall or uninstalls with errors, do the following to manually remove software:

☐ Delete the software folder in the C:\Program Files folder.
☐ Using the Registry Editor, export this key to the Windows desktop:

HKLM\Software\Microsoft\Windows\CurrentVersion\Uninstall

☐ Scroll through the entries in this key looking for all references to the software. Delete each reference, and be sure to search the entire list, because there might be several entries.
☐ Reboot the PC, and check for errors. If you encounter errors, you can undo registry changes by double-clicking on the exported key.

Search these startup folders for unwanted startup processes:

☐ C:\Documents and Settings*username*\Start Menu\Programs\Startup
☐ C:\Documents and Settings\All Users\Start Menu\Programs\Startup
☐ C:\Windows\Profiles\All Users\Start Menu\Programs\Startup
☐ C:\Windows\Profiles*username*\Start Menu\Programs\Startup

Search these folders for startup processes put there by Group Policy:

☐ C:\WINDOWS\System32\GroupPolicy\Machine\Scripts\Startup
☐ C:\WINDOWS\System32\GroupPolicy\Machine\Scripts\Shutdown
☐ C:\WINDOWS\System32\GroupPolicy\User\Scripts\Logon
☐ C:\WINDOWS\System32\GroupPolicy\User\Scripts\Logoff

Search this folder for startup processes put there Task Scheduler as scheduled tasks:

☐ C:\Windows\Tasks

Do the following to clean up services, drivers, and the registry:

☐ Use the Services Console (Services.msc) to look for unwanted services launched at startup.
☐ Use Device Manager to uninstall or disable unwanted devices.
☐ Using Appendix J as your reference, search the registry for other unwanted startup processes.

 For a complete list of registry keys and other entry points for startup processes, go to Appendix J, *Entry Points for Startup Processes*.

If Windows 2000/XP still starts or runs slowly, do the following:

☐ Verify the hard drive has enough free space (at least 15%) and use Disk Cleanup to clean the drive. Use Check Disk to repair the drive and Defrag to optimize it.
☐ If you don't have enough free hard drive space, consider adding a second drive. Purchase the fastest drive the motherboard can support.
☐ Use System Information to verify you have enough RAM (at least 512 MB, but more is better). Consider upgrading RAM.

Removing Malware from Windows 2000/XP

Here is a list of symptoms that suggest malicious software is at work:

Symptom: Pop-up ads plague you when surfing the Web.

Symptom: The system runs slowly, and programs take a long time to load.

Symptom: The number and length of disk accesses seem excessive for simple tasks. The number of bad sectors on the hard drive continues to increase.

Symptom: The access lights on the hard drive and floppy drive turn ON when there should be no activity on the devices. (However, sometimes Windows XP performs routine maintenance on the drive when the system has been inactive for a while.)

Symptom: Strange or bizarre error messages appear. Programs that once worked now give errors.

Symptom: Less memory than usual is available, or there is a noticeable reduction in disk space.

Symptom: Strange graphics appear on your computer monitor, or the computer makes strange noises.

Symptom: The system cannot recognize the optical drive, although it worked earlier.

Symptom: In Windows Explorer, file names now have weird characters or their file sizes seem excessively large. Files mysteriously disappear or appear.

Symptom: Files constantly become corrupted.

Symptom: The OS begins to boot but hangs before getting a Windows desktop.

Symptom: Your antivirus software displays one or more messages.

Symptom: You receive e-mail messages telling you that you have sent someone an infected message.

Symptom: Task Manager shows unfamiliar processes running.

Symptom: When you try to use your browser to access the Internet, strange things happen, and you can't surf the Web. Your Internet Explorer home page has changed, and you see new toolbars you didn't ask for.

Symptom: A message appears that a downloaded document contains macros, or an application asks whether or not it should run macros in a document. (It is best to disable macros if you cannot verify that they are from a trusted source and that they are free of viruses or worms.)

Follow these steps to rid the system of malware:

☐ If antivirus software is already installed on your system, download the latest malware definitions, and run the software.
☐ If you cannot run the antivirus software, boot into Safe Mode, and run the software from there.
☐ If antivirus software is not already installed, run the setup program on the antivirus software CD. During installation, the setup program scans for malware.
☐ Scan the system again to make sure everything is caught.

If the problem persists, do the following:

☐ If you can connect to the Internet, run antivirus software from its Web site. Try HouseCall Free Scan by Trend Micro, Inc. (*us.trendmicro.com/us/products/personal/*).
☐ Run an adware removal tool such as Windows Defender by Microsoft (*www.microsoft.com*) or Ad-Aware by Lavasoft (www.lavasoft.com). For best results, run both products.

If the problem persists, do the following:

☐ Use Msconfig.exe to search for startup processes left there by malware.
☐ For each registry entry, using the Registry Editor, back up the high-level registry key, and then delete the entry point. Also delete the program file.
☐ For each entry in a startup folder, delete the shortcut to the program file (if there is one) and also delete the program file.
☐ Delete Internet Explorer temporary files: In the drive C Properties window, click Disk Cleanup, and then delete Temporary Internet Files.

Sometimes a program file will not delete because it has been tagged as a system file. Do the following:

☐ Open a command prompt window, and go to the folder where the file is located.
☐ Use the Attrib command to change the file attributes. For example, for the program file int0094.exe, use this command: Attrib -h -s int0094.exe.
☐ Delete the file using the Del command. For example: Del int0094.exe
☐ Malware can hide in restore points. To purge all restore points, turn off System Restore, reboot the system, and turn on System Restore. All restore points are deleted.
☐ Use software such as Autoruns for Windows by Microsoft Sysinternals (*www.microsoft.com/technet/sysinternals*) to clean the registry of unwanted startup entries.
☐ Use software such as RootkitRevealer by Microsoft Sysinternals (*www.microsoft.com/technet/sysinternals*) to search for a rootkit (malicious software that can successfully hide from regular AV software products).

General Instructions for Problems with Windows 9x

☐ For Windows 98, if the problem is with one of the following subsystems, begin with the Windows 98 Troubleshooter. It has these 15 components:
  - Active Desktop Troubleshooter
  - Advanced Power Management Troubleshooter
  - DirectX Troubleshooter
  - Display Troubleshooter
  - DriveSpace Troubleshooter

- Hardware Troubleshooter
- Internet Connection Sharing Troubleshooter
- Memory Troubleshooter
- Modem Troubleshooter
- Network Troubleshooter
- Solving MS-DOS Program Problems with Windows 98
- Solving Problems Connecting to the Microsoft Network in Windows 98
- Solving PC Card Problems in Windows 98
- Sound Troubleshooter
- Startup and Shutdown Troubleshooter

☐ To access a troubleshooter, select Start and then Help. Type the name of one of the troubleshooters.

☐ Use the Windows 98 Registry Checker to verify and fix the registry. Select Start, Programs, Accessories, System Tools, and System Information. From this window, select Tools and Registry Checker.

☐ From the System Information window (see above), select Tools, System, and File Checker to verify system files. If changed, deleted, or corrupted system files are found, this tool restores them from the original Windows 98 CD-ROM.

☐ Use System Monitor to check for an application that is causing a performance problem or has a memory leak. Select Start, Programs, Accessories, System Tools, and System Monitor.

☐ From the Control Panel, double-click System and click the Performance tab. Verify that all file systems and virtual memory are using 32-bit drivers. Windows reports this status by saying that the system is running at optimal performance. If 32-bit drivers are not being used, Windows reports that a drive is using an MS-DOS compatibility mode file system.

☐ Research the problem and solutions at the Microsoft support site *support.microsoft.com/search*.

☐ Delete all files and folders in the \Windows\Temp folder.

☐ Run ScanDisk and Defragmenter.

Symptom: During a normal shutdown, the system hangs on the shutdown screen.

The fast shutdown feature might not be compatible with your system.

☐ To disable it, access the System Configuration Utility. Select the General tab, and click the Advanced button. Select the check box to Disable fast shutdown.

Symptom: The wrong font displays in Windows or Microsoft applications.

☐ Windows 9x has standard embedded fonts that should be included in every installation (Courier New, Arial, Times New Roman, Symbol, Wingdings, MS Serif, and MS Sans Serif). If these are missing, rerun Windows setup.

Symptom: Errors occur when trying to uninstall software using Add/Remove Programs.

Errors can occur if you have already deleted the software folders and files for a program that is listed in the Install/Uninstall list in the Add/Remove Programs window.

☐ To remove a program from this list, delete its key from the following registry key: HKEY_LOCAL_MACHINE\Software\Microsoft\Windows\CurrentVersion\ Uninstall.

General Instructions for Problems with Hardware

- ☐ Trade good for suspected bad, or install the suspected bad in a known good system.
- ☐ Uninstall and reinstall the hardware's device drivers.
- ☐ Check Device Manager for resource conflicts.
- ☐ Using Device Manager, disable other devices that you suspect might be in conflict.

 For more information about resolving conflicts, see *Resolving Resource Conflicts Using Legacy Devices* (page 114).

- ☐ Check Event Viewer for logged errors.
- ☐ Check CMOS setup for disabled ports, expansion slots, or IRQ values.
- ☐ Download and apply the latest device drivers from the hardware manufacturer's Web site.
- ☐ If you are trying to get newly downloaded drivers to work, consider that you might have downloaded the wrong driver file. Recheck the manufacturer Web site for the correct drivers.
- ☐ Make sure Windows updates are current.
- ☐ For internal devices that use a power cord from the power supply, check the voltage output from the power cord with a multimeter.

 TO LEARN MORE about how to use a multimeter to check voltage output, see page 1129 of Appendix E in *A+ Guide to Managing and Maintaining Your PC* or on page 689 of Appendix C in *A+ Guide to Hardware*.

- ☐ Check all internal connections (data cable, power cord). Reseat expansion cards.
- ☐ Check jumpers and DIP switches and any CMOS settings for the device.
- ☐ Suspect the applications software using the device. Try another application or reinstall the software.
- ☐ Verify that the applications software using the device is configured correctly using the correct serial port, parallel port, hardware device, and so forth.
- ☐ For Windows 9x, from the Windows 9x Startup menu, select Step-by-Step Confirmation. Look for error messages about the device.
- ☐ Install the device in a known good system, or install a known good device in this system. In so doing, you can decide if the problem is related to the device or the system. If the device works in a known good system, reinstall it in the original system. Loose connections might have been the problem.
- ☐ When updating the drivers, consider you might have downloaded the wrong device drivers. Verify the device manufacturer and model and double-check the Web site.

When Your System Has an Intermittent Problem

An intermittent problem is one that comes and goes, and you cannot reproduce the problem at will. The approach is to provide the cleanest possible environment for the system and then to look for a pattern as to when the problem appears so as to identify its source.

Symptom: The system reboots or crashes intermittently.

- ☐ Eliminate malware as the source. Scan for viruses and clean up the hard drive.
- ☐ Eliminate the power supply as the source. Check the voltage output of the power supply. Install a line conditioner and/or replace the power supply.
- ☐ Check Event Viewer for a history of hardware or software problems.
- ☐ Eliminate the unnecessary. Too many devices on a system might be overtaxing the power supply. Too many background processes running might be interfering

with software. Check Task Manager and the taskbar for extraneous processes. Use Msconfig to reduce startup to a minimum.

☐ Remove all unnecessary devices and cards (modem, network, sound, printer, scanner, etc.) from the computer and reboot.

☐ Reseat the CPU and memory modules.

☐ Check the motherboard for damage, shorts, frayed traces, bad connections, or faulty capacitors.

☐ Exchange RAM.

☐ Suspect overheating. Check the internal temperature of the system, and install additional coolers or fans. Tie cables up and out of the way of airflow. Clean out the dust from inside the case. Install bay covers and faceplates on all empty bays and expansion slots.

> **TO LEARN MORE** For more information about overheating and what to do about it, see page 170 of Chapter 4 of *A+ Guide to Managing and Maintaining Your PC* or page 118 of Chapter 3 in *A+ Guide to Hardware*.

Symptom: The system hangs or gives error messages intermittently.

☐ Check all Event Viewer logs for a history of hardware or software problems.

☐ Run drive Error Checking and Defragmenter. (For Windows 9x, run ScanDisk.)

☐ Run a current version of antivirus software to check for a virus. If the software finds a virus, run the antivirus software a second time to totally eliminate any malware problems. Run one or more anti-adware products such as Ad-Aware and Windows Defender.

☐ Make sure the latest Windows updates are installed.

☐ For software problems, if the PC is old and the OS has been installed for some time, reinstall the OS.

☐ For software problems, if you have the time, completely rebuild the entire hard drive, reformatting the drive, reinstalling the OS and applications. Back up the data first and then restore it after you have rebuilt the drive.

☐ For suspected hardware problems, reseat expansion cards, and check cable and power cord connections.

☐ Remove the hardware device's drivers, and reinstall the device.

☐ For hardware problems, trade good for suspected bad, and leave the good device in place long enough that the problem should have recurred.

☐ Suspect overheating. Check the internal temperature of the system and install additional coolers or fans and take other measures to control overheating.

> **TO LEARN MORE** For more information about overheating and what to do about it, see page 170 of Chapter 4 of *A+ Guide to Managing and Maintaining Your PC* or page 118 of Chapter 3 in *A+ Guide to Hardware*.

☐ Ask the user to keep a log of when the problems occur and exactly what messages appeared on the screen. Show the user how to get a printed screen of the error messages when they appear. From this log, search for an emerging pattern.

TROUBLESHOOTING FLOPPY DRIVES

If a floppy drive does not work, try the following:

☐ Remove the floppy disk. Does the shuttle window move freely?

☐ Do you see any dirt, hair, or trash on the disk's Mylar surface?

☐ Sometimes the shuttle window just needs a little loosening. Put the disk back in the drive and try again.

☐ Does the light on the correct drive go on when you try to access it? Maybe you are trying to access the B drive, but the disk is in the A drive.

☐ Will another disk work in the drive? If so, the problem is probably caused by the disk, not the drive. There is an exception: the drive might be out of alignment, which can cause it to be able to read only disks that it has formatted. Test this possibility by trying several disks, some formatted by this drive and some by others. If you conclude the drive is out of alignment, replace the drive.

☐ Does the drive light come on at all? If not, try to access the disk with a different software program or with the OS.

☐ Does the light stay on? If so, the data cable on the drive is reversed.

☐ Reboot the PC and try again.

☐ Check CMOS setup. Is the drive configured correctly?

☐ Verify that the disk is formatted.

☐ Check every connection from the motherboard to the drive. Check the power cable connection. Use a different power cable.

☐ If the drive uses a controller card, remove the card. Using a clean white eraser, erase and clean the edge connector, and reseat the card.

☐ Use a different power cable.

☐ Replace the data cable.

☐ Replace the drive.

☐ If the drive still does not work, suspect the motherboard or the ROM BIOS on the motherboard.

Symptom: An error message is displayed when trying to use the floppy drive.

Table 4-13 contains a list of error messages pertaining to floppy drives, what they mean, and what to do about them.

Table 4-13 Floppy drive error messages and what to do about them

Error	Description of the problem and what to do
General failure reading A: Abort, Retry, Fail?	The floppy drive is not accessible. See the list above for things to do.
Non-system disk or disk error. Replace and strike any key when ready.	The disk is not bootable. Remove the disk and boot from the hard drive, or replace the disk with one that is bootable.
Invalid or missing COMMAND.COM	Copy COMMAND.COM to the disk.
Invalid drive specification	The OS does not recognize that the floppy disk drive exists. See the list at the beginning of this section for items to check and do.
Not ready reading drive A: Abort, Retry, Fail?	• The disk in drive A is not readable. Reinsert the disk in the drive. • Suspect a corrupted boot record, FAT, or directory. Run a current version of antivirus software on the disk.
"Track 0 bad, disk not usable" message appears while trying to format a disk	You are using the wrong disk type switch with the Format command. Verify the disk type.
Write-protect error writing drive A	The switch on the disk is set to write-protect. Change the switch.

TROUBLESHOOTING THE HARD DRIVE AFTER BOOTING

Symptom: An important data file is missing or corrupted.

☐ If the file has been erased using Windows, look in the Recycle Bin.

☐ If an application cannot read or open one of its data files, the file header might be corrupted. Try renaming the file with a TXT file extension and importing the file as a text file.

☐ On the Tools tab of the Windows 2000/XP drive Properties window, run Check Now to repair lost clusters to files. (For Windows 9x, run ScanDisk.) Look in the newly created files for the data. The files are in the root directory of the hard drive.

☐ For a FAT file system, use the COPY command to copy the file to another media. When the error message "Unable to read from Drive C: Abort, Retry, Ignore" displays, choose Ignore. The OS ignores the corrupted sector and moves on to the next sector. You should be able to recover some of the data with this approach.

☐ For Windows 9x, if the file has been erased using MS-DOS or the Windows Recycle Bin has been emptied, try the DOS UNDELETE command: Restart the computer in MS-DOS mode (real mode). At the DOS prompt, type LOCK to make the FAT available to DOS. Use the UNDELETE command to recover the file. Type UNLOCK to release the file system to applications. Type EXIT to relaunch Windows 9x.

☐ Try using Norton Utilities or EasyRecovery by Ontrack to recover the file.

☐ Consider consulting a professional data-recovery service.

Symptom: Drive retrieves and saves data slowly.

☐ Make sure there is enough free space on the drive. Windows needs at least 15% of the drive free in order to run Defrag.

☐ Run Defragmenter to rewrite fragmented files to contiguous sectors.

☐ Run a current version of antivirus software.

☐ Clean up startup: Remove applications from the Windows Startup folder, and remove icons from the system tray. Use Msconfig.exe to find out what processes are loaded at startup. Then reduce the system to essentials.

☐ For Windows 9x, from Control Panel, double-click System and click the Performance tab. Check that 32-bit drivers are in use.

☐ Verify that CMOS settings are correct for the drive.

See Appendix B (page B-1) to understand CMOS settings for hard drives .

☐ If you are using disk caching software, verify that the software loads and is operational.

☐ If the drive is an IDE Ultra ATA/66 drive or higher, the new 80-conductor IDE cable is required. Sometimes the connector on the drive is blue to indicate this standard is used. Verify the correct type cable is used. Using the wrong cable can hinder performance.

TROUBLESHOOTING CD OR DVD DRIVES

Symptom: Cannot read the CD or DVD in the optical drive.

☐ Check both surfaces of the disc for scratches, dirt, and so on. Try cleaning it with soft cloth and window cleaner. Deep scratches on the bottom side can sometimes be removed with a CD cleaning kit, plastic cleaners, or polishes. Scratches on the top of the disc are actually more of a problem than those on the underside because the top side is not protected with a plastic coating as is used on the bottom side. Top-side scratches most likely mean the disc is ruined.

☐ Is the disc inserted upside down?

☐ Try a known good audio CD-ROM disc. Perhaps you are trying to use a DVD or CD-RW disc in a CD-ROM drive that is not designed to read that type of disc.

☐ Use a CD cleaning kit to clean inside the drive.

☐ Reboot the computer, and try again.

☐ Some CD-ROM drives cannot read CDs that were not properly closed when written to by a CD writer. Try another CD-ROM drive in another machine.

☐ If the CD-RW was created in more than one session, the drive must be MultiRead in order to read the CD. Try another CD-ROM drive in another machine.

☐ Check the data cable and power cord connections to the drive.

☐ Scan for viruses. Some viruses disable the optical drive.

Symptom: Burning a CD does not work.

☐ A CD can hold about 700 MB of data. Be sure your total file sizes don't exceed this amount.

☐ The hard drive needs some temporary holding space for the write process. Make sure you have at least 5 GB of free space for Windows to work.

☐ Disable any screen saver or other program that might interrupt the write process.

☐ If several CDs give you problems, try a different brand of CDs.

☐ A sluggish Windows system can cause a CD to not burn. Try a slower burn rate. To do that, right click the CD drive and select Properties. On the Recording tab, select a slower burn speed.

Symptom: Cannot load Windows 9x device drivers for the CD-ROM drive.

☐ Try loading drivers from DOS. Real-mode CD-ROM drivers can be loaded from the AUTOEXEC.BAT and CONFIG.SYS files. See the CD-ROM installation guide for specific commands for your drive. Here is one example:

In the CONFIG.SYS file: `DEVICE=C:\CDSYS\SLCD.SYS /D:MSCD001`

In AUTOEXEC.BAT: `C:\DOS\MSCDEX.EXE /D:MSCD001 /L:D /M:8`

☐ Try creating a bootable disk with these commands and the referenced files. (Modify the paths to point to drive A.)

 TO LEARN MORE about the parameters in the above command lines, see page 828 of Chapter 16 in *A+ Guide to Managing and Maintaining Your PC* or page 388 of Chapter 7 in *A+ Guide to Software*.

☐ Once the drive is working in DOS, try to install the Windows 9x drivers.

Symptom: The error message "Invalid Drive Specification" appears while trying to access the drive.

☐ Does the eject button work on the drive? If not, then check the power connection to the drive.

☐ For DOS installations, check these things:
  ▪ Check for errors in the command lines in the CONFIG.SYS or AUTOEXEC.BAT file according to the documentation that came with the CD-ROM. Did you get an error message during booting such as "Bad Command" or "File Not Found"? Verify that all driver files referenced are present at the correct location as specified in these two files.
  ▪ Verify that the MSCDEX.EXE command line is not placed too late in AUTOEXEC.BAT after the command to load Windows.
  ▪ Try a different version of MSCDEX. Look for this file in the \DOS directory, and change the path in front of the filename in AUTOEXEC.BAT to point to that version.
☐ Reseat the adapter card, if one is used, and check cable connections.
☐ For IDE drives, verify the jumper settings on the drive. Check that the IDE connection on the motherboard is enabled in CMOS setup.
☐ For SCSI drives, verify that termination and the SCSI ID are set correctly.
☐ For drives connected to sound cards, try uninstalling the drive and the sound card. Then install first the sound card and then the CD drive.

 TO LEARN MORE about SCSI configurations, see page 324 of Chapter 8 in *A+ Guide to Managing and Maintaining Your PC* or page 272 of Chapter 7 in *A+ Guide to Hardware*.

☐ For Windows, check that the driver is loaded correctly. Does Device Manager report a conflict or a problem with the driver?
☐ Uninstall and reinstall the drivers. Check the Web site of the drive manufacturer for updated driver files.

Symptom: The install process is terminated with the message "MSCDEX.EXE not found" during a DOS installation.

☐ MSCDEX.EXE must be copied onto the hard drive. Put it in the \DOS directory, and then restart the install process. Sometimes MSCDEX is placed in the Windows directory, and sometimes a copy is put in the newly created CD-ROM directory.
☐ Verify that the path to the file is correct in AUTOEXEC.BAT.

Symptom: The error message "Not Enough Drive Letters" appears during booting for a DOS installation.

☐ Increase the number of allowed drive letters with the LASTDRIVE line in CONFIG.SYS: LASTDRIVE=Z.

Symptom: Computer does not recognize CD-ROM (no D: prompt in MS-DOS or no drive D listed in Windows Explorer)

☐ Check the following configurations:
  ▪ For Windows, has the CD-ROM driver been installed? Look in Device Manager.
  ▪ Check to see whether or not another device is using the same port settings or IRQ number. Look in Device Manager.
☐ Check the following connections:
  ▪ Is the power cable attached to the CD-ROM?
  ▪ Is the data cable attached to the CD-ROM and to the controller?
  ▪ Is the stripe on the data cable correctly aligned to Pin 1? (Look for an arrow or small 1 printed on the drive. For a best guess, Pin 1 is usually next to the power connector.)

☐ For IDE drives, is the correct master/slave jumper set? For example, if both the hard drive and the CD-ROM drive are hooked up to the same ribbon cable, set the hard drive as master and the CD-ROM drive as slave.
☐ For IDE drives, check that the IDE connection is not disabled in CMOS setup.
☐ For SCSI drives, check that the proper ID is set and the device is terminated if it's on the end of the SCSI chain.
☐ Suspect a boot virus. Run a current version of an antivirus program.

TROUBLESHOOTING SOUND CARDS

Symptom: No sound.

☐ Verify that the speakers are connected and turned ON.
☐ Check that the volume is turned up on the speakers.
☐ Check that the Windows volume control is turned up and not muted.
☐ Verify that the speakers are plugged into the "Line Out" or "Spkr" port of the sound card.
☐ Verify that the transformer for the speaker is plugged into an electrical outlet on one end and into the speakers on the other end.
☐ Check the mixer settings. Is mute selected or are the volume settings set too low? Increase the master volume setting.
☐ Reboot the computer and try it again.
☐ Try a different application. Try to produce sound using Windows only.
☐ If the sound card has a "diagnose" file on the installation CD, use this diagnostic utility to check the sound card. On the installation CD, look for a technical manual with troubleshooting guidelines.
☐ Verify that the audio cable is attached between the CD-ROM and the analog audio connector on the sound card.
☐ Use Device Manager to check for a resource conflict. Verify that Device Manager does not report an error with the device driver installation. Look for a conflicting DMA channel, I/O address, or IRQ number.

> **GO TO** For more information on resolving conflicts, see *Resolving Resource Conflicts Using Legacy Devices* later in this section (page 114).

☐ Uninstall and reinstall the sound card drivers.
☐ To check for a bad connection, remove and reinstall the sound card.
☐ Replace the sound card with one you know is good.

Symptom: One or both speakers are making a humming noise.

☐ Move the speakers, making sure that speaker cables are not entangled with other cords.
☐ Move the sound card to a different expansion slot, as far from other components as possible.
☐ Try new, upgraded speakers.

Symptom: A game doesn't have sound.

☐ Download and apply the latest sound card drivers from the sound card manufacturer.
☐ Disable all background programs such as a screen saver or antivirus software. If this solves the problem, enable first one and then the next until you discover the one causing the problem.

☐ Try reducing sound acceleration. Open the Sounds and Audio Devices applet in Control Panel. On the Volume tab, Speaker settings, click Advanced. On the Performance tab, move the Hardware acceleration side to the left one click. Try the game again. You might have to move it all the way to the left.

TROUBLESHOOTING MICROPHONES

Symptom: The microphone does not work.

☐ Is the microphone plugged into the right port? Check volume settings in the Volume Control applet in Control Panel. Is the Mute checkbox checked?

☐ Are you picking up a lot of background noise? Try using a unidirectional microphone.

☐ Check your voice-recognition software. Is the recording volume set correctly in the control mixer? Is the microphone turned on in the software?

TROUBLESHOOTING A SCANNER

Symptom: Scanner does not work.

Isolate the problem by finding the answers to the following questions:

☐ Is the scanner plugged in and turned ON?

☐ Try the Scan button on the front of the scanner. If this works, then you know the problem is with the computer, the software on the computer, or the cable.

☐ Inspect the cables; are they securely connected?

☐ If the scanner is connected to a USB port, check Device Manager to make sure the port is enabled and working. To verify the port is working, try another USB device on the same port.

☐ If the scanner is connected to a parallel port, is it a bidirectional port? Sometimes this can be changed in CMOS setup.

☐ If the scanner is a SCSI device, is the ID of the scanner the same as another device? If so give the scanner an unused ID.

☐ Is the charge-coupled device unlocked? This is locked to prevent damage during shipping.

☐ Try uninstalling and reinstalling the scanner software.

Symptom: Scanner does not produce high-quality images.

A scanner that is not working properly might produce dirty images or no image at all. You can isolate the problem by finding the answers to the following questions:

☐ Is the scanner set to scan at a minimum of 300 dpi? If not, it can affect the quality of a printed image.

☐ Is your monitor set to 256 colors? If so, this could cause a spotted image. Set your monitor to 24-bit color or higher. Check first to see if your video card can handle the higher setting.

☐ Is the scanner image distorted with a blue color? This can be the result of a bad charge-coupled device (CCR). Send the scanner to an authorized service facility.

☐ Is the glass on the scanner clean? Use a soft cloth and glass cleaner to clean the surface.

□ Is the original image relatively free of imperfections? Optical character recogni-
   tion (OCR) software is affected by imperfections. Reducing the scanner settings
   might be helpful. Manually zoning might help by eliminating some of the
   imperfections.
□ Have the settings been altered from the default settings? If so, restore the default
   settings.
□ Does moving the scanner produce a clearer image? Scanners are sometimes
   affected by electrical noise.

Symptom: Cannot "acquire" from software.

□ There might be a problem with your TWAIN-compliant software. Check the
   applications documentation for help.
□ Turn OFF the PC and scanner. Turn ON the scanner, reboot the PC, and
   try again.
□ Try different software to acquire the image.

RESOLVING RESOURCE CONFLICTS USING LEGACY DEVICES

Windows 9x supports legacy devices, but Windows 2000/XP does not. Under
Windows 9x, resource conflicts will appear during booting as error messages, or
they will cause a device to fail to operate.

□ First remove the newly installed device that is in conflict.
□ Reboot the PC, and determine the resources currently used by other devices.
   From a DOS prompt, use the MSD utility, or from Windows 9x, use Device
   Manager. List on paper or print a report showing the DMA channels, IRQs, I/O
   addresses, and upper memory addresses used by each device on your system.
□ Determine the resources needed by the new device. Read its documentation,
   look for the information written on the device housing, or check the Web site
   of the device manufacturer.
□ Change the resources needed by the new device so as not to conflict with those
   used by other devices. If the device is not Plug and Play, use software to change
   the resources or modify the jumpers or DIP switches on the device.
□ If the device requires a resource that is currently in use, try reconfiguring the old
   device that uses this resource to force it to use a different resource. For PCI
   devices in conflict, try enabling PCI bus IRQ steering. For ISA devices in conflict, try disabling the feature.
□ If your motherboard supports it, use CMOS setup to reserve an IRQ for a PCI
   slot or to reserve an IRQ for an ISA device.

□ After resolving the conflict, reinstall the new device, reboot, and run the Add New Hardware wizard.

□ To determine the type of bus that a device is using, see Figures 4-8 and 4-9. Figure 4-8 shows four outdated bus connections on expansion cards (ISA, MCA, EISA, and VESA), and Figure 4-9 shows the four types of PCI expansion slots and the six types of PCI cards to use these slots.

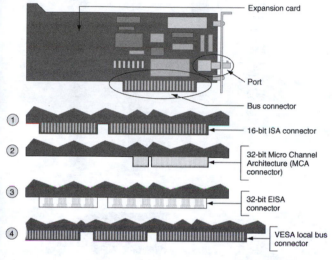

Figure 4-8 Four outdated bus connections on expansion cards

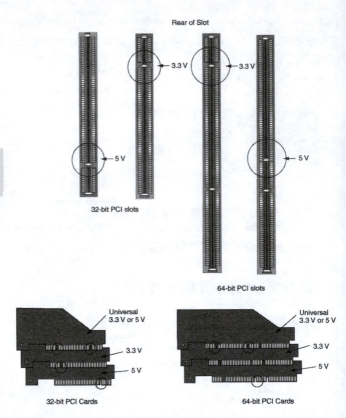

Figure 4-9   Four types of PCI slots and six differently configured PCI expansion
cards to use these slots

TROUBLESHOOTING PRINTERS

Begin by using Flowchart 4-6 to help isolate the problem, which can be caused
by the PC, the application attempting to use the printer, the OS and printer
drivers, connectivity between the PC and the printer, or the printer.

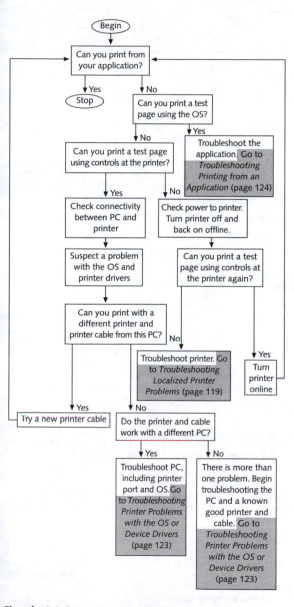

Flowchart 4-6 How to isolate a printer problem

Do the following to isolate the source of the problem:

☐ Try printing a test page using the OS to verify that all is working between the OS and the printer. To print a Windows test page, open the Printers or Printers and Faxes window. Right-click the printer icon and select Properties from the shortcut menu. (Be sure you select the right printer.) The Printer Properties dialog box appears. Click Print Test Page.

☐ If the OS test page is successful, then the OS, the printer drivers, connectivity to the printer, and the printer are all working properly.

Go to *Troubleshooting Printing from an Application* (page 124).

☐ If the OS test page effort was not successful and you are using a network printer, try printing from another computer on the network. If you cannot print from any computer on the network to this network printer, then consider the problem a localized printer problem. Troubleshoot the printer.

Go to *Troubleshooting Localized Printer Problems* (page 119).

☐ If you can print from another computer, the problem is with the PC or its connectivity with the network. Can the PC find other resources on the network? If so, then you have isolated the problem to the network printer configuration on this one PC.

Go to *Network Printer Problems* (page 126).

☐ If the OS test page effort was not successful and you are using a local printer, attempt to print a test page using controls on the printer. See the printer documentation for instructions. The test page generally lists information about the printer, including how much memory is on board.

☐ If the printer test page effort was not successful, then troubleshoot the printer.

Go to *Troubleshooting Localized Printer Problems* (page 119).

If you cannot print an OS test page, but you can print a printer test page, do the following to check simple problems with printing from the OS:

☐ Verify the printer is plugged in and turned on. Is the printer online?

☐ Delete any files in the print spool. From the Printers or Printers and Faxes window, double-click the printer icon. From the menu at the top of the window, click Printer, Cancel All Documents. (In Windows 9x, click Printer, Purge Print Documents.)

☐ Does the printer have paper?

☐ Is the paper damp, or is the paper jammed?

☐ Are you using the right kind of paper? Is it too heavy?

☐ Is the cable connected to the right port on the PC? Some SCSI connectors have 25-pins and look like a parallel port. For USB printers, is the USB port driver in Device Manager working without errors?

☐ Turn off the printer and turn it back on.

☐ Reboot the PC. Is the port enabled in CMOS setup?

- ☐ If you receive a memory overflow or printer overrun error, you either need to add memory to the printer or simplify your document.
- ☐ If the device prints gibberish, it might be because of a wrong printer driver. Replace the driver with the correct driver.

Go to *Troubleshooting Printer Problems with the OS or Device Drivers* (page 123).

TO LEARN MORE about troubleshooting printer problems, see Chapter 21, beginning with page 1171 in *A+ Guide to Managing and Maintaining Your PC* or Chapter 12, beginning with page 617 of *A+ Guide to Hardware* or Chapter 11, beginning with page 627 in *A+ Guide to Software*.

Troubleshooting Localized Printer Problems

Symptom: **Printing a test page using controls on the printer failed.**

- ☐ If the printer failed to successfully print a self-test page, turn the printer OFF and disconnect it from the PC. Turn the printer back ON, and try to print another self-test page.
- ☐ Check that the printer has paper. Verify that the paper is installed correctly.
- ☐ Search for jammed paper in the printer mechanism.
- ☐ Is the paper damp or wrinkled, causing it to refuse to feed?
- ☐ Verify that the printer cover and any rear-access doors to the printer are properly closed and locked.
- ☐ Reset the printer.
- ☐ For a laser printer, check that a toner cartridge is installed. Make sure the protective tape on the cartridge was removed when the cartridge was installed. For an ink-jet printer, check that ink cartridges are installed and that the protective pieces of tape have been removed from the print cartridges. For a dot matrix printer, check that the ribbon is in the correct position and is not jammed.
- ☐ Check that power is getting to the printer. Try another power source.
- ☐ Try another power cable.
- ☐ Search the printer documentation for troubleshooting tables. Check the Web site of the printer manufacturer for suggestions and things to try.
- ☐ For laser printers, replace the toner cartridge. For ink-jet printers, replace the ink cartridges.
- ☐ Check whether or not the printer is still under warranty. Contact the printer manufacturer or an appropriate printer service center for help.

Laser Printer Problems

Symptom: **Printer never leaves warm-up mode.**

The warming-up message should disappear as soon as the printer establishes communication with the PC. If it doesn't, try the following:

- ☐ Turn the printer OFF, and disconnect the cable to the computer.
- ☐ Turn on the printer. If it now displays a Ready message, the problem is communication between the printer and the computer.
- ☐ Verify that the cable is connected to the correct printer port.
- ☐ Verify that data to the installed printer is being sent to the correct port. For example, access the Properties dialog box of the installed printer as described above. Verify that the print job is being sent to LPT1 for a parallel port.
- ☐ Check that the USB, parallel, or serial port the printer is using is enabled in CMOS setup and is set to the correct mode.

- ☐ For a network printer, print a test page at the printer, which should report the IP address of the printer. Is the PC configured to use this same IP address for this printer?
- ☐ For a network printer, compare how the printer is installed on this PC to how it is installed on another PC on the network. Search the printer manufacturer Web site for instructions on how to install this network printer. Uninstall and install the printer carefully following these instructions.
- ☐ Replace the cable.

Symptom: A "Paper Out" message is displayed.

- ☐ Remove the paper tray. Be sure there is paper in the tray. Carefully replace the tray, being certain that the tray is fully inserted in the slot.
- ☐ Check the lever mechanism that falls into a slot on the tray when no paper is present. Is it jammed or bent?
- ☐ Turn the printer OFF and then back ON.
- ☐ When you insert the tray in the printer, does the printer lift the plate as the tray is inserted? If not, the lift mechanism might need repairing.

Symptom: A "Toner Low" message is displayed, or print is irregular or light.

- ☐ If you suspect that the printer is overheated, unplug the printer and allow it to cool.
- ☐ Remove the toner cartridge from the printer and gently shake it from side to side to redistribute the toner supply across the bottom of the bin. Replace it in the printer. To avoid flying toner, don't shake the cartridge too hard. This solution is really just a temporary fix for a cartridge that is low on toner. Plan to replace the cartridge soon.
- ☐ Extreme humidity might make the toner clump in the cartridge and cause the same error message. If this is a consistent problem, consider a dehumidifier for the room where the printer is located.
- ☐ EconoMode (a mode that uses less toner) might be ON; turn it OFF.
- ☐ On some laser printers, you can clean the mirror. Check the user guide for directions.
- ☐ A single sheet of paper might be defective. Try new paper.
- ☐ The paper might not be of high enough quality. Try a different brand of paper. Only use paper recommended for use in a laser printer.
- ☐ Try flipping over the stack of paper in the tray.
- ☐ Clean the inside of the printer with a dry, lint-free cloth. Don't touch the transfer roller.
- ☐ If the transfer roller is dirty, the problem will probably correct itself after printing several sheets.
- ☐ Replace the toner cartridge.
- ☐ Does the printer require routine maintenance? Check the Web site of the printer manufacturer for how often to perform the maintenance and to purchase the required printer maintenance kit.
- ☐ If none of these steps are productive, take the printer to an authorized service center.

Symptom: A "Paper Jam" message is displayed.

- ☐ If paper is jammed inside the printer, follow the directions in the printer documentation to remove the paper. Don't jerk the paper from the printer mechanism, but pull carefully and evenly on the paper.

☐ Check for jammed paper from both the input tray and the output bin. Check both sides.

☐ If there is no jammed paper, then remove the tray and check the metal plate at the bottom of the tray. Can it move up and down freely? If not, replace the tray with a new tray or replace the lifting mechanism. See the printer documentation for instructions and part numbers.

☐ When you insert the tray in the printer, does the printer lift the plate as the tray is inserted? If not, the lift mechanism might need repairing.

Symptom: White streaks appear in the print.

☐ Remove the toner cartridge, shake it from side to side to redistribute the toner supply, and replace the cartridge.

☐ This is usually caused by a dirty developer unit or corona wire. The developer unit is contained in the toner cartridge. Replace the cartridge or check the printer documentation for specific directions on how to remove and clean the developer unit. Allow the corona wire to cool, and clean it with a lint-free swab.

Symptom: Print appears speckled.

☐ Try replacing the cartridge. If the problem persists, the power supply assembly might be damaged.

☐ Install the printer's maintenance kit.

☐ Replace the laser drum. Is the printer still under warranty?

Symptom: Printed images are distorted.

☐ Check for debris that might be interfering with the printer operation.

☐ Is the paper damp? If the paper is damp or stored in a humid environment, it can create printer problems.

☐ If loose toner comes out with your printout, the fuser is not reaching the proper temperature. Professional service is required.

☐ If the page has a gray background or gray print, the photoreceptor drum is worn out and needs to be replaced.

☐ Replace the toner cartridge.

☐ Replace the laser drum.

Dot Matrix Printer Problems

Symptom: Print quality is poor.

☐ Begin with the ribbon. Does it advance normally while the carriage moves back and forth? Is it placed correctly in the ribbon guide?

☐ Adjust the print head spacing. There is usually a lever adjustment that can alter the distance between the print head and the plate.

☐ Replace the ribbon.

☐ If the new ribbon still does not advance properly, check the printer's advance mechanism.

☐ Check the print head for dirt. Make sure that it's not hot before you touch it. If you see buildup, wipe each wire with a cotton swab dipped in alcohol or contact cleaner.

Symptom: The top or bottom of each line prints faintly or not at all.

☐ This problem is caused by the print head alignment. Adjust the print head so that it hits the ribbon evenly on top and bottom.

Symptom: Print head moves back and forth, but nothing prints.

☐ Check that the ribbon is installed correctly between the plate and the print head.

☐ Check that the ribbon advances properly.
☐ Adjust the print head so that it is the correct distance from the ribbon.
☐ Try a new ribbon.

Symptom: Print head jams on movement.

☐ Check the print head transport bar for dust, dirt, or signs of wear or uneven lubrication.
☐ Clean the print head transport bar with a cotton swab or cloth soaked in alcohol. Lubricate it with a light coating of general-purpose oil along the entire length.
☐ If this step doesn't solve the problem, the motor driver is probably worn out. Have it serviced or replace the printer.

Ink-Jet Printer Problems

Symptom: Print quality is poor.

☐ Is the correct paper for ink-jet printers being used? The quality of paper determines the final print quality, especially with ink-jet printers. In general, the better the quality of the paper used with an ink-jet printer, the better the print quality. Do not use paper lighter than 20 lb. in any type of printer, unless the printer documentation specifically says that a lower weight is satisfactory.
☐ Is the ink supply low, or is there a partially clogged nozzle? (This problem might arise if the printer has been idle for several days.)
☐ Remove and reinstall each cartridge. Follow the printer documentation to align the print cartridges.
☐ Follow the printer's documentation to clean each nozzle.
☐ Change the print quality selection for the printer. (Use the Printer Properties dialog box.)
☐ Is the print head too close to or too far from the paper?
☐ If you are printing on transparencies, try changing the fill pattern in your application.

Symptom: Printing is intermittent or absent.

☐ Make sure that the correct printer driver is installed.
☐ Is the ink supply low?
☐ Are nozzles clogged? Follow the instructions in the printer documentation to clean the nozzles using either a manual method or the printer software.
☐ Replace the ink cartridges or replenish the ink supply. Follow the directions in the printer documentation.
☐ Sometimes leaving the printer on for a while will heat up the ink nozzles and unclog them.

Symptom: Ink is streaked.

☐ Follow the printer manufacturer's directions to clean the print cartridge assemblage. You will be directed to use clean distilled water and to be careful to not touch the nozzle plate. Print a self-test page at the printer to check the quality. This procedure should be followed until normal print quality returns. Don't leave the print cartridges out of their cradle for longer than 30 minutes to prevent the nozzles from drying out.
☐ There is a little sponge in some printers near the carriage rest that can become clogged with ink. It should be removed and cleaned.

Troubleshooting Printer Problems with the OS or Device Drivers

Symptom: Cannot print an OS test page, but printing a self-test page at the printer is successful.

☐ The print spool might be stalled. Try deleting all print jobs in the printer's queue. Double-click the printer icon in the Printers or Printers and Faxes window. For Windows 2000/XP, select Printer, Cancel All Documents. For Windows 9x, select Printer, Purge Print Documents. (It might take a moment for the print jobs to disappear.)

☐ If you still cannot print, reboot the PC. Verify that the printer cable or cable connections are solid.

☐ Verify that the printer is online. See the printer documentation for information on how to determine that status from the control panel of the printer.

☐ Verify that the proper printer cable is used. Parallel port printers require an IEEE-1284 compliant bidirectional parallel cable.

☐ Verify that data to the installed printer is being sent to the correct port. Access the Properties dialog box of the installed printer. For a local printer using a parallel port, verify that the print job is being sent to LPT1. For a network printer, compare the port configuration to another computer on the network.

☐ Try removing and reinstalling the printer driver. To uninstall the printer driver, right-click the printer icon in the Printers or Printers and Faxes window, select Delete to remove the printer, and then reinstall the printer.

☐ For Windows 9x, verify that the printer is able to communicate to the OS. Access the Printer Properties dialog box, click the Services tab, and then Test printer communications. If communication is not bidirectional, the printer should still print, but you will not have all features of the printer available to the OS.

☐ For Windows 9x, in the printer's Properties dialog box, click Disable bidirectional support for this printer. The PC and printer might have a problem with bidirectional communication.

☐ Check the configuration of the USB, serial, or parallel port in CMOS setup that the printer is using.

☐ Check the parallel port mode in CMOS setup. If ECP mode is selected, verify that a DMA channel is available and not conflicting with another device. Try setting the port to bidirectional.

TO LEARN MORE about parallel port modes, see page 399 of Chapter 9 in *A+ Guide to Managing and Maintaining Your PC* or page 347 of Chapter 8 of *A+ Guide to Hardware*.

☐ Try a different cable.

☐ Try printing using the same printer and printer cable but a different PC. If this step works, then the problem is with the PC or the OS.

☐ Try printing from the PC using a different printer and printer cable. If this step works, then the problem is with the printer or printer cable.

☐ If you cannot print to a different printer and you have access to a port tester, test the port. If you don't have a port tester, try connecting another device to this port.

See Appendix L (page L-1) for information about a port tester.

☐ Try another printer driver. It might not print graphics correctly, but if another driver does work at all, then you can conclude that you have a faulty driver. For example, if you have an HP LaserJet 970Cxi, try using the HP LaserJet 970Cse driver.

☐ Check the Web site of the printer manufacturer for a newer printer driver. Download and install the correct driver.

☐ Verify printer properties. Try lowering the resolution or printing in draft mode.

☐ For a parallel port, check the resources assigned to the port. Open Device Manager, select LPT1, and click Properties. Verify that the resources are assigned correctly for LPT1. Make sure that Device Manager reports "No conflicts."

☐ For Windows 9x, in the printer Properties dialog box, try disabling "Check Port State Before Printing."

☐ Verify printer properties. Try lowering the resolution.

☐ Try disabling printer spooling. Go to the printer Properties dialog box and select Print Directly to the Printer. (For Windows 2000/XP, this option is on the Advanced tab.) Spooling holds print jobs in a queue for printing, so if spooling is disabled, printing from an application can be slower.

☐ For Windows 9x, if you are having trouble printing from an application, the application might be incompatible with Windows. One way to try to solve this problem is to click Start, Run, and type mkcompat.exe. This utility enables you to troubleshoot and solve problems that might make an application incompatible with a certain version of Windows.

☐ If you are having trouble printing from an application, you can also bypass spooling by selecting Print from the File menu in the application, selecting the option to print to a file, and then dragging that file to the icon representing your printer.

☐ Check the hard drive for errors. For Windows 2000/XP, use Error Checking and for Windows 9x, use ScanDisk.

☐ Verify that enough hard drive space is available for the OS to create temporary print files.

☐ Boot Windows in Safe Mode and attempt to print. (For a network printer, use Safe Mode with Networking.) If this step works, then there might be a conflict between the printer driver and another driver or application.

☐ Check the printer documentation for troubleshooting steps to solve printer problems.

☐ When updating the drivers, consider that you might have downloaded the wrong printer drivers. Verify the printer manufacturer and model, and double-check the Web site.

Troubleshooting Printing from an Application

Symptom: Cannot print from an application, but printing an OS test page is successful.

☐ Verify that the correct printer is selected in the Print setup dialog box.

☐ Try printing a different file within the same application.

☐ Delete any files in the print spool. Select Start, Settings, Printers. From the Printers window, double-click the printer icon. From the menu at the top of the window, click Printer, Purge Print Documents.

☐ Reboot the PC. Immediately enter NotePad or WordPad, type some text, and print.

☐ Reopen the application giving the print error, and attempt to print again.
☐ Try creating new data in a newly created file and printing it. Keep the data simple.
☐ Try printing from another application.
☐ If you can print from other applications but not this application, consider reinstalling the application.
☐ Remove and reinstall the printer drivers.
☐ For a DOS application, remove and reinstall the printer. During the installation, verify that the printer is configured to print from DOS programs.

Symptom: Only part of a page prints to a laser printer, or nothing prints.

☐ For some laser printers, if the printer does not have enough memory to hold the entire page, an error occurs. For others, only a part of the page prints.
☐ For some HP LaserJet printers that don't have a control panel on the front of the printer, an error message displays as a flashing amber error light. For some HP LaserJet printers that have a control panel, the error message, "20 Mem Overflow," displays. This indicates that there is not enough memory. The solution is to install more memory or print only simple pages with little graphics.
☐ Print a self-test page to verify how much memory is installed. Check the user guide for the printer to determine how much memory the printer can support and what kind of memory to buy.

Symptom: Printing is very slow.

☐ Reboot the PC. After a reboot, use Task Manager to verify that only necessary processes are running.
☐ Delete any spooled print jobs still pending.
☐ Clean up the hard drive, deleting temporary files.
☐ Use Disk Defragmenter to optimize the hard drive.
☐ Verify that enough hard drive space is available for the OS to create temporary print files.
☐ Close any applications that are not currently being used.
☐ Uninstall and reinstall the printer driver.
☐ Add more memory to the printer. See the printer manual for directions. A printer self-test page usually states how much printer memory is installed.
☐ Lower the printer resolution and the print quality (which lowers the REt settings).
☐ For Windows 9x, verify that EMF spooling is enabled. Access the Printer Properties dialog box. Click the Detail tab, and then click Spool Settings. In the Spool data format box, select EMF. Select Spool print jobs so that the program finishes printing faster.
☐ Upgrade the computer's memory or the CPU.

Symptom: Images don't print correctly, or garbage prints.

☐ Start the computer in Safe Mode, and try to print again.
☐ Try printing only a single page at a time.
☐ For laser printers, if only a part of the page prints, the printer might be low on memory. Add printer memory, or print only simple pages with few graphics.
☐ For Windows 9x, try disabling EMF spooling. Access the Printer Properties dialog box. Click the Detail tab, and then click Spool Settings. In the Spool data format box, select RAW. Select Print Directly to the Printer.

Network Printer Problems

Symptom: Cannot print to a network printer.

Problems with network printing might be caused by the printer, the network to the printer, or the computer trying to use the printer. You can isolate the problem by finding the answers to the following questions:

☐ Is the printer online?

☐ Is the correct network printer selected?

☐ Verify the correct drivers for the printer are installed.

☐ Does the user have rights to use the printer? Log in as an administrator. In the Printers or Printers and Faxes window, open the printer Properties window and click the Security tab. Make sure that the user group or user account is in the list of those allowed to use the printer. If appropriate, add Everyone to the list.

☐ If you are using a printer connected locally to another computer on the network, try accessing a shared folder on the remote PC. If you cannot, you might not be logged on to your PC with a user ID and password that the remote PC recognizes.

☐ Can you print from the computer that has the printer installed locally? If not, solve the problem at the local PC before attempting to solve the problem of printing over the network.

☐ Run the self-test on the printer; does it print? If not, there is a problem with the printer.

> **TO LEARN MORE** about how to share folders and printers on a network using Windows, see page 1003 of Chapter 19 in *A+ Guide to Managing and Maintaining Your PC* or page 549 of Chapter 10 of *A+ Guide to Software*.

☐ Turn the printer OFF and back ON. Try rebooting the PC.

☐ Using the Printers or Printers and Faxes window, delete the printer. Using Windows 2000/XP My Network Places or Windows 9x Network Neighborhood, reconnect the printer.

☐ Is the printer shared on the PC to which it is connected? If so, is the PC running?

☐ Can you print to another network printer? If so, there might be a problem with the printer's configuration.

☐ Can the PC that has the printer locally connected (the host PC) view shared files and folders on the computer from which you're trying to print (the remote PC)?

☐ Is enough hard disk space available on the remote PC?

☐ Can you print successfully from another application on the remote PC?

☐ Can you print successfully from the host PC using the identical application?

☐ If you print to a file and then send the file to the host PC, does it print successfully? If this step works, then the problem lies with data transmission to the network printer. If it does not work, then the problem involves the application or print driver on the remote PC.

☐ Try running diagnostic software provided by the printer manufacturer.

☐ For DOS applications, you might need to exit the application before printing will work. Verify the printer is configured to handle DOS printing over the network.

☐ For a printer connected directly to the network, try Pinging the printer. If the Ping does not work, print a test page at the printer, which should show you the IP address of the printer. Is the IP address correct?

□ Check the PC's configuration of the network printer. Is it set to use a TCP/IP port using the correct IP address?

□ Look on the printer manufacturer Web site for directions to install the network printer. Uninstall and reinstall the printer, carefully following these directions. Try the Ping command again.

□ Can another PC on the network print to the network printer? If so, carefully compare the printer configurations, and look for differences that you can fix.

TROUBLESHOOTING PDA AND PC CONNECTIONS

For problems connecting a PDA to a PC, check the following:

□ Is the PDA software installed on the PC? Does the software have to be launched manually before the connection will work?

□ Is the USB or serial cable plugged in at both ends?

□ For a USB connection, verify that the USB controller is working in Device Manager with no conflicts.

□ Is the USB or serial port enabled in CMOS setup?

□ Is the PDA turned ON?

□ For Bluetooth wireless connections, set the PDA close to the computer. Reinstall the Bluetooth driver on the PC. Bluetooth connections should immediately work without any special configuration as soon as the two devices are close to each other.

□ Check the PDA documentation for other things to do and try.

□ Uninstall and reinstall the PDA software on the PC.

□ Check the Web site of the PDA manufacturer for problems and solutions.

TROUBLESHOOTING NOTEBOOKS

Symptom: Notebook appears to be "dead."

□ Maybe the battery is dead. Connect the AC adapter. Do you hear fans spinning or see lights?

□ Maybe the problem is just with the display. Try connecting an external monitor.

□ Check the AC adapter connections at the notebook and at the power outlet. Check the power cords connected to the adapter itself.

□ Does the outlet have power? Try connecting a lamp or other device.

□ Unplug the AC adapter. Remove the battery and any PC Cards or other peripherals. Press the reset button (if you have one). Reconnect power and try again. Don't use the touch pad while restarting.

□ Remove all but one RAM module and try again. Reinstall all RAM modules and try again.

□ The problem might be caused by a faulty AC adapter, RAM, CPU, or motherboard. First try a known good AC adapter.

Symptom: Battery pack does not work, but the AC adapter does.

□ Check that the battery is installed correctly.

□ Charge the battery.

□ Try a known good battery.

Symptom: Cannot boot from a CD or floppy disk.

□ Make sure that the CD or floppy is bootable. Try booting on another computer.

□ Check the boot sequence in CMOS setup.

Symptom: Forgotten password.

☐ Notebook manufacturers can reset power-on passwords, but how they do this is strictly protected. Contact an authorized service center for your notebook, and ask how to proceed.

Symptom: The battery pack discharges too quickly.

☐ If a battery is old and begins to discharge quickly, replace the battery.

☐ Turn down the brightness of the LCD panel.

☐ Check power management settings in Control Panel, and adjust the "Running on batteries" options. Verify that the Portable/Laptop power scheme is selected.

☐ Check power management settings in CMOS setup. Consider using default options.

☐ The battery gauge might need to be calibrated. Try calibrating the battery. Your notebook might include a utility to do this. Check the Start menu, or see the notebook documentation for instructions.

☐ Some applications might be drawing too much power and CPU time. Use Task Manager to identify processes that are hogging resources.

☐ When playing a movie on DVD, make sure the Portable/Laptop power scheme is selected in the power management options of Control Panel.

☐ When using applications such as MS Word that automatically save files, extend the time to automatically save. This will reduce hard disk access.

☐ Remove PC Cards when you're not using them. Some draw power even when they are not in use.

☐ Surfing the Internet using a modem can draw excess power. Consider using a wireless or Ethernet connection instead.

☐ Reading and writing to CDs or DVDs and games use a lot of power. Try limiting these tasks when running on battery power.

Symptom: Notebook turns OFF immediately after it is turned ON.

☐ The battery might be very low. Try recharging the battery.

Symptom: Battery will not charge.

☐ Make sure you're using the correct AC adapter with the proper power rating.

☐ Check that the battery is installed correctly and the AC adapter is connected at all points.

☐ Move the notebook away from any heat source. Allow the battery to cool. Check that all air vents are clear of obstructions.

Symptom: Notebook does not enter standby mode or hibernation.

☐ If the problem started after new software was installed, try uninstalling the software. Contact the software manufacturer for a fix.

☐ Is there a connection to another computer that is active? If the notebook is busy, it will not suspend.

☐ Check that hibernation is enabled in CMOS setup. Verify the power management settings in Control Panel are correct. Is hibernation enabled in this window?

Symptom: Dark or dim LCD display.

☐ Adjust the brightness of the LCD panel.

☐ Press the Fn key and other keys to toggle between display devices several times.

☐ Try an external monitor.

☐ Reseat memory modules.

☐ If the problem persists, it might be caused by faulty RAM, LCD panel, inverter, motherboard, internal video cables, or the CPU.

Symptom: Using an external monitor or projector does not work.

- ☐ Use the Fn key and other keys to toggle display to an external device.
- ☐ Check all connections.
- ☐ Does the monitor or projector have power? Is it turned ON?
- ☐ Try a lower screen resolution.
- ☐ Try another external device.

Symptom: Hard drive doesn't spin up or gives errors.

- ☐ Try removing and reinstalling the drive.
- ☐ The problem might be with the hard drive or the motherboard. Try installing the hard drive in another computer. For a desktop computer, you can use a USB converter kit to install the hard disk using a USB port on the desktop computer.

Symptom: Hard disk makes strange noises.

- ☐ Backup all data immediately.
- ☐ Remove and reinstall the drive.
- ☐ Are you sure the noise is coming from the hard disk? Check for other noises from a fan, PC card drive, or other device.
- ☐ Replace the hard drive.

Symptom: Files on the hard drive are corrupted.

- ☐ Run antivirus software to check for malware.
- ☐ Use the hard drive Properties window to check for drive errors.
- ☐ If the notebook has diagnostic software, run it.
- ☐ Recover as much data as you can. Then reformat the drive and reinstall the system.

Symptom: A CD or DVD does not work.

- ☐ Check the disc for dirt, smudges, scratches, or other damage. Clean it with a soft dry cloth. Try another disc. Make sure the disc is correctly inserted in the drive.
- ☐ Restart the notebook and try again.
- ☐ For a DVD that has a region code error, know that most DVD drives allow only a limited number of region codes to be used by the drive. After this number is exceeded, DVDs with other region codes won't work. See the documentation for your DVD player software for help.

Symptom: One or more keys on the keyboard don't work.

- ☐ Check the keyboard applet in Control Panel for errors. If Windows reports the keyboard is giving problems, try updating device drivers.
- ☐ Is the numeric keypad enabled or disabled? See notebook documentation for how to toggle this setting using the Fn key.
- ☐ If certain keys don't work or the key caps are loose or missing, consider replacing the keyboard.

Symptom: Out of memory error.

- ☐ Make sure there is enough free space on drive C.
- ☐ Close some applications and background processes.
- ☐ Consider upgrading memory.

Symptom: No sound.

- ☐ Check sound volume on keyboard and in Windows task bar. Is sound muted?
- ☐ Check Device Manager for errors with the sound device.
- ☐ If the notebook has diagnostic software, run it.

Symptom: A USB port does not work.

- ☐ Check USB device connections. Try a different USB device.
- ☐ Restart the notebook.
- ☐ In Device Manager, check for errors under Universal Serial Bus controllers (the controller that manages the USB port).
- ☐ Check CMOS setup. Is the port enabled?
- ☐ If the notebook has diagnostic software, run it.
- ☐ Using Device Manager, try updating the USB drivers for the port
- ☐ Try another USB port.

Symptom: Modem port does not work.

- ☐ Check the dial-up connection properties and settings.
- ☐ Check Device Manager for errors. Is the modem enabled?
- ☐ If you're in a hotel, ask for a data line. Don't use a digital line or a PBX.
- ☐ Try disabling data compression and error correction.
- ☐ If your notebook has diagnostic software, run it.

Symptom: Network port does not work.

- ☐ Check all cable connections.
- ☐ Check the light beside the port (if there is one). A steady light indicates a connection and a blinking light indicates activity.
- ☐ If your notebook has diagnostic software, run it.

> **GO TO** For more things to do and check when troubleshooting a network connection, go to *Troubleshooting Wired Networks* (page 132).

Symptom: Cannot connect to a wireless network.

- ☐ Check that the wireless switch on the keyboard is turned ON. There might also be a wireless switch turned ON or OFF using Fn and a function key.
- ☐ Move the notebook to a better position within the wireless access area.
- ☐ After following the procedures to check TCP/IP and wireless settings, if you still are not able to make a connection and the notebook has diagnostic software, run it.

> **GO TO** To learn how to check TCP/IP settings and wireless settings, go to *Troubleshooting Wireless Networks* (page 133).

Symptom: PC Card device does not work.

- ☐ Restart the notebook.
- ☐ Try the card in another computer.
- ☐ Uninstall the card, and reinstall it using current device drivers downloaded from the card manufacturer Web site.
- ☐ When updating the drivers, consider you might have downloaded the wrong device drivers. Verify the device manufacturer and model, and double-check the Web site.

Symptom: Notebook overheats.

- ☐ Don't place notebook on blankets or other fabric that can prevent air from circulating underneath the notebook. All vents need to be free.
- ☐ Games use a lot of CPU power and can cause overheating.
- ☐ If the problem persists, consider a fan is not working.

Symptom: Notebook halts or runs sluggishly.

☐ Access Task Manager (press Ctl-Alt-Del) and look for an application that is not responding.

☐ Restart the notebook.

☐ Check the hard drive to make sure there is enough free space. Run Chkdsk and Defragmenter.

☐ Check for overheating.

To solve problems with Windows and applications starting or running slowly, go to *Speeding Up Windows 2000/XP* (page 101).

TROUBLESHOOTING SMALL NETWORKS

Small networks can be as simple as two PCs connected with a crossover cable. A network can have centralized hubs or switches with PCs connected to them using patch cables. Networks can be wired or wireless, and most networks are a combination of both. If Internet access is available on one PC, that PC can share it with others on the network, or the Internet access can be provided by a router connected to a DSL box or cable modem. A wireless network can use a wireless access point to access a wired network, or wireless PCs can connect in ad hoc mode with no wireless access point involved.

If a Windows XP or Windows 98 PC has an Internet connection, it can use Internet Connection Sharing (ICS) to allow other PCs on the network access to the Internet. ICS serves as a proxy server to others on the network. Third-party proxy software can also be used instead of ICS. A more common configuration is to use a router that connects to the Internet, which contains firmware that acts as the proxy server. Also, a firewall that protects the network from unauthorized access on the network can be software (for example, Windows XP Firewall) or hardware (for example, firmware on the router).

When wired and wireless networks and Internet access are involved, begin by troubleshooting problems with the network before tackling problems with Internet access. Begin by using Flowchart 4-7 to help isolate a network problem.

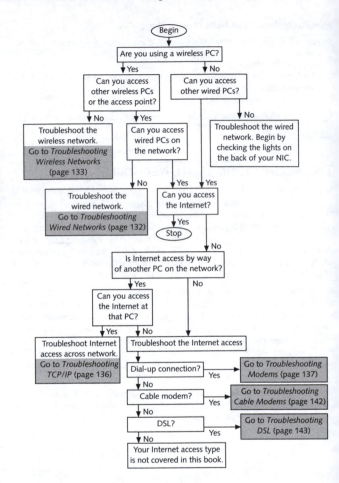

Flowchart 4-7 Troubleshooting network problems

Troubleshooting Wired Networks

Symptom: Computer cannot make a connection to the network.

- ☐ Are the indicator lights working on the NIC? This means the NIC is seeing the network. One steady light indicates connectivity, and one blinking light indicates activity on the network. If no lights, then consider the problem to be hardware related. Check the network cable connection.
- ☐ Are the indicator lights on the hub functioning, and are the cables connected?

☐ Are you sure you used a patch (straight-through) cable? A crossover cable will not work.

☐ Are all the cables connected?

☐ Check the network cable to make sure it is not damaged and that it does not exceed the recommended length for the type of network you are using.

☐ Go to Device Manager, and see if your NIC is listed and appears okay to Windows. If Device Manager reports errors, try uninstalling and reinstalling the NIC.

☐ Using the Network Connections window, make sure the network is enabled.

☐ Are other computers on the network unable to communicate with each other? If the entire network is down, the problem is not isolated to the PC and the NIC you are working on.

☐ If other computers on the network are working and the NIC lights are still not lit, consider replacing the NIC.

☐ Check My Network Places or Network Neighborhood, and look for resources on remote computers. Do you need to log on to a remote computer with a valid user ID and password?

☐ For peer-to-peer networking, do all computers need to share resources in the same workgroup?

TO LEARN MORE about how to share resources in the same Windows workgroup, see Chapter 17, beginning with page 897 in *A+ Guide to Managing and Maintaining Your PC* or Chapter 8, beginning with page 443, of *A+ Guide to Software*.

☐ Turn off all PCs that cannot connect and reboot each, one at a time.

☐ For a TCP/IP network, run ipconfig, and check to see if an IP number has been assigned.

☐ Is the firewall preventing communication? Some commercial firewalls can block access; check the documentation for configuration information. Are Windows XP Firewall settings correct? When using a router as a firewall, can you access the router firmware from any computer on the network? If so, check firewall settings. Try temporarily turning off the firewall to see if the problem is resolved. If so, turn it back on and resolve the firewall problem.

☐ Connect the network cable to a different port on the hub.

☐ Verify the user account name and the computer name are not the same. Sometimes this can cause problems.

☐ Is your motherboard BIOS current? Flash BIOS if an upgrade is available.

If your problem is still not solved, go to *Troubleshooting TCP/IP* (page 136).
GO TO

Troubleshooting Wireless Networks
Symptom: A wireless PC cannot connect to a wireless network.

☐ Just like radios, wireless connections are susceptible to interference. Are any cordless phones, microwave ovens, or other wireless networks nearby causing interference?

☐ For notebooks, check that the wireless switch on the keyboard is turned ON. Also look for a software switch turned ON using Fn and a function key.

☐ Open the Wireless Network Connection window. From this window, you can select the access point you want to connect to. Make sure you are in range of the access point. If available, try a different access point.

☐ Have you assigned a computer name and a workgroup name to all PCs on the network? The workgroup must be the same for all computers on the network.

☐ If a new device is added to the network and it doesn't work, it might be using the 802.11a standard instead of the more common 802.11b/g/n standards.

☐ Verify the TCP/IP or NetBEUI settings are correct.

 For troubleshooting TCP/IP network settings, go to *Troubleshooting TCP/IP* (page 136).

☐ If you are attempting to connect two wireless PCs in ad hoc mode, do the following:

- Verify that both NICs are set to the same mode.
- Verify the service set identifier (SSID) is set to ANY, indicating the PC can connect to any access point it finds.
- Verify the transmission rate (Tx Rate) is set to fully automatic.
- Disable encryption until you have the connection working.
- Try uninstalling and reinstalling the NIC drivers.
- Try connecting the PC to an access point device.

☐ If you are using a wireless access point (AP), do the following:

- Make sure the AP device is ON and has power.
- Verify that other PCs on the wireless LAN can connect to the AP.
- Make sure the correct SSID is used, which is case sensitive. Check that encryption is not being used, or, if it is used, the correct type (WEP, WPA, or WPA2) is selected and the correct passphrase is used.
- If you use the AP to connect to a wired LAN, check the network cable looking for a frayed or broken cable or connectors, and verify the connectors are secure.
- If your AP connects you to the Internet and you lose the connection, consider the AP device to be the problem before troubleshooting the computer.
- Check the Web site of the AP manufacturer for more things to check and try.

 TO LEARN MORE about configuring wireless LANs, see Chapter 17, beginning with page 905 in *A+ Guide to Managing and Maintaining Your PC* or Chapter 10, beginning with page 494 of *A+ Guide to Hardware* or Chapter 8, beginning with page 451, of *A+ Guide to Software*.

☐ If a device fails to work, it might have a bad transceiver in the NIC. Try a different NIC.

Symptom: A new wireless network does not work.

If you are setting up a new wireless network, be sure to check the following:

☐ Is there a cross-over cable between the AP and the cable modem or DSL router? You might need a straight-through cable.

☐ Is the AP using the same channel that the computers are using?

☐ Disable all security features for the AP, and try to connect again. After you get the connection working, then enable one security feature at a time until you find the one giving problems.

☐ When using encryption, are all users using the same passphrase? When using MAC filtering, have you entered the NIC's MAC address in the MAC table of the AP?

☐ If you are using static IP addressing from your ISP and the AP is connected to the Internet, did you enter the following values at the AP setup screen: IP address, Subnet mask, Default Gateway, and ISPs DNS IP addresses?

☐ Be sure all the power and network cables are properly connected and that the LEDs are lit.

☐ Run ipconfig, and check to see if an IP number has been assigned.

☐ Try releasing and renewing the IP address.

☐ Have you chosen the same type of WLAN for all devices on the network? The choices are Infrastructure Mode or Ad-Hoc Mode. Use Infrastructure Mode if an AP is used. Use Ad-Hoc Mode if PCs connect to each other without the use of an access point (AP).

☐ If you can connect to the wireless network, but cannot access resources on the network, check that you have assigned a computer name and a workgroup name to all PCs on the network. The workgroup must be the same for all computers on the network.

TO LEARN MORE about configuring and using Windows workgroups, see Chapter 17, beginning with page 897, in *A+ Guide to Managing and Maintaining Your PC* or Chapter 8, beginning with page 443, of *A+ Guide to Software*.

☐ If a new device is added to the network and it doesn't work, it might be using the 802.11a standard instead of the more common 802.11b/g/n standards.

☐ Verify the TCP/IP or NetBEUI settings are correct.

GO TO For troubleshooting TCP/IP network settings, go to *Troubleshooting TCP/IP* (page 136).

Symptom: The wireless network is not secured.

The first step is to secure the router or access point by changing the username and password so that others cannot access and control the device. Here are three other ways a wireless network can be secured:

☐ Disable SSID broadcasting so that a user must know the name of the wireless network in order to use the network. (This method secures which users can use the network. However, know that savvy users can use sniffer software to discover the SSID.)

☐ Enable MAC-address filtering so that a computer cannot use the network unless its MAC address has been entered into a table in the wireless access point. (This method secures which computers can use the network.)

☐ Encrypt data being sent over the network so that it cannot be read. (This method secures the data sent over the network.)

Do the following to secure a wireless network:

☐ To disable SSID broadcasting, connect to the setup utility on the access point by way of the wired network. Using the setup utility windows, disable SSID broadcasting, and change the SSID to a secret name. Distribute the name to those authorized to use the network.

☐ Use the wireless access point's setup utility to enable MAC-address filtering. Enter the MAC address of each computer authorized to use the wireless network.

☐ To encrypt data, enable an encryption method that is supported by the access point and every computer using the network. WPA2 is stronger than WPA, which is stronger the WEP. Use the strongest method supported by all devices. Enter a passphrase, and distribute it to all authorized users.

Troubleshooting TCP/IP

Symptom: Cannot connect to a network or ISP using TCP/IP.

One useful tool to diagnose TCP/IP problems is Ping, which tests connectivity by sending a signal to a remote computer. If the remote computer is online and it hears the signal, it will respond, unless it is configured to not respond for security reasons. Two other useful tools are IPConfig under Windows 2000/XP and WinIPcfg under Windows 9x, which test the TCP/IP configuration. Try these things:

☐ For Windows 2000/XP, at the command prompt, enter *Ipconfig /all*. For Windows 9x, click Start, Run, enter *Winipcfg* in the Run dialog box, and then click OK. If the TCP/IP configuration is correct and an IP address is assigned, the IP address, subnet mask, and default gateway appear along with the adapter address.

☐ For dynamic IP addressing, if the PC could not reach the DHCP server, then it will assign itself an IP address. This is called IP autoconfiguration. The results of the Ipconfig command and the Winipcfg window both show the IP address as the IP Autoconfiguration Address, and the address will begin with 169. In this case, suspect that the PC is not able to reach the network or the DHCP server is down.

☐ Try to release the current IP address and lease a new address. To do this with Ipconfig, first use the *Ipconfig /release* command, and then use the *Ipconfig /renew* command. Using Winipcfg, with the network card selected, click the Release button, and then click the Renew button.

☐ Next try the loopback address test. At a command prompt, enter the command *Ping 127.0.0.1* (with no period after the final 1). This IP address always refers to your local computer. It should respond with a reply message from your computer. If this works, TCP/IP is likely to be configured correctly.

☐ If you get any errors up to this point, then assume that the problem is on your PC. Check the installation and configuration of each component such as the network card and the TCP/IP protocol suite. Remove and reinstall each component and watch for error messages, writing them down so that you can recognize or research them later as necessary. Compare the configuration to that of a PC that is working on the same network.

☐ Next Ping the IP address of your default gateway. If it does not respond, then the problem might be with the gateway or with the network to the gateway.

☐ Now try to Ping the host computer you are trying to reach. If it does not respond, then the problem might be with the host computer or with the network to the computer.

☐ If you have Internet access and substitute a domain name for the IP address in the Ping command, and Ping works, then you can conclude that DNS works. If an IP address works, but the domain name does not work, the problem lies with DNS. Try this command: *ping www.course.com*.

 If the Ping command works, but Internet Explorer still cannot connect, then go to *Troubleshooting Internet Explorer* (page 144).

☐ Make sure the NIC and its drivers are installed correctly by checking the NIC in Device Manager.

☐ Try uninstalling and reinstalling the NIC. If the drivers install with errors, download new drivers from the manufacturer and try again. Look on the CD that came with the NIC for a setup program or diagnostic software. Try them, but before you use the setup program, be sure to first uninstall the NIC.

☐ When a network drive map is not working, first check My Network Places and verify that you can access other resources on the remote computer. You might need to log onto the remote computer with a valid user ID and password.

☐ Traceroute (Tracert in Windows) is used to show all intermediate hops, and it can be used to locate where a connect problem is occurring. At the command prompt, enter *Tracert* and then an IP address.

 TO LEARN MORE about how to configure a TCP/IP network, see page 881 of Chapter 17 in *A+ Guide to Managing and Maintaining Your PC* or page 426 of Chapter 8 of *A+ Guide to Software*.

☐ When updating the drivers, consider you might have downloaded the wrong device drivers. Verify the device manufacturer and model, and double-check the Web site.

TROUBLESHOOTING CONNECTIONS TO THE INTERNET

You have gotten to this point in the Troubleshooting Tool if the following is true:

☐ You are working from a PC that is connected directly to the Internet by way of a modem, cable modem, DSL box, or router.

☐ You can boot to the Windows desktop, but you cannot access the Internet.

 If you connect to the Internet by way of a local network, and you cannot access others on the network, then go to *Troubleshooting Small Networks* (page 131).

 If you connect to the Internet by way of a DSL connection, and your PC is connected to the DSL box by way of a network, network cable, or USB cable, then go to *Troubleshooting DSL* (page 143).

 If you connect to the Internet by way of a cable modem, and your PC is connected to the cable modem by way of a network, network cable, or USB cable, then go to *Troubleshooting Cable Modems* (page 142).

 If you can Ping a server on the Internet, but Internet Explorer does not work, then go to *Troubleshooting Internet Explorer* (page 144).

Troubleshooting Modems

You have gotten to this point in the Troubleshooting Tool if the following is true:

☐ You cannot connect to the Internet, and you are using a modem to make the connection.

☐ You can boot successfully to the Windows desktop.

First verify the modem is working. To do that, attempt to make a call using the modem. If you hear the modem dial the number and begin making the handshaking sounds, then you can assume the modem is working and the problem is with Dial-Up Networking, the ISP, or your TCP/IP settings on your PC.

If your modem is working and you still cannot connect to the Internet, then go to *Troubleshooting Problems with Dial-Up Networking and Connecting to the Internet* (page 140).

Symptom: The modem does not respond.

To address this problem, answer the following questions and try the following approaches:

- ☐ Is the modem plugged into the phone jack?
- ☐ Is the external modem plugged into the computer? Is the connection solid?
- ☐ There are two jacks on a modem. Are the lines reversed?
- ☐ Is the phone line working? Plug in a phone. Is there a dial tone?
- ☐ Try a different phone cable.
- ☐ Do you need to dial an extra character to get an outside line, such as 9 or 8?
- ☐ Does Windows recognize the modem in Device Manager? If not, uninstall it and install it again.
- ☐ Click Diagnostics in the Modems Properties dialog box, and then click More Info. Windows will give you information about the problem if it can talk to your modem.
- ☐ Try a known good modem.
- ☐ Is your modem using the V.92 standard? There are still some K56flex, x2, and V.90 modems around. Replace the old modem with a V.92 modem.
- ☐ Has the modem ever worked, or is this a new installation? If it is a new installation, check these things:
  - Is the computer short on RAM or hard drive space? Try closing all other applications currently running.
  - For Windows 98 installations, is the modem set to the same COM port and IRQ to which the software is set?
  - Is the COM port working? Test it using third-party software. Is it disabled in CMOS setup?
  - For Windows 98, is another device also configured to the same COM port or IRQ that the modem is using?
  - For an internal legacy modem, check the DIP switches and jumpers. Do they agree with the modem properties in the OS?
  - Try moving an internal modem to a different expansion slot. For an external modem using a serial port card, move the serial port card to a different slot.
  - For a USB modem, check the connection at the PC or hub.
  - For an external modem, use a different cable. (For a serial port, you need an RS-232 cable).
- ☐ Are the lights on an external modem working? The lights can tell you if the modem is working and if it is responding to commands.
- ☐ For a PC Card or PCMCIA card, reinsert the card. In Windows, an icon should be present on the taskbar.
- ☐ Did the software correctly initialize the modem? If you did not give the correct modem type to the software, it might be trying to send the wrong initialization command. Try AT&F. (For Windows 2000/XP, in Control Panel, double-click Phone and Modem Options. Click Modems, Properties, Advanced. Enter the AT command under Extra initialization commands. Under Windows 9x, in Control Panel, double-click Modem. Select the modem and click Modem Properties, Connections, Advanced Connection Settings. Enter the AT command under Extra Settings.) Retry the modem.

Symptom: The modem says that there is no dial tone, even though you can hear it.

□ The modem might not be able to detect the dial tone, even if you can hear it. Try unplugging any other equipment plugged into the same phone line such as a fax machine.

□ Try giving the ATX0 command before you dial. Enter the command under Modem Properties as described above.

□ Straighten your phone lines! Don't let them get all twisted and crossed up with other heavy electrical lines.

Symptom: The modem dials and then says that the other end is busy, even when you know that it is not.

□ This problem can arise with international calls; the modem does not recognize the signal as a ring. Try entering the ATX0 command before entering the command to dial.

□ Straighten the phone lines and remove extra equipment, as described above.

Symptom: The sending modem and the receiving modem take a very long time to negotiate the connection.

□ This problem is probably due to a noisy phone line. Try calling again or using a different number.

□ Remove other equipment from your line. A likely suspect is a credit card machine.

□ Turn off data compression, and try again.

□ Turn off error correction, and try again.

□ Try forcing your modem to use a slower speed.

Symptom: During a connection, it sounds as if the handshaking starts all over again.

□ Called retraining, modems normally do this if the phone line is noisy and causes much data to become corrupted. Do the things listed above to clear your line of equipment and twisted phone lines.

Symptom: File transfers are too slow.

□ If your modem supports data compression, verify that the modem is configured to use it.

Symptom: The modem loses the connection at odd times or is slow.

□ Check the port speed and line speed assigned to the modem.

□ For Windows 2000/XP, in the Modem Properties box, click Advanced, Change Default Preferences to make sure the Disconnect a Call If Idle More Than option is not checked. For Windows 9x, open the Modems Properties dialog box and click the Connections tab; make sure that the option is not checked.

□ Make sure call waiting is turned off. Usually *70 enables and disables call waiting.

□ You might have a noisy phone line. Try the connection using two modems of the same brand and model. If performance is better, the problem is most likely the phone line, because two modems of the same brand and model are best able to compensate for a noisy phone line.

□ Is the phone line from the modem to the jack too long? Electromagnetic interference might be the problem.

□ Straighten the phone lines, and clear the line of any extra equipment.

☐ Uninstall and reinstall the modem. Allow Windows to detect the modem for you and install its own drivers.

☐ Search the Web site of the modem manufacturer for a new driver, and install that.

Symptom: The modem drops the connection and gives the NO CARRIER message.

☐ Most likely the connection was first dropped by the remote modem. Check that no one is trying to use a phone extension on this line.

☐ Disable call waiting by putting *70, before the dialing number in the string. Some communication software has a setting to disable call waiting. If not, you can put these four characters in the Windows 2000/XP Extra initialization commands under the Advanced tab of Modem Properties or the Windows 9x Extra Settings box of Advanced Connections Settings.

☐ Remove extra equipment from the line, and straighten the phone lines.

Symptom: When the weather is bad, the connection often disconnects.

☐ This problem is caused by a dirty phone line. Remove any extra equipment and straighten the lines.

Symptom: Whenever large files are downloaded, some data is lost.

☐ Make sure that hardware flow control is ON and that software flow control is OFF for the software, the COM port, and the modem.

Symptom: The connection fails whenever large files are uploaded or downloaded.

There might be a buffer overflow. Try these things to gain better control of data flow:

☐ Make sure that hardware flow control is ON and that software flow control is OFF for the software, the COM port, and the modem.

☐ Is the serial port speed set too high for the UART chip you have? Lower the port speed.

☐ For an external modem, try a different serial port cable.

Symptom: You get nothing but garbage across the connection.

☐ Check the port settings. Try 8 data bits, no parity, and one stop bit (8, No, and 1).

☐ Slow down the port speed.

☐ Slow down the modem speed.

Troubleshooting Problems with Dial-Up Networking and Connecting to the Internet

Symptom: Using a modem, you cannot connect to an Internet service provider or to a network.

Because dial-up networking involves so many different components, first find out what works and what doesn't. Find out the answers to these questions:

☐ Does the modem work? Try calling any working phone number. You should hear the modem attempt a handshake before it disconnects.

☐ Perform a modem diagnostic test. For Windows 2000/XP, open Device Manager, right-click on the modem, and select Properties from the shortcut menu. Click Diagnostics, Query Modem. For Windows 9x, in the Control

Panel, click the Modems icon. Select the COM port the modem is installed on, and click More Info.

☐ Compare the printout of a modemlog.txt file that was made during a successful connection at another PC with the modemlog.txt file of this PC so as to identify the point in the connection at which an error occurs. For Windows 2000/XP, logging is always turned ON. To view and print the log file, click the Diagnostics tab on the modem's Properties box. Then click View log. The log file will open in Notepad. For Windows 9x, to log modem events to the modemlog.txt file, double-click Modems in Control Panel, then select the modem, click Properties, Connection, Advanced, and turn ON Recording to a log file.

☐ Are all components installed? Check for the Dial-Up Adapter and TCP/IP, and check the configuration of each.

☐ Check the Dial-Up Networking connection icon for errors. Is the phone number correct? Does the number need to include a 9 to get an outside line? Has a 1 been added in front of the number by mistake?

☐ Reboot your PC, and try again.

☐ Try dialing the number manually from a phone. Do you hear beeps on the other end?

☐ Try removing and reinstalling each network component. Begin with TCP/IP.

☐ Try another phone number.

☐ For Windows 9x, sometimes older copies of the Windows socket DLL might be interfering with the current Windows 9x socket DLL. (Windows 9x might be finding and executing the older DLL before it finds the newer one.) Search for and rename any files named WINSOCK.DLL except the one in the Windows\System directory.

☐ Open a command prompt window and use the Ping command. Try *Ping www.course.com.* If the Ping command works, then suspect problems with Internet Explorer.

GO TO Go to *Troubleshooting Internet Explorer* (page 144).

Symptom: You can connect, but you get the message "Unable to resolve hostname."

This error message means that TCP/IP is not able to determine how to route a request to a host. Right-click the Dial-Up Networking connection icon, select Properties, and check for these things:

☐ Under Server Type, try making the only network protocol allowed TCP/IP.

☐ Under TCP/IP settings, check the IP addresses of the DNS servers.

☐ Make sure Using the default gateway is selected.

☐ Try not selecting IP header compression.

Symptom: After connecting, you get the error message "Unable to establish a compatible set of network protocols."

This error is most likely to be caused by a problem with the installation and configuration of Dial-Up Networking and/or TCP/IP. Try these things:

☐ Verify that Dial-Up Adapter and TCP/IP are installed and configured correctly.

☐ Remove and reinstall TCP/IP. Be sure to reboot after the installation.

☐ Try putting the two computers in the same workgroup.

☐ For Windows 9x computers, try putting them in different workgroups.

☐ Windows can write the events of PPP processing a call to a log file. Create the file on a PC that makes a successful connection, and compare it with the log file of your bad connection to see exactly when the problem began. Do the following:

■ For Windows 2000/XP, logging is always ON. To view the log file, on the modem's Properties box, click Diagnostics, View log. The log file is named ModemLog_*modemname*.txt.

■ For Windows 9x, to turn ON the logging of events to the file, double-click the Network icon in Control Panel. Click Dial-Up Adapter, click Properties, select the Advanced tab, and select Record a log file. On the Value list, click Yes, and then click OK. Reboot the PC. The file PPPLog.txt is created in the Windows folder as the connection is made and used.

Symptom: When you double-click on the Web browser, the modem does not dial automatically.

☐ Right-click the Web browser icon, and select Properties on the drop-down menu. Under the Connection tab, check Connect to the Internet as needed.

Symptom: The connection works but immediately fails again.

☐ Check to see if PPP is enabled. Go to Properties in Dial-Up Networking.

Troubleshooting Cable Modems

This type of connection uses a cable modem that is connected to the TV cable outlet using coaxial cable and is also connected to a NIC in your PC using a network cable. Some cable modems connect to your PC using a USB cable and port. Find out the answers to these questions:

☐ Check all cable connections between your PC and the modem and between the modem and the cable TV outlet.

☐ Look at the coaxial cable. Are there any breaks or bends of 90° or more? If so replace the cable.

☐ Is the cable television working? If not, contact your cable company.

☐ If your Internet connection suddenly disconnects, either your service is disrupted or your browser has crashed. Try restarting your browser or rebooting your PC.

☐ Unplug the cable modem, and wait five minutes before plugging it back in. Reboot your PC. If that fails, contact your service provider.

☐ If you are using a router, unplug the router and the cable modem. Wait five minutes. Plug up the cable modem, and wait until the lights settle. Then plug up the router.

 TO LEARN MORE about cable modem installations, see page 934 of Chapter 18 in *A+ Guide to Managing and Maintaining Your PC* or page 480 of Chapter 9 in *A+ Guide to Software*.

☐ Open a command prompt window, and use the Ping command. Try *Ping www.course.com*. If the Ping command works, then suspect problems with Internet Explorer.

 Go to *Troubleshooting Internet Explorer* (page 144).

Troubleshooting DSL

This type of connection uses a high-speed phone line between the DSL converter box or router and a network cable between the converter box or router and the NIC in your PC. You can also install your own router between the DSL box and your network. DSL connections are always on. Find out the answers to these questions:

- ☐ Check all connections to the DSL box, router, and switches. Reset the DSL box.
- ☐ Look at both the phone line and the network cable. Are there any breaks, and are the connectors secure? If you see damage, replace the line or cable.
- ☐ Is the telephone working? If not, contact your phone company or DSL provider.
- ☐ Verify that DSL filters are installed at all telephones on this phone line.
- ☐ Is the router functioning? Try turning OFF the router and turning it back ON. Using your browser, you can access the router's firmware by entering the IP address of the router.
- ☐ Try releasing and renewing your IP address. For Windows XP, in the Network Connections window, right-click on the connection icon, and select Repair from the shortcut menu. For Windows 2000, use *Ipconfig/release* and *Ipconfig/renew*. For Windows 9x, use *Winipcfg*.
- ☐ Has your PC been in sleep mode? Sometimes your connection will not survive sleep mode, and you'll have to reboot. Manually disconnect from the Internet if you are going to be away from your PC for any length of time.
- ☐ If the connection suddenly disconnects, either your service is disrupted or your browser has crashed. Try restarting your browser or rebooting your PC.
- ☐ Unplug the router and the DSL box. Wait five minutes. Plug up the DSL box, and wait until the lights settle. Then plug up the router.
- ☐ If you still have a problem, contact your service provider.
- ☐ Did you previously use a modem for a dial-up connection? If so, in Windows 9x, examine the value for the registry key RWIN. It should be at least 32KB.
- ☐ Open a command prompt window and use the Ping command. Try *Ping www.course.com*. If the Ping command works, then suspect problems with Internet Explorer.

Go to *Troubleshooting Internet Explorer* (page 144).

TO LEARN MORE about DSL installations, see page 938 of Chapter 18 in *A+ Guide to Managing and Maintaining Your PC* or page 484 of Chapter 9 in *A+ Guide to Software*.

Troubleshooting Firewalls

Symptom: There is a problem with a hardware or software firewall.

- ☐ If you install a firewall and ICS fails, check the documentation. Some firewalls do not support ICS. For Windows XP, use Windows XP Internet Connection Firewall.
- ☐ If you plan to connect more than two PCs behind the firewall using a 56K modem, know that your connection will be slower with the firewall than without it.
- ☐ Some hardware firewall devices have only a single port for a PC. If you plan to connect more than two PCs behind the firewall, you need a multiport device or an additional switch or hub.
- ☐ Some ISPs might restrict the sharing of an Internet connection. Check with your ISP for details.

☐ When you connect the firewall, make sure you use the right type of Ethernet cable.

☐ When you connect the cable to the firewall, a link light should come on. If it doesn't, either the cable is bad or you used the wrong type of cable.

☐ Be careful configuring the router. A mistake can create a security hole that could make the router useless. Be sure to read the manual.

☐ Try resetting the router to default settings. After you do this, be sure to change the administrator password to the router to prevent unauthorized access.

☐ Be sure to set up to enable DHCP or PPPoE, if your ISP provides either. Check with your ISP to see what it provides.

☐ You will have to set rules for the firewall. The simplest set of rules is to let all outgoing requests through and not allow any incoming requests through.

☐ If you use software that allows incoming requests for communication from the Internet to computers on your network, you must change the rules to open ports, which then increases your security risks.

 TO LEARN MORE about configuring a hardware firewall, see page 958 of Chapter 18 in *A+ Guide to Managing and Maintaining Your PC* or page 504 of Chapter 9 in *A+ Guide to Software*.

 TO LEARN MORE about configuring a software firewall, see page 951 of Chapter 18 in *A+ Guide to Managing and Maintaining Your PC* or page 497 of Chapter 9 in *A+ Guide to Software*.

Troubleshooting Internet Explorer

You have reached this point in the Troubleshooting Tool if the following is true:

☐ You have verified you can connect to the Internet by using the Ping command to reach a server on the Internet.

☐ Internet Explorer cannot access the Internet or gives errors.

Internet Explorer is a highly integrated component of Windows XP, so know that you cannot uninstall, install, or update it without doing the same for Windows XP.

Symptom: Internet Explorer gives errors, your Internet Explorer home page has changed, you cannot access a Web site, or you see new toolbars you didn't ask for.

Suspect malicious software is at work. Do the following:

☐ Run a current version of antivirus software. Use more than one AV product. Also use more than one anti-adware product such as Ad-Aware and Windows Defender.

 If the problem is not solved, go to *Removing Malware from Windows 2000/XP* (page 103).

Symptom: You cannot access a Web site using Internet Explorer.

☐ Apply all Windows updates; this action also updates Internet Explorer.

☐ In Internet Explorer, click Tools, Internet Options, to open the Internet Options window. Empty the Internet Explorer cache by clicking Delete Files.

☐ To further empty the cache of hidden files, delete the cache folder which is:

C:\Documents and Settings\username\Local Settings\Temporary Internet Files

☐ Consider the Hosts file might have an error. Go to the C:\Windows\System32\ Drivers\Etc folder, and unhide files in this folder. Open the Hosts file with Notepad. Look for a line that doesn't begin with # that is pointing a domain name to a wrong IP address.

☐ Use System File Checker (sfc.exe) to verify Windows system files.

Symptom: Internet Explorer freezes or crashes.

☐ Apply all Windows updates; this action also updates Internet Explorer.

☐ Slow video might cause an Internet game to crash. Try updating your video drivers.

☐ To make your system stable, decrease hardware acceleration. In the Display Properties window, select the Troubleshoot tab. Move the Hardware acceleration meter to the left one notch. If this doesn't help, keep moving it one notch to the left until the system becomes stable.

☐ Try uninstalling and reinstalling add-ons that the Web site might be using.

☐ Use System File Checker (sfc.exe) to verify Windows system files.

☐ Consider repairing a corrupted Windows installation. Go to *Performing a Reinstallation (Repair) of Windows 2000/XP* (page 80). Because you might lose Windows settings when you do this, a better option might be to install a different Web browser such as Firefox by Mozilla (*www.mozilla.com/firefox*).

BEEP CODES AND POST CODES

This appendix contains the beep codes and error messages for the major BIOS manufacturers. For more information, see the particular manufacturer's Web site. Many are listed in Appendix H, *Important URLs*.

AMIBIOS BEEP CODES

Before video is active, AMIBIOS communicates errors with beep codes listed in Table A-1.

Table A-1 AMIBIOS beep codes

Beeps	Description	Things to try and do
1 beep	Refresh failure	• Reset the memory modules • Replace modules
2 beeps	Parity error	Same as for 1 beep
3 beeps	Base 64 KB memory failure	Same as for 1 beep
4 beeps	Timer not operational	Indicates a serious problem that might be caused by expansion cards or the motherboard: • Remove all expansion cards except the video card. If the problem goes away, reinstall one card first and then another until you find the card causing the problem. • The motherboard is faulty and must be replaced or sent in for repair
5 beeps	Processor error	Same as for 4 beeps
6 beeps	8042—gate A20 failure	• Replace the keyboard • If the problem persists, see directions for 4 beeps
7 beeps	Processor exception interrupt error	Same as for 4 beeps
8 beeps	Display memory read/write failure	• Replace the memory on the video card • Replace the video card
9 beeps	ROM checksum error	Same as for 4 beeps
10 beeps	CMOS shutdown register read/write error	Same as for 4 beeps
11 beeps	Cache memory bad	Same as for 4 beeps

AWARD BIOS ERROR MESSAGES

Award BIOS does not use beep codes to communicate errors unless the error has to do with the video subsystem. After video is working, errors are communicated as POST codes that can be read by a POST diagnostic card and as error messages displayed on the screen.

TO LEARN MORE about POST diagnostic cards, see Appendix L, *Where to Go for More Help: Hardware Resources* (page L-2). For a list of POST codes and their meanings, see the Phoenix Web site at *www.phoenix.com*. (Award BIOS is owned by Phoenix).

Table A-2 provides a list of error messages that Award BIOS might display during POST.

Table A-2 Award BIOS error messages

Error message	Description	Things to do
1 long, 2 short beeps	There is a problem with video	• Reset the video card • Replace the video card
BIOS ROM checksum error—system halted	BIOS code is corrupted	Replace the BIOS chip
CMOS battery failed	Bad CMOS battery	Replace the battery
CMOS checksum error—defaults loaded	CMOS may be corrupted or battery may be weak	Replace the battery
CPU at nnnn	The running speed of CPU is displayed	This is not an error
Display switch is set incorrectly	A switch on the motherboard that can be set to color or monochrome is set differently than setup	Either change the switch or change setup so they agree
Press ESC to skip memory test	User option	This is not an error
Floppy disk fail	BIOS can't find or initialize the floppy disk	• Install a floppy disk drive or change setup so none is expected • Troubleshoot the floppy drive
Hard disk initializing…	For information only	This is not an error
Hard disk install failure	BIOS can't find or initialize the hard drive controller	• Install a hard drive or change setup so none is expected • Troubleshoot the hard drive subsystem
Hard disk(s) diagnosis fail	A hard drive has failed a diagnostic test	Troubleshoot the hard drive subsystem

(continued)

Table A-2 Award BIOS error messages (continued)

Error Message	Description	Things to Do
Keyboard error or no keyboard present	BIOS can't find the keyboard	• Check keyboard connection • Check that no keys are pressed
Keyboard is locked out—unlock the key	One or more keys are pressed	Check that nothing is resting on the keyboard
Memory test	Memory is being counted	This is not an error
Memory test failed	Memory error—more information may follow	• Reseat memory modules • Replace modules
Override enabled—defaults loaded	BIOS was unable to boot with current CMOS settings so default settings were loaded	Check previous CMOS setup for errors
Press TAB to show POST screen	Motherboard OEM may replace Award BIOS screen with its own	Press TAB to show original Award BIOS screen
Primary master hard drive fail Primary slave hard drive fail Secondary master hard drive fail Secondary slave hard drive fail	POST detected a hard drive failure	Troubleshoot the IDE hard drive subsystem

Phoenix has three general categories of BIOSs: AwardBIOS, FirstBIOS, and PhoenixBIOS. Within each category, there are several BIOS products and versions. See the Phoenix Web site for more information on these products.

Phoenix BIOS

Phoenix BIOS communicates problems during POST and error conditions with beep codes and POST codes that can be read by diagnostic cards (Table A-3).

Table A-3 POST/beep codes for Phoenix BIOS 4.x

Beep code	POST Code	Description
1–1–1–3	02	Verify real mode
1–1–2–1	04	Get CPU type
1–1–2–3	06	Initialize system hardware
1–1–3–1	08	Initialize chipset registers with initial POST values

(continued)

Table A-3 POST/beep codes for Phoenix BIOS 4.x (continued)

Beep Code	POST Code	Description
1-1-3-2	09	Set in POST flag
1-1-3-3	0A	Initialize CPU registers
1-1-4-1	0C	Initialize cache to initial POST values
1-1-4-3	0E	Initialize I/O
1-2-1-1	10	Initialize power management
1-2-1-2	11	Load alternate registers with initial POST values
1-2-1-3	12	Jump to UserPatch0
1-2-2-1	14	Initialize keyboard controller
1-2-2-3	16	BIOS ROM checksum
1-2-3-1	18	8254 timer initialization
1-2-3-3	1A	8237 DMA controller initialization
1-2-4-1	1C	Reset programmable interrupt controller
1-3-1-1	20	Test DRAM refresh
1-3-1-3	22	Test 8742 keyboard controller
1-3-2-1	24	Set ES segment to register to 4GB
1-3-3-1	28	Autosize DRAM
1-3-3-3	2A	Clear 512K base RAM
1-3-4-1	2C	Test 512 base address lines
1-3-4-3	2E	Test 512K base memory
1-4-1-3	32	Test CPU bus-clock frequency
1-4-2-1	34	CMOS RAM read/write failure (this code commonly indicates a problem on the ISA bus such as a card not seated correctly)
1-4-2-4	37	Reinitialize the chipset
1-4-3-1	38	Shadow system BIOS ROM
1-4-3-2	39	Reinitialize the cache
1-4-3-3	3A	Autosize cache
1-4-4-1	3C	Configure advanced chipset registers
1-4-4-2	3D	Load alternate registers with CMOS values
2-1-1-1	40	Set initial CPU speed
2-1-1-3	42	Initialize interrupt vectors
2-1-2-1	44	Initialize BIOS interrupts
2-1-2-3	46	Check ROM copyright notice
2-1-2-4	47	Initialize manager for PCI options ROMs
2-1-3-1	48	Check video configuration against CMOS
2-1-3-2	49	Initialize PCI bus and devices
2-1-3-3	4A	Initialize all video adapters in system
2-1-4-1	4C	Shadow video BIOS ROM
2-1-4-3	4E	Display copyright notice
2-2-1-1	50	Display CPU type and speed
2-2-1-3	52	Test keyboard

(continued)

Table A-3 POST/beep codes for Phoenix BIOS 4.x (continued)

Beep Code	POST Code	Description
2-2-2-1	54	Set key click if enabled
2-2-2-3	56	Enable keyboard
2-2-3-1	58	Test for unexpected interrupts
2-2-3-3	5A	Display prompt "Press F2 to enter SETUP"
2-2-4-1	5C	Test RAM between 512 K and 640 K
2-3-1-1	60	Test expanded memory
2-3-1-3	62	Test extended memory address lines
2-3-2-1	64	Jump to UserPatch1
2-3-2-3	66	Configure advanced cache registers
2-3-3-1	68	Enable external and CPU caches
2-3-3-2	69	Initialize SMI handler
2-3-3-3	6A	Display external cache size
2-3-4-1	6C	Display shadow message
2-3-4-3	6E	Display nondisposable segments
2-4-1-1	70	Display error messages
2-4-1-3	72	Check for configuration errors
2-4-2-1	74	Test real-time clock
2-4-2-3	76	Check for keyboard errors
2-4-4-1	7C	Set up hardware interrupt vectors
2-4-4-3	7E	Test coprocessor if present
3-1-1-1	80	Disable onboard I/O ports
3-1-1-3	82	Detect and install external RS232 ports
3-1-2-1	84	Detect and install external parallel ports
3-1-2-3	86	Reinitialize onboard I/O ports
3-1-3-1	88	Initialize BIOS data area
3-1-3-3	8A	Initialize extended BIOS data area
3-1-4-1	8C	Initialize floppy controller
3-2-1-1	90	Initialize hard drive controller
3-2-1-2	91	Initialize local bus hard drive controller
3-2-1-3	92	Jump to UserPatch2
3-2-2-1	94	Disable A20 address line
3-2-2-3	96	Clear huge ES segment register
3-2-3-1	98	Search for option ROMs
3-2-3-3	9A	Shadow option ROMs
3-2-4-1	9C	Set up power management
3-2-4-3	9E	Enable hardware interrupts
3-3-1-1	A0	Set time of day
3-3-1-3	A2	Check key lock
3-3-3-1	A8	Erase F2 prompt
3-3-3-3	AA	Scan for F2 key stroke

(continued)

Table A-3 POST/beep codes for Phoenix BIOS 4.x (continued)

Beep Code	POST Code	Description
3-3-4-1	AC	Enter setup
3-3-4-3	AE	Clear in-POST flag
3-4-1-1	B0	Check for errors
3-4-1-3	B2	POST done—prepare to boot operating system
3-4-2-1	B4	1 beep
3-4-2-3	B6	Check password (optional)
3-4-3-1	B8	Clear global descriptor table
3-4-4-1	BC	Clear parity checkers
3-4-4-3	BE	Clear screen (optional)
3-4-4-4	BF	Check virus and backup reminders
4-1-1-1	C0	Try to boot with INT 19
4-2-1-1	D0	Interrupt handler error
4-2-1-3	D2	Unknown interrupt error
4-2-2-1	D4	Pending interrupt error
4-2-2-3	D6	Initialize option ROM error
4-2-3-1	D8	Shutdown error
4-2-3-3	DA	Extended block move
4-2-4-1	DC	Shutdown 10 error
4-2-4-3	DE	Keyboard controller failure (most likely problem is with RAM or cache unless no video is present)
4-3-1-3	E2	Initialize the chipset
4-3-1-4	E3	Initialize refresh counter
4-3-2-1	E4	Check for forced flash
4-3-2-2	E5	Check hardware status of ROM
4-3-2-3	E6	BIOS ROM is okay
4-3-2-4	E7	Do a complete RAM test
4-3-3-1	E8	Do OEM initialization
4-3-3-2	E9	Initialize interrupt controller
4-3-3-3	EA	Read in bootstrap code
4-3-3-4	EB	Initialize all vectors
4-3-4-1	EC	Boot the Flash program
4-3-4-2	ED	Initialize the boot device
4-3-4-3	EE	Boot code was read okay

Table A-4 provides a list of POST/beep codes for Phoenix ROM BIOS PLUS and Phoenix BIOS Version 1.xx.

Table A-4 POST/beep codes for Phoenix ROM BIOS PLUS and Phoenix BIOS Version 1.xx

Port 80h Value	Beep Code	Error/Test Description
01h	None	80286 register test in progress
02h	1-1-3	CMOS write/read test in progress or failure
03h	1-1-4	BIOS ROM checksum in progress or failure
04h	1-2-1	Programmable interval timer test in progress or failure
05h	1-2-2	DMA initialization in progress or failure
06h	1-2-3	DMA page register write/read test in progress or failure
08h	1-3-1	RAM refresh verification in progress or failure
09h	None	1st 64 K RAM test in progress
0Ah	1-3-3	1st 64 K RAM chip or data line failure—multibit
0Bh	1-3-4	1st 64 K RAM odd/even logic failure
0Ch	1-4-1	1st 64 K RAM address line failure
0Dh	1-4-2	1st 64 K RAM parity test in progress or failure
10h	2-1-1	1st 64 K RAM chip or data line failure—bit 0
11h	2-1-2	1st 64 K RAM chip or data line failure—bit 1
12h	2-1-3	1st 64 K RAM chip or data line failure—bit 2
13h	2-1-4	1st 64 K RAM chip or data line failure—bit 3
14h	2-2-1	1st 64 K RAM chip or data line failure—bit 4
15h	2-2-2	1st 64 K RAM chip or data line failure—bit 5
16h	2-2-3	1st 64 K RAM chip or data line failure—bit 6
17h	2-2-4	1st 64 K RAM chip or data line failure—bit 7
18h	2-3-1	1st 64 K RAM chip or data line failure—bit 8
19h	2-3-2	1st 64 K RAM chip or data line failure—bit 9
1Ah	2-3-3	1st 64 K RAM chip or data line failure—bit A
1Bh	2-3-4	1st 64 K RAM chip or data line failure—bit B
1Ch	2-4-1	1st 64 K RAM chip or data line failure—bit C
1Dh	2-4-2	1st 64 K RAM chip or data line failure—bit D
1Eh	2-4-3	1st 64 K RAM chip or data line failure—bit E
1Fh	2-4-4	1st 64 K RAM chip or data line failure—bit F
20h	3-1-1	Master DMA register test in progress or failure
21h	3-1-2	Slave DMA register test in progress or failure
22h	3-1-3	Master interrupt mask register test in progress or failure
23h	3-1-4	Slave interrupt mask register test in progress or failure
25h	None	Interrupt vector loading in progress
27h	3-2-4	Keyboard controller test in progress or failure
28h	None	CMOS power-fail and checksum checks in progress
29h	None	CMOS config info validation in progress

(continued)

Table A-4 POST/beep codes for Phoenix ROM BIOS PLUS and
Phoenix BIOS Version 1.xx (continued)

Port 80h Value	Beep Code	Error/Test Description
2Bh	3-3-4	Screen memory test in progress or failure
2Ch	3-4-1	Screen initialization in progress or failure
2Dh	3-4-2	Screen retrace tests in progress or failure
2Eh	None	Search for video ROM in progress
30h	None	Screen believed operable: screen believed running with video ROM
31h	None	Monochromatic screen believed operable
32h	None	40-column color screen believed operable
33h	None	80-column color screen believed operable
34h	4-2-1	Timer tick interrupt test in progress or failure
35h	4-2-2	Shutdown test in progress or failure
36h	4-2-3	Gate A20 failure
37h	4-2-4	Unexpected interrupt in protected mode
38h	4-3-1	RAM test in progress or failure above address 0FFFFh
3Ah	4-3-3	Interval timer channel 2 test in progress or failure
3Bh	4-3-4	Time-of-day clock test in progress or failure
3Ch	4-4-1	Serial port test in progress or failure
3Dh	4-4-2	Parallel port test in progress or failure
3Eh	4-4-3	Math coprocessor test in progress or failure

Phoenix has three BIOSs that are based on the older Phoenix BIOS: FirstBIOS
Desktop Pro, FirstBIOS Workstation Pro, and FirstBIOS Notebook Pro. See the
Phoenix Web site for more information on these products.

DELL BIOS

Dell BIOS communicates problems during POST as beep codes (Table A-5) or
as error messages on screen (Table A-6).

Table A-5 Dell BIOS beep codes at start-up

Beep code	Description	Things to do
1-2	Video card not found	• Reseat the video card • Replace the video card • Try a different slot (instead of using the AGP slot, try a video card in a PCI slot)
1-2-2-3	ROM BIOS failure	Replace the ROM BIOS chip

(continued)

Table A-5 Dell BIOS beep codes at start-up (continued)

Beep code	Description	Things to do
1-3-1-1 1-3-3-1 1-3-4-1 1-3-4-3 1-4-1-1	Memory failure	• Reseat memory modules • Replace memory modules
1-3-1-3	Keyboard controller failure	Reseat the keyboard connector on the motherboard

Table A-6 Dell BIOS error messages at start-up

Error message	Description	Things to do
Bad Command or File Name	Command file does not exist or is in the wrong path	Check Autoexec.bat and Config.sys files for errors
Battery is extremely low. Replace it immediately.	Notebook computer has low battery	Switch to AC power, replace the battery, or turn OFF the notebook and charge the battery
Checksum error	CMOS RAM is corrupted	Try restoring CMOS default settings by running CMOS setup
Data error Sector not found Seek error	Problem with reading from a floppy disk or hard drive	Run Chkdsk on the disk or drive
Decreasing available memory Gate A20 failure Memory address line failure Memory data line failure Memory odd/even logic failure Memory write/read failure	Memory failure	• Reseat memory modules • Move modules to a different slot • Replace memory
Disk C failed initialization Hard-disk drive failure	Hard drive failure	• Check CMOS setup to verify the drive configuration • Troubleshoot the hard drive subsystem
Diskette drive [0,1] seek failure Diskette read failure Diskette subsystem reset failed	Floppy drive failure	• Check CMOS setup to verify the floppy drive configuration • Troubleshoot the floppy drive subsystem

(continued)

Table A-6 Dell BIOS error messages at startup (continued)

Error Message	Description	Things to Do
Invalid configuration information–please run setup program	CMOS setup is inconsistent	• Run the setup program
Keyboard clock line failure Keyboard data line failure	Keyboard failure	• Check the keyboard connection • Replace the keyboard
No boot device available Nonsystem disk or disk error	Cannot boot from hard drive or floppy disk	• Remove the floppy disk • Verify the partitions on the hard drive are intact (Run Diskpart or Fdisk) • Troubleshoot booting from the operating system
Time of day clock stopped	CMOS battery has failed	• Replace the CMOS battery
Unexpected interrupt in protected mode	Keyboard or memory failure	• Check the keyboard connection • Replace the keyboard • Reseat memory modules • Replace memory

B

USING CMOS SETUP

This appendix describes how to use your CMOS setup. Typical settings for Award, AMI, and Phoenix BIOSes are covered. For specific information concerning your CMOS setup, see the documentation for your motherboard.

 If your motherboard documentation is not available, check the Web site of the motherboard manufacturer. See Appendix H for important URLs (page H-1).

HOW TO IDENTIFY YOUR MOTHERBOARD AND BIOS

For newer motherboards, to identify your motherboard and BIOS, do the following:

- [ ] Turn the system power OFF.
- [ ] Turn the power ON. While the memory count is displaying on the screen, press the Pause/Break key.
- [ ] Look for the long string of numbers in the lower-left corner of your screen, which identifies the motherboard.
- [ ] Look for the BIOS manufacturer and version number somewhere near the top of the screen.
- [ ] You can also find the BIOS manufacturer and version number on the CMOS setup utility screen.

For older motherboards, to identify your motherboard and BIOS, do the following:

- [ ] Turn the system power OFF and unplug the keyboard.
- [ ] Turn the power ON. You will get a keyboard error, which stops the start-up process.
- [ ] Look for the long string of numbers in the lower-left corner of your screen, which identifies the motherboard.
- [ ] Look for the BIOS manufacturer and version number somewhere near the top of the screen.
- [ ] You can also find the BIOS manufacturer and version number on the CMOS setup utility screen.

If you cannot find the motherboard or BIOS information on the screen during boot, do the following:

- [ ] Enter CMOS setup and look for the BIOS and version number on the main menu screen.
- [ ] Open the computer case and look for the motherboard brand and model number imprinted on the board (see Figure B-1).

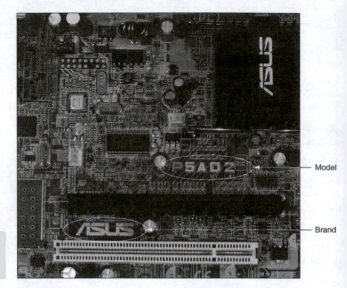

Figure B-1   The motherboard brand and model are imprinted somewhere on the board

How to Access CMOS Setup

Table B-1 explains how to access setup for BIOSes that have built-in setup programs. For older PCs that don't have a built-in setup program, use a setup program stored on floppy disk. If you don't have a setup disk, check the Web site of the motherboard manufacturer or the BIOS manufacturer for a replacement disk.

Table B-1 How to access CMOS setup

BIOS	Keys to press during POST to access setup
AMI BIOS	DEL
Award BIOS	DEL
Older Phoenix BIOS	CTL-ALT-ESC or CTL-ALT-S
Newer Phoenix BIOS	F2 or F1
Dell computers using Phoenix BIOS	CTL-ALT-ENTER
Older Compaq computers like the Deskpro 286 or 386	Place the diagnostics disk in the disk drive, reboot your system, and choose Computer Setup from the menu
Newer Compaq computers like the ProLinea, Deskpro, Deskpro XL, Deskpro XE, or Presario	Press the F10 key while the cursor is in the upper-right corner of the screen, which happens just after the 2 beeps when booting*
All other older computers	Setup is accessed by using a setup program on the diskette that came with the PC. If the diskette is lost, see the next section for information on obtaining a new setup program.

* For Compaq computers, the CMOS setup program is stored on the hard drive in a small, hidden partition of about 3 MB. If this partition becomes corrupted, you must run setup from a floppy disk. If you cannot run setup by pressing F10 at startup, suspect a damaged partition.

SETUP PROGRAMS FOR OLDER PCS

Older PCs were not built with the setup program contained in the BIOS programs as they are today but rather with the program stored on a diskette provided by the motherboard manufacturer. Do the following to access setup on an older PC when the original setup diskette from the manufacturer is lost:

For Any Older PC

First try to contact the motherboard manufacturer.

See Appendix H for URLs of motherboard manufacturers (page H-2).

For Phoenix BIOS on 286 and 386 Systems

Phoenix provides a setup program but does not provide any support for it and recommends that you first try the setup program from the motherboard manufacturer. The program changes only Standard settings.

Try Clearing CMOS Setup

If you can't locate a program, try clearing CMOS setup, which should restore setup to default values. Try each of the following in order:
1. Look for a jumper on the motherboard that clears CMOS setup when closed. If you find it, turn OFF the PC, close the jumper, wait about 30 seconds, remove the

jumper cap, and turn the PC back ON. Enter CMOS setup, and apply the option to return CMOS to default settings.

2. On some PCs, you can clear CMOS by unplugging the PC, unplugging the battery that powers CMOS, and disconnecting the power supply connections to the motherboard. Leave the motherboard without any power for a couple of days.

3. If you can boot from a Windows 9x startup disk, use DEBUG to clear CMOS. Enter these commands:

`A:\> DEBUG`	Access DEBUG from the floppy disk
`- o 70 2E`	At DEBUG's hyphen prompt, enter the o command: Output to I/O port 70 the value 2E
`- o 71 FF`	Output FF to I/O port 71
`- q`	Exit DEBUG

Hard boot the PC. You should get an error message about CMOS and then default values should load.

4. If you are trying to clear CMOS setup to erase a forgotten power-on password, you can use software to identify the password or remove it. Search the Internet for these programs, called cracks. Be certain that you understand how to use the software before you try it and that the software provider is reputable.

5. As a last resort, replace the CMOS RAM chip. When you reboot with the new CMOS chip, a CMOS error message is displayed and default settings are restored.

CMOS Settings

Table B-2 is a list of CMOS setup settings and what they mean. For an excellent, more detailed description of setup fields for Award BIOS, see the Phoenix Web site at *www.phoenix.com*.

Table B-2   CMOS settings and descriptions

Setting	Description
System time	Real-time clock can also be set with DOS TIME command.
System date	Real-time clock can also be set with DOS DATE command.
Quick boot	Enable/disable. Enable to cause POST to skip some tests and speed up booting. Disable this feature when installing or testing a motherboard to get a thorough POST.
Above 1 MB memory test	Disables POST check of this memory to speed up booting; the OS checks this memory anyway.

(continued)

Table B-2 CMOS settings and descriptions (continued)

Setting	Description
Password checking option	Establishes a start-up password. Use this only if you need to prevent someone untrustworthy from using your PC. Sometimes there are two passwords, each with different levels of security.
Voice messages at POST	Enable/disable. Enable to cause error messages during POST to be communicated as voice messages.
Boot sequence	Possible options: A, C; A, CDROM, C; USB device, C, A; D, A; E, A; F, A; C only; ZIP, C; C, A • This option determines where the system looks to find an OS.
HDD sequence	Options: IDE first, SCSI first • This option selects the hard drive to which the system looks first for an OS. Default is IDE.
Processor settings	
Processor speed	Sets the appropriate speed for your processor; used for throttling and overclocking.
I/O voltage	Sets the appropriate I/O voltage for the processor.
Core voltage	Sets the appropriate core voltage for the processor.
External clock	Sets the system bus speed.
Legacy diskette A: or B:	Options: Floppy disk types 360 KB, 720 KB, 1.2 MB, 1.44 MB, 2.88 MB, Not Installed • Default is usually 1.44 MB.
Primary master Primary slave Secondary master Secondary slave	ID string from the IDE drive is displayed when BIOS sees the drive present. You cannot make an entry for this setting. • The motherboard has two or more built-in IDE interfaces, each supporting one SATA device or two IDE devices, one master and one slave, sharing a data cable. Master and slave settings are determined by jumpers on the drives. • Most likely, the primary interface is set to IRQ 14 and I/O address 1F0, and the secondary interface is set to IRQ 15 and I/O address 170. Resources are shared by the two drives on the interface.
IDE type	Options: Auto, User • Select Auto to enable autodetection if the drives support it. Drive type will then be automatically detected. Select manual for older drives that don't support autodetect and then enter the drive parameters manually. • Drive specifications include: Cylinders: (0–65535) Heads: (1–16) Sectors: (0–63) Maximum capacity: Will be calculated based on number of cylinders, heads, and sectors. Look for these values written on top of the drive housing or in the drive documentation, or see the Web site of the drive manufacturer.

(continued)

Table B-2 CMOS settings and descriptions (continued)

Setting	Description
IDE drive options	These hard drive options should all be set automatically when autodetection is enabled:
Multisector transfers or Block mode	Options: Max, Disabled, 2, 4, 8, 16, and 32 • Most drives, except older drives, can use this feature, which allows multisectors to be read on a single transfer. • Set to Max unless the drive is giving errors, then reduce the number of sectors to read at one time. • Try disabling this option if a hard drive still gives errors.
LBA mode	Options: Enable, Disabled • This option works only on large drives (larger than 500 MB) that support LBA mode.
Large disk access mode	Options: DOS, Other (default: DOS) • This option enables translation for large drives. Normally keep set to DOS for DOS and all versions of Windows.
32-bit transfer mode	Options: Standard, Fast PIO 1, Fast PIO 2, Fast PIO 3, Fast PIO 4, FPIO 3/DMA 1, FPIO 4/DMA 2, Multiword DMS, Ultra ATA-33, Ultra ATA-66, Ultra ATA-100, and others. • These options should autodetect if supported by the drive. They speed up data transfer. • If you are having problems with the drive, try setting this mode to Standard.
Translation mode	Options: ECHS, Assisted LBA • Allow autodetection to make the selection.
SMART monitoring	Enable/disable. Enable to monitor the hard drive for failure.
Sound	Option: Enabled, Disabled • If the speaker does not work, verify that this option is enabled.
Joystick	Option: Enabled, Disabled • If the joystick does not work, verify that it is enabled.
Serial ports A, B	Options for each serial port: Enabled, Disabled • When enabled, you can force the port to use a specific IRQ and I/O address or allow the BIOS to make its own selections. • Normally, allow BIOS to make the selection, unless you are trying to resolve a resource conflict.
Base I/O address	Options: Auto, 3F8, 2F8, 3E8, 2E8
Interrupt	Options: Auto, IRQ3, IRQ4
Parallel port	Options: Auto, Enabled, Disabled, OS Controlled • Allow the BIOS to automatically select options below unless you are trying to resolve a resource conflict.
Base I/O address	Options: 378, 278, 3BC
Interrupt	Options: IRQ7, IRQ5

(continued)

Table B-2 CMOS settings and descriptions (continued)

Setting	Description
Mode	Options: Bidirectional, Output Only, ECP, EPP • When mode is set to EPP, the base address options change to 178, 278, and 378. • When mode is set to ECP, an option for DMA channel appears, which can be set to DMA 1 or DMA 3.
Fixed disk boot sector	Options: Normal, Write-protect (default: Normal) • Write-protect to protect the boot sector against a virus, but you must remove the protection when installing an OS or for software that must write to the boot sector.
Power management options	You can set all power management options to disabled and allow Windows to handle power management.
Standby timeout	Options: Off, 1, 2, 4, 6, 8, 12, 16 minutes • Minutes of inactivity before the system enters standby mode. According to Energy Star standards, when in standby mode, a system must reduce 92% of its power consumption.
Auto suspend timeout	Options: Off, 5, 10, 15, 20, 30, 40, 60 minutes • Minutes of inactivity before the system enters suspend mode. According to Energy Star standards, when in suspend mode, a system must reduce 99% of its power consumption.
Hard disk timeout	Options: Disabled, 10, 15, 30, 45 seconds, 1, 2, 4, 6, 8, 10, 15 minutes • The amount of time of inactivity before the hard drive shuts down.
Video timeout	Options: Disabled, 10, 15, 30, 45 seconds, 1, 2, 4, 6, 8, 10, 15 minutes • The amount of time of inactivity before the video signal is shut down.
Resume on modem ring	Options: Off, On • Set on to allow a phone call to activate a modem, which in turn can power up the PC. Use this option to receive an incoming fax when the PC is not in use.
Resume on time	Options: Off, On • Use this setting to power up the PC at a specified date and time, such as to perform a scheduled backup.
Resume time	Can be set to any time.
Resume date	Can be set to any date from 1981 to 2099.
Resume on LAN	Options: On, Off • Allows the system to be powered up remotely over a LAN.
Resume on keyboard	Allows you to power up your PC by pressing a certain key combination.
Video ROM BIOS shadow	Options: Enable, Disable • Allows ROM BIOS to be copied to RAM and executed from there, which improves performance because RAM is faster than ROM.

(continued)

Table B-2 CMOS settings and descriptions (continued)

Setting	Description
C8000-CBFFF to DC000-DFFFF	Options: Enabled, Disabled • With this option you can shadow the ROM on expansion cards to RAM. To use it, you must know the memory addresses of the ROM on the expansion cards.
Onboard FDC controller	Options: Enable, Disable • Normally enabled, but disable it to use a floppy drive controller on an expansion card.
Onboard PCI IDE	Options: Enable, Primary, Secondary, Disable • This option allows you to enable or disable the primary and secondary IDE channels. Disable a channel to use an IDE channel on an expansion card.
PnP and PCI setup	
Plug and Play (PnP)	Enable/disable. Enable for Windows 9x, which uses PnP data from BIOS. Disable for Windows 2000/XP/Vista, which does all the PnP configuration.
Secured setup configurations	Options: Yes, No • Setting this option to No prevents PnP from changing CMOS values.
PCI/PNP ISA IRQ resource exclusion IRQ3 IRQ4 IRQ5 IRQ7 IRQ9 IRQ10 IRQ11	Options for each IRQ: Available, Reserved • This option allows you to reserve an IRQ so that PnP cannot assign the IRQ to PCI for the PCI controller to assign to a PCI slot. • Reserve an IRQ when a legacy ISA card needs it and PnP does not recognize the need.
DMA x used by ISA	Options for each DMA channel: Yes, No • Reserve a DMA channel for a legacy ISA device that needs it when BIOS does not recognize the need.
ISA MEM block BASE	Options: No/ICU, Yes • Allows you to reserve upper memory addresses in the C800H–DFFFH address range for a legacy ISA device. • Default value is No/ICU, which means that no memory is reserved. ICU stands for ISA configuration utility, which can reserve the memory without involving this BIOS feature. • When you set the value to Yes, you must then select an address range from the available options and a block size from 8 K to 64 K.
PnP OS installed	Options: Yes, No • When set to Yes, the OS can use PnP to reassign IRQs to the PCI bus slots (called PCI bus IRQ steering). Set to No to prevent these reassignments.

(continued)

Table B-2 CMOS settings and descriptions (continued)

Setting	Description
PCI latency timer	Default value: 32 clocks • The number of PCI clock cycles that a device can hold the PCI bus when another has requested it. The lower the value, the quicker a device can get the bus, but lower values can also lower overall bandwidth of the bus. Leave the value at the default unless expansion cards are unstable; in that case, try a slightly lower value.
Reset configuration data	Options: Enable, Disable • Enabling this feature causes PnP data in BIOS (ESCD) to be reset. • Normally leave this option disabled. • If you cannot boot after installing a new device, enable this feature and reboot to cause BIOS to rebuild the ESCD data.
USB device IRQ preference	Options: Auto, IRQ5, IRG9, IRQ10, IRQ11 • Specifies IRQ assignment to a USB device. • Use Auto unless you are trying to resolve a resource conflict.
Language	Select the language used by the CMOS utility
Event logging	Enable/disable. Enable to log system errors and/or boot errors. On the event logging menu, you can view logged events, mark events as having been read, and clear the log.
LAN controller	Enable/disable. Enable to use an onboard network port.
Wireless LAN	Enable/disable. Enable to use an onboard wireless network component.
Hard drive passwords	Enable/disable. Enable to require one or two passwords to access the hard drive. Used mostly on laptops to protect data when the laptop is stolen.

WINDOWS AND DOS COMMANDS

This appendix contains a list of the most valuable Windows and DOS commands used at the command prompt while troubleshooting.

ATTRIB +R -R +A -A +S -S +H -H Drive:\Path\Filename /S /D

☐ **Purpose:** Displays or changes the read-only, archive, system, and hidden attributes of a file. If a file has a hidden or system attribute, you must remove these attributes before you can change the R or A attributes of the file. Wildcard characters are allowed in the command line. The ATTRIB command can be used from a command prompt window or from the Windows 2000/XP Recovery Console.

☐ **Parameters:**

+H or -H	Sets or removes the hidden-file attribute.
+R or -R	Sets or removes the read-only status of the file.
+S or -S	Sets or removes the system status of the file.
+A or -A	The archive attribute marks a file as having been changed since the last backup. The XCOPY command can use and change this attribute. Also see XCOPY.
/S	Includes subdirectories found within the specified path.
/D	Applies the ATTRIB command to directories.

☐ **Syntax with examples:**

ATTRIB +H +R filename.ext	Makes the file a hidden, read-only file.
ATTRIB -H -R filename.ext	Unhides the file and removes read-only status.
ATTRIB filename.ext	Displays the file's attributes.
ATTRIB +A C:\data*.doc /S	Turns on the archive attribute for all files with a .doc file extension in the C:\data folder and its subfolders. This command can be useful when used along with the XCOPY command to select files for copying. See XCOPY.

CHKDSK Drive:\Path\Filename /F /V

☐ **Purpose:** Examines a hard drive or disk for lost and cross-linked clusters and repairs them. For Windows 2000/XP, use the command in a command window, from the Recovery Console, or from the Windows desktop. From the desktop, on the disk Properties window, Tools tab, use the Check Now command to access the CHKDSK command. For Windows 9x, rather than using CHKDSK, use ScanDisk, which checks more issues than does CHKDSK.

□ **Parameters for Windows 2000/XP:**

/F	Fixes errors in the NTFS or FAT file system on a drive. The drive must be locked. If the drive is in use, a message appears offering to check the drive during the next computer restart.
/R	Fixes file system errors and also recovers data from bad sectors. The drive must be locked.
Path and filename	Use the path and filename only with the FAT file system to check a specific file or group of files for fragmentation.

□ **Syntax with examples:**

CHKDSK C:	Examines drive C for lost and cross-linked clusters, and reports errors found.
CHKDSK C: /R	Examines drive C for file system errors and fixes them. Also attempts to recover data from bad sectors.

□ **Parameters for Windows 9x:**

/F	Fixes errors in the FAT on a drive.
/V	Displays each file as it's being checked. V stands for verbiage.

□ **Syntax with examples:**

CHKDSK C:	Examines drive C for lost and cross-linked clusters, and reports errors found.
CHKDSK C: /R	Examines drive C for file system errors and fixes them. Also attempts to recover data from bad sectors.

CONVERT Volume FS:NTFS /V

Windows 2000/XP command that converts a volume or drive using the FAT file system to the NTFS file system. Files and folders on the volume are not affected. The volume must be locked. If the volume is in use, CONVERT will ask permission to perform the operation at the next computer restart.

□ **Parameters**

Volume	Specify the logical drive or volume letter.
/V	Displays detailed information during the operation. V stands for verbiage.

☐ **Syntax with examples**

CONVERT D: FS:NTFS	Converts drive D: from FAT to NTFS file system.
CONVERT D: FS:NTFS /V	Converts drive D: from FAT to NTFS file system, displaying details of the operation.

COPY /D /V /N /A /

☐ **Purpose:** Copies a file or group of files from one location to another.
☐ **Parameters:**

/D	Copies an encrypted file and decrypts it at the new locations.
/V	Verifies the source file and the destination file are the same.
/Y	Does not prompt you when overwriting an existing file.

☐ **Syntax with examples**

COPY Myfile.txt C:\Data	Copies the file Myfile.txt to the C:\Data folder.
COPY *.* \TEMP /Y	Copies all files to the \TEMP folder without asking for confirmation.

DEFRAG Drive: /A /V /F

☐ **Purpose:** Examines a volume (logical drive) for fragmented files, and rewrites these files to the disk or drive in contiguous clusters. Use this command to optimize a hard drive, improving the hard-drive performance. DEFRAG requires at least 15% of the drive to be free; this space is used to sort fragmented files. If you don't have adequate space on the drive, clean up the drive before defragging. DEFRAG takes time to work; to interrupt the command in progress, press Ctrl-C. DEFRAG skips over corrupted files and sectors. Therefore, for best results, run CHKDSK before you run DEFRAG. Also see CHKDSK.
☐ **Paramaters:**

/A	Analyzes the logical drive or volume and displays a report.
/V	Displays a complete analysis and/or defragmentation report. Without this parameter, DEFRAG displays only a summary report.
/F	Forces defragmentation even when disk space is low.

□ **Syntax with examples:**

DEFRAG C:	Optimizes drive C.
DEFRAG C: /V	Optimizes the drive and displays a detailed report.

DEL or ERASE Drive:\Path\Filename [...] /P /F /S/ Q/ A

□ **Purpose:** Deletes a file or group of files. You can use more than one filename separated by spaces, commas, or semicolons.

□ **Parameters:**

/P	Prompts for confirmation before deleting a file.
/F	Forces deletion of read-only files.
/S	Deletes files from current directory and its subdirectories.
/Q	Quit mode does not prompt you before deleting.
/A	Deletes files with specified attributes.

□ **Syntax with examples:**

DEL Myfile.*	Deletes all files in the current directory with the filename Myfile.
DEL *.txt /A +A	Deletes all files with the .txt file extension that has the archive attribute set.

DIR Drive: \Path\Filename /P /Q /W /D

□ **Purpose:** Lists files and subdirectories in the current directory.

□ **Parameters:**

/P	Lists files and subdirectories and their sizes a page at a time.
/Q	Lists file ownership information.
/W	Lists files and subdirectories in a wide-screen format.
/D	Lists in wide-screen format and files are sorted by column.

□ **Syntax with examples:**

DIR A:	Lists all files in the root directory of drive A:.
DIR C: /P /W	Lists all files in the C: root directory, one page at a time across the screen.
DIR C:\temp*.txt	Lists all files in the C:\temp folder that have a .txt file extension.

EDIT Drive:\Path\Filename

□ **Purpose:** A text editor that is handy to use at a command prompt when editing text files such as Autoexec.bat, Config.sys or Boot.ini.

□ **Syntax with examples:**

`EDIT C:\autoexec.bat`	Allows you to view and edit the contents of this file.

FDISK /Status /MBRs

□ **Purpose:** Windows 9x command that creates partitions and logical drives on a hard drive, displays partition information, and restores a damaged master boot record.

□ **Syntax with examples:**

FDISK	Use the FDISK menu to display partition information, create a primary partition and one logical drive on it, and create an extended partition with one or more logical drives.
FDISK/MBR	Repairs a damaged master boot record (MBR) program stored at the beginning of the partition table.
FDISK/Status	Displays partition information for all hard drives in the system.

FORMAT Drive: /FS:filesystem /V:volumename /Q /C /S

□ **Purpose:** Formats a disk or hard drive. For a hard drive, first partition the drive and create each logical drive. To partition the drive in Windows 2000/XP, use DISKPART, and in Windows 9x, use FDISK. Then use FORMAT to format each logical drive. It creates an OS boot record, file system, and root directory for each logical drive so that files can be copied to the drive.

□ **Parameters:**

/FS:filesystem	Specifies the file system to use, FAT or NTFS. Floppy disks can only use the FAT file system.
/V:volumename	Assigns a volume name to the drive.
/Q	Quick format rewrites the file table and root directory only. Use on disks that have already been formatted.
/C	For NTFS only; files written to the new volume will be compressed.
/S	Windows 9x option only. Places operating system files on the disk necessary to boot.

□ **Syntax with examples:**

FORMAT A:	Formats a floppy disk. Creates a boot record, FAT, root directory, and sector and track markings on the disk.
FORMAT E:	Formats the volume, naming the volume FILESERVER.

GETMAC

☐ **Purpose:** Windows XP utility that displays the MAC address of the network adapter.

IPCONFIG /All /Release /Renew /?

☐ **Purpose:** Displays, releases, and renews IP address, subnet mask and default gateway. IPCONFIG is used with Windows 2000/XP. For Windows 9x, see WINIPCFG.

☐ **Parameters:**

/All	Use to display detailed host information.
/Release	Use to release (clear) all of the adapter's TCP/IP settings.
/Renew	Use to renew all of the adapter's TCP/IP settings.
/?	Displays information about IPCONFIG.

MEM /C /M <filename> |More

☐ **Purpose:** Gives you a status report on the system's DOS-related memory, how much memory is currently free, and the largest executable program size. Use it to help manage memory in a DOS environment.

☐ **Syntax with examples:**

MEM /C	Lists status of programs in conventional and upper memory.
MEM /M myfile.exe	Displays how much memory the program file allocates for itself and its data.
MEM /C |MORE	Lists status of memory one page at a time.

MIRROR /Partn

☐ **Purpose:** An older DOS 5.0 command that is used today only to save the partition table of a hard drive to floppy disk. Use the UNFORMAT command to restore the table to a hard drive.

☐ **Syntax with examples:**

MIRROR /Partn	Saves partition table to disk.

NETSTAT –a –n –r -s

☐ **Purpose:** Displays active TCP connections, port information, and the IP routing table.

☐ **Parameters:**

NETSTAT -a	Displays all active connections and ports.
NETSTAT -n	Displays active connections, but the addresses and port numbers are listed numerically.
NETSTAT -r	Displays the IP routing table.
NETSTAT -s	Displays connection statistics by protocol.

PING −t −a −n Target

☐ **Purpose:** To test the connection between two hosts on the Internet.

-t	The Ping command continues to send echo requests until it is interrupted by your pressing Ctrl-Break (statistics will display) or Ctrl-C (command will halt with no display).
-a	The host name of the destination IP address displays.
-n Count	Specifies how many echo requests are sent. The default is four.
Target	The target can be given as a host name or IP address.

☐ **Syntax with examples:**

PING www.course.com	Uses the host's fully qualified domain name.
PING 198.107.178.152	Uses the host's IP address.
PING −n 10 www.course.com	Make 10 echo requests.
PING −a 198.107.178.152	Request and display the host name of the given IP address.

ScanDisk Drive: /A /N /P

☐ **Purpose:** For Windows 9x, examines a hard drive for errors and repairs them if possible. ScanDisk checks the FAT, long filenames, lost and cross-linked clusters, directory tree structure, bad sectors, DriveSpace or DoubleSpace file structure, and compression structure. For a badly damaged hard drive, use ScanDisk and then reformat the drive. For Windows 2000/XP, see CHKDSK.

☐ **Parameters:**

/A	Scans and repairs all drives on the system.
/P	Displays problems found and does not make any changes to the disk.
/N	Does not prompt the user while processing.

☐ **Syntax with examples:**

SCANDISK C:	Scans drive C and fixes problems where possible.
SCANDISK C: /P	Preview mode only reports errors but makes no changes to drive C.

ScanReg

☐ **Purpose:** Restores or repairs the Windows 98 Registry. It uses backups of the registry that Windows 98 Registry Checker automatically makes each day.

☐ **Syntax with examples:**

ScanReg /Restore	Restores the registry from a previous backup. A menu displays asking you which backup to use.
ScanReg /Fix	Repairs a corrupted registry.
ScanReg /Backup	Creates a new backup of the registry. Don't use this command if the registry is giving problems.
ScanReg /Opt	Optimizes the registry by deleting unused entries.
ScanReg /?	Help feature of ScanReg.

SYS Drive:

☐ **Purpose:** The Windows 9x SYS command copies the system files needed to boot to a disk or hard drive. Use the command if the Windows 9x or DOS system files on a drive are corrupted. You can access the drive, but you can't boot from it.

☐ **Syntax with examples:**

SYS C:	Copies files needed to boot to drive C.
SYS A:	Copies files needed to boot to drive A.

TRACERT Targetname or IP Address

☐ **Purpose:** The TRACERT command is used to trace the route taken to a destination.

☐ **Syntax with examples:**

TRACERT www.course.com	Uses the host's fully qualified domain name to trace the route.
TRACERT 198.107.178.152	Uses the host's IP address to trace the route.

UNFORMAT Drive: /Partn

☐ **Purpose:** Windows 9x command that reverses the effect of an accidental format or repairs a corrupted partition table if it has previously been saved with the MIRROR command.

☐ **Syntax with examples:**

| UNFORMAT C: | Reverses the effect of an accidental format. |
| UNFORMAT/Partn | Repairs a damaged partition table if the table has previously been saved with the MIRROR /PARTN command and the PARTNSAV.FIL file is available. |

WINIPCFG

☐ **Purpose:** The Windows 9x command to display, release, and renew IP address, subnet mask and default gateway. For Windows 2000/XP, see IPCONFIG. To use the command, enter WINIPCFG at a command prompt or from the Run dialog box.

XCOPY Source Destination /A /C /D:mm-dd-yyyy /C /E /F /H /I /K /M /N /O /P /Q /R /S /T /U /W /Y /-Y

☐ **Purpose:** Copies directories, their subdirectories, and files (not including hidden or system files unless the /H parameter is used). Use a valid drive, path, and filename (wildcards are allowed) for source and destination. If the destination is omitted, the current drive and path are assumed. XCOPY is generally faster and offers more options than COPY.

☐ **Parameter:**

/A	Copies source files that have their archive attribute set and does not change the archive setting.
/C	Ignores errors as it copies. Without this parameter, if XCOPY encounters an error, it halts, which can be very frustrating if you're copying a long list of files.
/D:date	Copies source files that have been created or edited since the specified date.
/E	Copies source subdirectories, even if they are empty. Use with the /S parameter.
/F	Displays filenames as it copies.
/H	Copies files with the hidden or system attribute. By default, XCOPY does not copy these files.
/I	Does not prompt you when the destination is a directory that does not yet exist. By default, XCOPY asks permission before creating the directory.
/K	Retains the read-only attribute for destination files. By default, the read-only attribute is lost.
/M	Copies source files that have their archive attribute set and turns the archive setting off.
/N	Allows copying from an NTFS volume to a volume using the FAT file system.
/O	Copies file ownership information.
/P	Prompts the user before copying each file.
/Q	Suppresses displaying file names while copying.
/R	Copies read-only files.
/S	Copies source subdirectories unless they are empty.
/T	Copies source subdirectories, but not the files in these subdirectories. To include empty subdirectories, also use the /E parameter.

/U	Copies files from the source that already exist in the destination.
/V	Verifies that copied files are identical to source files.
/W	Displays a prompt and waits for a response before copying begins.
/Y	Overwrites existing files without asking for confirmation.
/-Y	Asks for confirmation before overwriting an existing file. This is the default setting.

XCOPY A:*.* C:\Windows/S	Copies all files on the disk in drive A to the C:\Windows directory. Files in subdirectories are included.
XCOPY A:*.* C:\Windows	Same as above, but subdirectories are not included.
XCOPY C:\data*.doc C:\test /U /Y	Copy files with the .doc file extension in the C:\data folder to the C:\test folder. Only copy files that are already in the C:\test folder and do not ask permission before overwriting these files.
XCOPY *.* \Data > mylist.txt	Rather than actually copying the specified files, create a list of files to be copied in the text file mylist.txt.

Accessing Extended Memory and CD-ROM Drive While in Real Mode

For troubleshooting problems with Windows 95, when working at a command prompt, you are likely to need access to extended memory and the CD-ROM drive during a troubleshooting session. By default, Windows 95 does not include these abilities on a Windows 95 startup disk, but you can add these options to the disk.

On your system disk, include this command in AUTOEXEC.BAT:

MSCDEX.EXE /D:MYTAG /L:E /M:10	Real mode extender for CD-ROM drive. Requires a driver loaded from CONFIG.SYS. MYTAG identifies that driver.

Include these commands in CONFIG.SYS on your system disk. Also put the CD-ROM drivers, MSCDEX.EXE, and HIMEM.SYS on the disk.

DEVICE=HIMEM.SYS	Provides access to extended memory.
DEVICE=MTMCDAI.SYS /D:MYTAG	Device driver for CD-ROM drive. Other real mode drivers are included on the Windows 98 emergency start-up disk.

APPENDIX

D

RECOVERY CONSOLE

The Recovery Console can be used to repair and troubleshoot problems in both Windows 2000 and Windows XP. All information in this appendix pertains to both Windows 2000 and Windows XP, unless otherwise noted.

LAUNCHING THE RECOVERY CONSOLE

The three ways to launch the Recovery Console are:

- From the Windows 2000 or Window XP setup CD
- From the operating system startup menu if the Recovery Console has previously been installed
- By booting from the Windows 2000/XP boot disks

 TO LEARN MORE about the six Windows XP boot disks and to obtain the executable file needed to create them, see the Microsoft Knowledge Base Article 310994 at the Microsoft Web site, *support.microsoft.com*.

Loading Recovery Console from the Windows XP Setup CD:

Do the following to launch Recovery Console from the Windows XP setup CD:

1. Insert the Windows XP setup CD into your CD-ROM drive.
2. Reboot your computer and enter **CMOS setup**. (Typically, press **F1** or **F2** during the first few seconds of the boot process.)
3. Set the first boot device in the CMOS to be the CD-ROM drive.
4. Save and exit CMOS. The computer will automatically reboot.
5. When prompted, press any key to boot from the Windows XP setup CD.
6. Select **R to Repair Windows XP using the Recovery Console**.
7. Once inside the Recovery Console, select the Windows installation (for example, C:\Windows) that you would like to log onto and repair. (Typically, type **1** and press **Enter**.)
8. Type the local administrator password and press **Enter**.

Loading Recovery Console from the Windows 2000 Setup CD:

Do the following to launch Recovery Console from the Windows 2000 setup CD:

1. Insert the Windows 2000 setup CD into your CD-ROM drive.
2. Reboot your computer and enter CMOS setup. This can typically be accomplished by pressing **F1** or **F2** during the first few seconds of the computer booting process.
3. Set the first boot device in the CMOS to be the CD-ROM drive.
4. Save and exit CMOS. The computer will automatically reboot.
5. When prompted, press any key to boot from the Windows 2000 CD-ROM.
6. Select **R** to Repair the Windows 2000 installation.
7. Select **C** to Repair the Windows 2000 installation by using the Recovery Console.
8. Once inside the Recovery Console, select the Windows installation (for example, C:\Windows) that you would like to log on to and repair. (Typically, type **1** and press **Enter**.)
9. Type the local administrator password and press **Enter**.

Installing the Recovery Console on the Hard Drive

Do the following to install the Recovery Console on the hard drive so that it is an option in the Windows startup menu:

1. Insert the Windows 2000/XP setup CD in the CD-ROM drive.
2. Click **Start**, then click **Run**.
3. Type **E:\I386\Winnt32.exe /cmdcons** (substitute the correct letter of the CD-ROM drive for E if necessary).
4. Click **OK**.
5. If prompted, click **Yes** to begin the Recovery Console installation process.

The installation process creates a hidden and read-only folder named Cmdcons on the %SystemDrive% (usually C:\) and the following line is added to the Boot.ini file:

```
C:\CMDCONS\BOOTSECT.DAT="Microsoft Windows Recovery Console" /cmdcons
```

This results in a boot selection menu with a 30-second boot timer displaying each time you boot.

Removing the Recovery Console from the Windows Startup Menu

Do the following to uninstall the Recovery Console from the hard drive, removing it from the Windows startup menu:

1. Delete the Cmdcons folder located at %SystemDrive% (usually C:\).
2. Remove the following line from Boot.ini (be very careful when editing Boot.ini):

```
C:\CMDCONS\BOOTSECT.DAT="Microsoft Windows Recovery Console" /cmdcons
```

After removing the line, make sure there is a carriage return after the last line in Boot.ini.

RECOVERY CONSOLE COMMANDS

This section lists and describes commands that can be used after you've logged onto the Recovery Console. Note that the commands are not case sensitive, but some command parameters can be case sensitive. This is especially true when using the Set command to modify environment variables.

HELP <Command>

- **Purpose:** Displays a list of all commands that can be used in the Recovery Console.
- **Syntax with examples:**

| HELP | Displays all commands in the Recovery Console. |
| HELP ATTRIB | Displays information about the ATTRIB command. |

ATTRIB −R +R −S +S −H +H −C + C Filename

- **Purpose:** Changes the attribute of a file or folder. Parameters can be used to apply or remove read-only, system, hidden, or compressed attributes. This command can be useful for removing system and hidden attributes from a corrupt swap file (C:\pagefile.sys) so that the file can be deleted. Or you remove read-only, system, and hidden attributes from the C:\Boot.ini file so that it can be edited.

- **Parameters:**

+H or −H	Sets or removes the hidden-file attribute.
+R or −R	Sets or removes the read-only status of the file.
+S or −S	Sets or removes the system status of the file.
+C or −C	Sets or removes the compressed file attribute.

- **Syntax with examples:**

| ATTRIB −rhs Boot.ini | Removes the read-only, hidden, system attribute from the Boot.ini file. |
| ATTRIB +H Boot.ini | Hides the Boot.ini file. |

BATCH Inputfilename Outputfilename

- **Purpose:** Runs Recovery Console commands that are listed in a text file. This technique is similar to using a batch file. The optional output parameter allows you to redirect the output to another source (other than the screen).

- **Syntax with examples:**

| Batch File1.bat | Execute the commands in the batch file, File1.bat |
| Batch File1.bat Myfile.txt | Execute the commands in the batch file, File1.bat, and store the results of the command in the text file, Myfile.txt. |

BOOTCFG/add/default/disablerdirect/list/rebuild /redirect/scan

- **Purpose:** Used to troubleshoot boot configuration and recovery issues with the Boot.ini file. This command is not available in the Windows 2000 Recovery Console.

- **Parameters:**

/add	Scans for and allows you to add other operating systems to Boot.ini.
/default	Sets the boot (default) operating system in Boot.ini.
/disableredirect	Disables redirection (port, baud rate) that may have been created in Boot.ini using the /redirect command.
/list	Displays a list of all entries in Boot.ini.
/rebuild	Scans for and automatically adds other operating systems to Boot.ini.
/redirect	Enables redirection of port and baud rate information in Boot.ini.
/scan	Scans for other operating systems that may exist on your hard drive.

- **Syntax with examples:**

BOOTCFG /rebuild	Rebuilds the Boot.ini, adding other operating systems to the startup menu. Before using this command, use the Copy command to make a backup of the Boot.ini file.
BOOTCFG /list	Displays entries in Boot.ini.

CD or CHDIR Drive: path

- **Purpose:** Changes current directory to a specified directory.
- **Syntax with examples:**

CD /Windows	Changes to the /Windows directory.
CD ..	Changes to the current parent folder.

CHKDSK Drive: /P/R

- **Purpose:** Used to scan, display, and correct errors on a hard drive. This useful command can solve issues associated with bad sectors and help recover readable data. You can use the command on any drive, but be sure to issue the command from the drive that contains Windows, because the command searches for the Autochk.exe file in the \%systemroot%\System32 folder.

- **Parameters:**

/P	Performs an extensive analysis of the drive but does not make any changes.
/R	Performs an analysis of the drive, marks bad sectors, and attempts to recover readable data.

- **Syntax with examples:**

| CHKDSK C: /R | Locates bad sectors and recovers readable data. |

CLS

- **Purpose:** Clears the screen.

COPY Source [Destination]

- **Purpose:** Copies files and folders from one location to another. Works similar to the DOS copy command.

DEL or DELETE Drive:\Path\Filename

- **Purpose:** Deletes a file or files. By default, the command only works in the Windows folder and subfolders, removable media, and the root directory of the hard drive. For other options, see the SET command.

DIR [Drive:\Path]

- **Purpose:** Displays a list of the contents (files and folders) of the specified directory. Wildcard characters are allowed only if the environment variable, AllowWildCards, has been set to true using the SET command.

DISABLE [ServiceName] [DeviceDriverName]

- **Purpose:** Used to disable a service or device driver that is set to automatically start when Windows 2000/XP loads. The service or driver might be corrupt and might need to be disabled in order for Windows 2000/XP to load properly. For example, if the Agp440 service (deals with video resolution) fails to load successfully and Windows 2000/XP will not load, it might be wise to disable Agp440. Use the LISTSVC command to list all services that can be disabled.

- **Syntax with examples:**

| DISABLE Agp440 | Disables the Agp440 service. |

DISKPART

- **Purpose:** Used to modify partitions on your hard drive. Do not use this command if you have upgraded your hard drive to a dynamic disk configuration. Use the MAP command to list devices (hard drives) that can be managed with DISKPART. For Windows 2000, type DISKPART without parameters to load a GUI for managing your partitions. For Windows XP, type DISKPART without parameters to get to a Diskpart prompt (DISKPART>). At the prompt, type HELP for a full list of Diskpart commands.

- **Parameters:**

| /Add | Creates a partition (if possible) on your hard drive. |
| /Delete | Removes a partition from your hard drive. |

- **Syntax with examples:**

DISKPART	For Windows 2000, loads a GUI interface that you can use to manage your partitions. For Windows XP, provides a Diskpart> prompt to enter Diskpart commands.
DISKPART /add \Device\HardDisk0 10240	Creates a partition on the hard drive and makes it 10240MB (10GB).

ENABLE [ServiceName] [DeviceDriverName]

- **Purpose:** Used to enable a service or device driver that can then start when Windows 2000/XP loads. Use the LISTSVC command to list services that qualify to be enabled.

EXIT

- **Purpose:** Used to exit the Recovery Console and reboot the computer.

EXPAND Source /F:filename [Destination] /D /Y

- **Purpose:** Used to expand compressed files from the Windows 2000/XP Setup CD. This is useful for troubleshooting issues with corrupt system files. For example, you can expand and automatically copy the Windows 2000/XP kernel (kernel32.dll) to the System32 folder.

- **Parameters:**

/F	Name the file you want to extract. Wildcard characters can be used to expand multiple files.
/D	Don't expand the compressed file. Displays a list of files that are contained within the compressed file.
/Y	Don't prompt if overwriting an existing file.
Source	The name of the cabinet file that contains the compressed files.
Destination	The location where the expanded file is to be written.

- **Syntax with examples:**

EXPAND D:\i386\Driver.cab /F:Msvideo.sys C:\Windows\system\drivers	Locates the compressed file Msvideo.sys in the Driver.cab file in the D:\i386 folder and writes the expanded file to the C:\Windows\system\driver folder.
EXPAND Driver.CAB /d	Shows the files contained within the compressed cabinet file.

FIXBOOT [Drive]

- **Purpose:** Used to create a new boot sector on the specified system partition.

- **Syntax with examples:**

FIXBOOT C:	Rewrites boot sector to drive C:.

FIXMBR [DeviceName]

- **Purpose:** Repairs the master boot record on the boot partition. This command is useful when the master boot record (MBR) has been damaged because of a virus or worm. Use the MAP command to get a list of hard drives that can be fixed by FIXMBR.

- **Syntax with examples:**

FIXMBR	Rewrites the MBR program to the boot device used to boot the primary operating system.
FIXMBR \Device\HardDisk1	Rewrites the MBR program to the hard drive specified.

FORMAT [Drive:] /Q /FS:filesystem

- **Purpose:** Used to format a hard drive. Parameters can be used to format the hard drive with FAT, FAT32, or NTFS file system types.

- **Parameters:**

/Q	Performs a quick format.
/FS:FAT	Formats a FAT16 logical drive or volume.
/FS:FAT32	Formats a FAT32 logical drive or volume.
/FS:NTFS	Formats a NTFS logical drive or volume.

- **Syntax with examples:**

FORMAT C: /FS:FAT32	Formats a FAT32 volume.
FORMAT C:	Formats the NTFS volume because NTFS is the default file system used if none is specified.

HELP [CommandName]

- **Purpose:** Displays information about the specified command. If no parameter is given, a list of commands available in the Recovery Console displays.

LISTSVC

- **Purpose:** Displays a list of all services in Windows 2000/XP and their state (Automatic, Manual, Disabled). Used with the DISABLE and ENABLE commands.

LOGON

- **Purpose:** Detects all installed operating systems and prompts for the local administrator password of each operating system. Used to log onto the Recovery Console.

MAP

- **Purpose:** Lists all drives and associated drive letters on a computer along with file system types and partition sizes. Use the command to list items that you can then refer to when managing partitions with the DISKPART command.

MD or MKDIR [Drive:]Path

- **Purpose:** Creates a specified directory. Works similar to the DOS MD command.

MORE or TYPE [Drive:][Path]Filename

- **Purpose:** Displays contents of a text file on the screen, one screen at a time.

- **Syntax with examples:**

MORE Readme.txt	Displays file contents on screen.
TYPE C:\Windows\Readme.txt	Displays file contents on screen.

NET

- **Purpose:** Cannot be used within the Windows 2000/XP Recovery Console because the TCP/IP protocol stack is not loaded in the Recovery Console. This command has been erroneously added to the Recovery Console.

RD or RMDIR [Drive:]Path

- **Purpose:** Deletes a specified directory. Works similar to the DOS RD command.

REN or RENAME [Drive:][Path]Filename1 Filename2

- **Purpose:** Renames a specified file. Works similar to the DOS REN command.

SET Variable = Value

Displays a list of all environment variables within the Recovery Console. Can be used to modify environment variables to add more flexibility to the Recovery Console.

• **Syntax with examples:**

SET	Displays list of variables and values.
SET AllowWildCards = TRUE	Enables support for wildcards (for example, *.*, which is useful when copying or deleting multiple files.
SET AllowAllPaths = TRUE	Enables access to all folders and files on the hard drive.
SET AllowRemovableMedia = TRUE	Enables file copy to a floppy or flash disk, which is normally disabled.
SET NoCopyPrompt = TRUE	Disables prompts when overwriting existing files and folders.

SYSTEMROOT

• **Purpose:** Sets the current directory to the system root (for example, C:\ WINDOWS).

ADDING MORE FLEXIBILITY TO THE RECOVERY CONSOLE

Using the Recovery Console, you have limited access to files and folders on the hard drive. You can only access the following directories:

- Files on the root directory (C:\)
- Files in the *%SystemRoot%* and its subdirectories (for example, C:\Windows, C:\Windows\System32)
- Files in the C:\Cmdcons directory (if you've installed the Recovery Console locally)
- Files and directories on removable disks (for example, floppy disk, Zip disk, and CD-ROM drive)

It's important to know that you cannot copy files from the hard drive to a floppy disk or Zip disk. However, you can copy files from a floppy disk, Zip disk, and CD-ROM drive to the hard drive. Therefore, the standard Recovery Console environment can be somewhat limiting. Fortunately, you can add more flexibility by modifying Recovery Console policies. Do the following to modify the Recovery Console policies:

1. Open the **Control Panel**.
2. Double-click **Administrative Tools** applet, and then double-click **Local Security Policy**.
3. Under Security Settings, click **Local Policies**, and double-click **Security Options**.
4. Scroll through the settings on the Policy pane until you find **Recovery console: Allow floppy copy and access to all drives and all folders**.
5. Double-click this Recovery Console setting, and click **Enable**.
6. Click **OK**.
7. Close all Windows.

Once inside the Recovery Console, type the following commands to add even more power to the Recovery Console. You must type the commands exactly as they are listed, with spaces and correct case.

- Set AllowWildCards = TRUE
- Set AllowAllPaths = TRUE
- Set AllowRemovableMedia = TRUE
- Set NoCopyPrompt = TRUE

WINDOWS 2000/XP STOP ERRORS

A STOP error, also known as a Blue Screen of Death (BSOD), occurs when Windows 2000/XP encounters a fatal error from which it cannot recover. As a result, the computer freezes (or stops), and an error message appears on a blue or black background. The error message contains information about the fatal error and provides details on how to troubleshoot the problem. There are many different kinds of STOP errors, but the basic form is:

STOP: 0X0000000A (0X00000001, 0X00000002, 0X00000003, 0X00000004)

0X0000000A: The name of the STOP error. An additional STOP error name may be provided.

Examples include KERNEL_DATA_INPAGE_ERROR, IRQL_NOT_LESS_OR_EQUAL, and INACCESSIBLE_BOOT_DEVICE.

One to four parameters follow. Each parameter can be a combination of letters and numbers. All four parameters (if they are present) are used to troubleshoot a fatal error.

0X00000001: Parameter one.

0X00000002: Parameter two.

0X00000003: Parameter three.

0X00000004: Parameter four.

Some STOP errors might list no parameters at all. When a STOP error occurs, it is very important to record the STOP error name and all displayed parameters exactly as they appear on your screen. If an additional STOP error name is provided, record it as well.

WHY DO STOP ERRORS OCCUR?

STOP errors occur because of the following:

- [ ] Virus infections
- [ ] Newly added hardware, software, or recently upgraded device drivers
- [ ] Hardware failure (for example, hard drive, RAM, or video adapter failure)
- [ ] Old BIOS, hardware, software, or device drivers that are not designed to run with your operating system
- [ ] Software failure
- [ ] Failed upgrade of the operating system

WHEN DO STOP ERRORS TYPICALLY OCCUR?

STOP errors typically occur at the following times:

☐ During the operating system boot process
☐ During the use of corrupt or outdated hardware, software, or device drivers
☐ During the operating system shutdown process
☐ During the installation or upgrade of a new operating system

WHY DOES THE PC SPONTANEOUSLY REBOOT?

Using Windows 2000/XP, some STOP errors are not displayed by default. If these STOP errors occur, the default action is to automatically reboot the computer. This behavior makes troubleshooting a STOP error very difficult. However, you can modify this setting so that a STOP error message is displayed instead of rebooting the computer by doing the following:

1. To change this setting, right-click **My Computer**, and select **Properties** from the shortcut menu.
2. Click the **Advanced tab**. Under the Startup and Recovery pane, click **Settings**.
3. In the Startup and Recovery dialog box, uncheck **Automatically Restart**. The next time a STOP error occurs, a screen will appear that describes the source of the error.

TROUBLESHOOTING STOP ERRORS

When a STOP error occurs, do the following:

☐ Record the STOP error exactly as it appears on your screen.
☐ Refer to Table E-1 for more information, or use a search engine such as Google (*www.google.com*) to search the Internet about the error.
☐ Update your virus definitions, and perform a full scan using antivirus software before using the information in Table E-1. Performing a full virus scan is the first step for troubleshooting *all* STOP errors. If the virus scan does not work, try running it in Safe Mode with Networking or Safe Mode.
☐ If any new software, hardware, or device drivers were recently installed, then uninstall or remove them. Read the STOP error screen carefully to see if the device driver for a particular device is listed by name. You might use the driver rollback feature or System Restore.
☐ If any hardware, software, or device drivers were recently upgraded, uninstall them. You might can use the driver rollback feature or System Restore.
☐ Perform a Last Known Good Configuration recovery by pressing F8 as your computer starts the boot process.
☐ If possible, run CHKDSK /R and the disk DEFRAG utilities.
☐ If possible, install the latest Windows updates. If the installation fails, try running it in Safe Mode.
☐ Disable all unneeded services that are set to automatically run when Windows loads.
☐ A device such as a hard drive, hard disk controller (on the motherboard), modem, video card, RAM, and so on might be failing. Begin replacing computer components such as the RAM, video adapter, modem, motherboard, or hard drive with known good components.
☐ Check to make sure that the hard drive is not full.
☐ Read all Event Viewer logs, and look for recent errors.

- [ ] Remove all unnecessary components in your computer including modems, sound cards, network cards, CD or DVD drives, Zip drives, scanners, and printers.
- [ ] Disable or uninstall your antivirus software.
- [ ] Disable all BIOS features related to Plug and Play, caching, shadowing, and virus protection.
- [ ] Consider upgrading the video adapter drivers using the latest drivers downloaded from the video adapter manufacturer's Web site.
- [ ] Consider upgrading your computer's BIOS.
- [ ] If you're going to upgrade to Windows XP, run D:\i386\winnt32 /checkupgradeonly (where D is the drive letter of your CD-ROM). This will help identify devices or software that may cause a STOP error.
- [ ] If you're currently using or planning to upgrade to Windows XP, visit the Windows XP Hardware Compatibility List at *winqual.microsoft.com/HCL/Default.aspx?m=x*.
- [ ] If you're currently using or planning to upgrade to Windows Vista, visit the Windows Vista Hardware Compatibility List at *winqual.microsoft.com/HCL*.
- [ ] To prevent STOP errors related to device drivers using Windows 2000/XP, be sure to install drivers that have been digitally signed by Microsoft. A digitally signed driver has been verified to work with the operating system. You will receive a warning prompt during the installation of device drivers that have not been digitally signed.

Table E-1 Common STOP error messages and what to do about them

Error Message	What It Means and What to Do
STOP 0X0000000A or IRQL_NOT_LESS_OR_EQUAL	Caused by faulty hardware or software that is attempting to access a protected memory area. Uninstall any newly installed hardware or software.
TIP See the Microsoft Knowledge Base Article 228888 at the Microsoft Web site *support.microsoft.com*.	
STOP 0X0000001E or KMODE_EXCEPTION _NOT_HANDLED	If this error occurs during the installation process, check the hard drive for free space.
TIP See the Microsoft Knowledge Base Articles 161703 (for Windows 2000) and 314451 (for Windows XP) at the Microsoft Web site, *support.microsoft.com*.	
STOP 0X00000023 or FAT_FILE_SYSTEM	Caused by a read or write failure to FAT16 or FAT32 file system drive. The FAT16 or FAT32 file system is corrupted. Immediately boot into the Recovery Console and copy important data files that have not been backed up to another media before attempting to recover the system. Run Chkdsk and Defrag utilities. Could be a hard drive failure.

(continued)

Table E-1 Common STOP error messages and what to do about them (continued)

Error Message	What It Means and What to Do
💡 **TIP** See the Microsoft Knowledge Base Article 228888 at the Microsoft Web site, *support.microsoft.com.*	
STOP 0X00000024 or NTFS_FILE_SYSTEM	The NTFS file system is corrupted. Immediately boot into the Recovery Console, and copy important data files that have not been backed up to another media before attempting to recover the system.
💡 **TIP** See the Microsoft Knowledge Base Article 228888 at the Microsoft Web site, *support.microsoft.com.*	
STOP 0X0000002E or DATA_BUS_ERROR	Caused by faulty memory (RAM, Level 2 cache, or video adapter memory) or hard disk corruption. Replace RAM and/or the video adapter. Run Chkdsk or Defrag on the hard drive.
STOP 0X0000003F or NO_MORE_SYSTEM_PTES	Caused by installing incompatible devices, device drivers, or software. Uninstall any newly added software, devices, and device drivers.
STOP 0X0000004E or PFN_LIST_CORRUPT	Caused by faulty RAM. Replace with known good RAM.
💡 **TIP** See the Microsoft Knowledge Base Article 291806 at the Microsoft Web site, *support.microsoft.com.*	
STOP 0X00000050 or PAGE_FAULT_IN_NONPAGED_AREA	Caused by faulty memory (RAM, Level 2 cache, or video adapter memory) or newly installed hardware or software. Replace RAM and uninstall newly added software, devices, and device drivers.
STOP 0X00000076 or PROCESS_HAS_LOCKED_PAGES	Bad sectors are on the hard drive, there is a hard drive hardware problem, or RAM is defective. Try running Chkdsk or Scandisk.
STOP 0X00000077 or KERNEL_STACK_INPAGE_ERROR	Hard drive corruption or failure. Could also be related to faulty memory (RAM, Level 2 cache, or video adapter memory) or a damaged motherboard.

(continued)

Table E-1 Common STOP error messages and what to do about them (continued)

Error Message	What It Means and What to Do
STOP 0X00000079 or MISMATCHED_HAL	Windows is using an incorrect version of the Hardware Abstraction Layer file. Copy Hal.dll from Windows setup CD to the hard drive. This error may also be caused by recent modifications to ACPI configuration. Undo recent modifications.
STOP 0X0000007A or KERNEL_DATA_ INPAGE_ERROR	There is a bad sector on the hard drive where the paging file is stored; there is a virus or defective RAM. Try running Chkdsk. You can use the Recovery Console to delete the page file (C:\Pagefile.sys) using the DEL command, but first use the ATTRIB command to remove the hidden and system attributes from the file.
STOP 0X0000007B or INACCESSIBLE_BOOT_DEVICE	There is a boot sector virus or fail ing hard drive or disk controller. Try Fixmbr from the Recovery Console.

> **TIP** See the Microsoft Knowledge Base Article 324103 at the Microsoft Web site, *support.microsoft.com*.

Error Message	What It Means and What to Do
STOP 0X0000007F or UNEXPECTED_KERNEL _MODE_TRAP	Caused by faulty memory (RAM, Level 2 cache, or video adapter memory) or newly installed hardware or software. Replace RAM and uninstall newly added software, devices, and device drivers. This error can also occur if you're overclocking your processor.
STOP 0X0000009F or DRIVER_ POWER_STATE_FAILURE	Uninstall newly added software, devices, and device drivers. If necessary, disable standby mode and hibernation mode.
STOP 0X000000BE or ATTEMPTED_WRITE_TO_ READONLY_MEMORY	Uninstall newly added software, devices, and device drivers.
STOP 0X000000C2 or BAD_ POOL_CALLER	Uninstall newly added software, devices, and device drivers. This problem may also be due to a faulty hard drive or hard disk controller.

(continued)

Table E-1 Common STOP error messages and what to do about them
(continued)

Error Message	What It Means and What to Do
STOP 0X000000CE or DRIVER_UNLOADED_WITHOUT_CANCELLING_PENDING_OPERATIONS	Uninstall newly added software, devices, and device drivers.
STOP 0X000000D1 or DRIVER_IRQL_NOT_LESS_OR_EQUAL	Uninstall newly added software, devices, and device drivers.
STOP 0X000000D8 or DRIVER_USED_EXCESSIVE_PTES	Uninstall newly added software, devices, and device drivers.
STOP 0X000000EA or THREAD_STUCK_IN_DEVICE_DRIVER	Uninstall newly added software, devices, and device drivers.
STOP 0X000000ED or UNMOUNTED_BOOT_VOLUME	If using high-speed devices (such as a hard drive), make sure you're using an 80-pin cable that is capable of handling high-speed transfer rates. Possible hard drive failure.
STOP 0X000000F2 or HARDWARE_INTERRUPT_STORM	Uninstall newly added software, devices, and device drivers. Upgrade BIOS.
STOP 0XC000021A or STATUS_SYSTEM_PROCESS_TERMINATED	Uninstall newly added software, devices, and device drivers.
STOP 0XC0000221 or 0XC000026C STATUS_IMAGE_CHECKSUM_MISMATCH or UNABLE_TO_LOAD_DEVICE_DRIVER	Uninstall newly added software, devices, and device drivers. May need to restore original files from Windows Setup CD.
Black screen with no error messages	This is likely to be a corrupted MBR, partition table, boot sector, or Ntldr file. Try using the Fixmbr and Fixboot commands from the Recovery Console.
While running Windows, a STOP error appears and then the system reboots. The reboot happens so fast you can't read the error message.	Set Windows to not reboot after a STOP error so that you have the chance to read the message to help you understand the root problem. See instructions earlier in this appendix. If you cannot boot to the Windows desktop to make the change, press F8 to boot to the Advanced Options menu and then select *Disable automatic restart on system failure.*

TO LEARN MORE: For additional information on Windows 2000 STOP error messages, visit *www.microsoft.com/technet/prodtechnol/windows2000 pro/proddocs/progs/pgsappb.mspx.*

CPUs AND CHIPSETS

This appendix, which lists major PC microprocessors and important facts about them, is organized by CPU manufacturer. In addition, you'll find information about Intel chipsets.

INTEL CPUs

Table F-1 is a list of microprocessors manufactured by Intel indicating the processor family name, processor number, speed, and description. For more information, see the Intel Web site at *www.intel.com*. Intel has two utilities to identify your CPU: one for Windows and one designed to work from a bootable floppy disk. They will identify an Intel processor. The Windows version also gives the processor speed. Download the utilities from:

www.intel.com/support/processors/tools/piu/

Older Intel Desktop Processors

Table F-1 Older Pentiums and Celeron processors

Processor	Processor speeds (MHz or GHz)	System bus speeds (MHz)	Description
Classic Pentium	60 to 200 MHz	60, 66	16 K L1 cache
Pentium MMX	133 to 300 MHz	66	32 K L1 cache
Pentium Pro	150 to 200 MHz	60, 66	16 K L1 and 256 K, 512 K or 1 MB L2 cache
Pentium II	233 to 450 MHz	66, 100	32 K L1 and 256 K or 512 K L2 cache
Pentium II Xeon	400 or 450 MHz	100	32 K or 512 K, 1MB, or 2 MB L2 cache
Pentium III	450 MHz to 1.33 GHz	100, 133	32 K L1 and 512 K unified, nonblocking L2 cache, or 256 K L2 Advanced Transfer Cache
Pentium III Xeon	600 MHz to 1 GHz	100 or 133	32 K L1 and 256 K, 1 MB, or 2 MB L2 Advanced Transfer Cache

(continued)

Table F-1 Microprocessors manufactured by Intel (continued)

Processor	Processor speeds (MHz or GHz)	System bus speeds (MHz)	Description
Celeron	850 MHz to 2.9 GHz	400, 533	32 K Execution Trace Cache (ETC) and 128 K or 256 K Advanced Transfer L2 cache. Uses FC-PGA2 package. Installs in an mPGA478 socket.
Celeron D 320 to 351	2.4 GHz to 3.2 GHz	533	ETC L1 and 256 K L2 cache. Uses an FC-LGA, FC-PGA478, FC-PGA4, or FC-LGA4 package. Installs in an LGA775 land socket or mPGA478 pin socket.

Current Intel Desktop Processors

Table F-2 lists the current desktop processors by Intel.

Table F-2 Current Intel desktop processors

Processor family	Processor number	Processor speeds (MHz or GHz)	System bus speeds (MHz)	Description
Core 2 Extreme	QX6800, QX6700, X6800	2.66 to 2.93 GHz	1066 MHz	Socket LGA775, chipset 975X
Core 2 Quad	Q6600	2.40 GHz	1066 MHz	Socket LGA775, chipset 975X
Core 2 Duo	E6700, E6600, E6420, E6400, E6320, E6300, E4400, E4300	1.80 to 2.66 GHz	800 MHz or 1066 MHz	Socket LGA775. Supported chipsets are 975X, P965, 946PL, 946GZ, Q965, Q963, or G965
Pentium Extreme	965, 955, 840	3.20 to 3.73 GHz	1066 MHz or 800 MHz	Socket LGA775. Chipset 975X or 955X. Uses Dual Channel DDR2 memory.
Pentium D	960, 950, 945, 940, 935, 930, 920, 915, 840, 830, 820, 805	2.80 to 3.60 GHz	800 MHz	Socket LGA775. Supported chipsets are 945, 975X, 955X, 965, 946PL, 946GZ, 945G, 945P, E7230. Uses DDR2 or Dual Channel DDR2 memory.

(continued)

Table F-2 Current Intel desktop processors (continued)

Processor family	Processor number	Processor speeds (MHz or GHz)	System bus speeds (MHz)	Description
Pentium 4 Extreme Edition with Hyper-Threading (HT)	Earlier Pentium 4s were not assigned processor numbers.	3.2 GHz to 3.73 GHz	800 or 1066 MHz	Uses a FC-LGA, mPGA478, or FC-PGA2 package. Installs in a LGA775-land or 478-pin socket. Uses the 975XE, 925X, 915P, 915G 875P, 865PE, 865G, or E7230 chipset. Uses Dual Channel DDR and Dual Channel DDR2 RAM.
Pentium 4 with HT	520, 521, 524, 530, 531, 540, 541, 550, 551, 560, 561, 570J, 571, 630, 631, 640, 641, 650, 651, 660, 661, 662, 670 and some earlier models that were not assigned model numbers.	2.4 GHz to 3.8 GHz	800 MHz	Installs in a LGA775-land or 478-pin socket. Uses these chipsets: 925X, 925XE, 915G, 915GV, 915GL, 915P, 915PL, 955, 945G, 945P, E7230, 875P, 865PE, 865GV, or 865G. Uses DDR, Dual Channel DDR, or Dual Channel DDR2 RAM.
Pentium 4	No processor numbers were assigned to these early processors.	1.3 GHz to 3.06 GHz	400, 533	Installs in a 423-pin or 478-pin socket. Uses these chipsets: 865GV, 910GL, 845G, 845E, 845GV, 845GE, 845PE, or 915P. Uses SDRAM, DDR SDRAM, DDR, Dual Channel DDR 400/333/266 SDRAM memory.

AMD CPUs

Processors by Advanced Micro Devices, Inc., or AMD (www.amd.com), are popular in the game and hobbyist markets, and they are generally less expensive than compatible Intel processors. Older and newer AMD processors are listed next.

Older AMD Processors

Table F-3 is a list of older AMD CPUs, their speeds, the socket or slot they run on, and the Intel Pentium microprocessor they most closely resemble.

Table F-3 Older AMD processors

Processor	Latest Clock Speeds (MHz or GHz)	Compares to (MHz)	System Bus Speed	Package Type	Socket or Slot
AMD–K6–2	166 to 500 MHz	Pentium II, Celeron	66, 95, 100	CPGA	Socket 7 or Super Socket 7
AMD–K6–III	350 to 450	Pentium II	100	CPGA	Super Socket 7
Duron	1 GHz to 1.3 GHz	Celeron	200	CPGA or OPGA	Socket A
Athlon	Up to 1.9 GHz	Pentium III	200	Card	Slot A
Athlon Model 4	Up to 1.4 GHz	Pentium III	266	CPGA	Socket A

Current AMD Processors

AMD processors currently sold by AMD are listed next:

☐ Processors designed for desktops include the Athlon 64 X2 Dual-Core (64-bit processor uses 939-pin socket), the Athlon 64 FX (64-bit processor uses a 939-pin or 940-pin socket), the Athlon 64 (64-bit processor uses a 754-pin or 939-pin socket), the Athlon XP (uses Socket A), and the 32-bit Sempron processor. The Sempron is comparable to the Celeron and uses Socket A or a 754-pin socket.

☐ Two processors designed for high-end workstations or servers are the Athlon MP, which uses Socket A, and the Opteron, which uses dual-core processing and Socket 940.

☐ Processors designed for notebooks include the Turion 64 X2 Dual-Core Mobile, Turion 64 Mobile, Mobile Athlon 64, Athlon 64 for Notebooks, Mobile Athlon XP-M, and Mobile Sempron.

VIA AND CYRIX CPUS

Table F-4 is a list of CPUs from VIA, the current owner of Cyrix, their processor speeds, the socket or slot they run on, and the Intel Pentium processor they most closely resemble. For more information, see the VIA Web site at *www.via.com.tw.*

Table F-4 VIA and Cyrix family of CPUs

Processor	Latest Clock Speeds (MHz)	Compares to	System Bus Speed (MHz)	Socket or Slot
Cyrix M II	300, 333, 350	Pentium II, Celeron	66, 75, 83, 95, 100	Socket 7
Cyrix III	433 to 533	Celeron, Pentium III	66, 100, 133	Socket 370
VIA C3	Up to 1.4 GHz	Celeron	100, 133or 200	Socket 370

PROCESSOR PACKAGES

Flat and thin processor packages used by Intel are listed below:

- ☐ *PPGA (Plastic Pin Grid Array).* The processor is housed in a square box designed to fit flat into Socket 370. Pins are on the underside of the flat housing, and heat sinks or fans can be attached to the top of the housing by using a thermal plate or heat spreader. The early Celeron processors used this package with 370 pins.
- ☐ *PPGA INT2 and PPGA INT3.* These packages are used by Pentium 4s and have 423 pins.
- ☐ *PGA (Pin Grid Array).* Pins on the bottom of this package are staggered and can be inserted only one way into the socket. It is used by the Xeon with 603 pins. When used by the Pentium 4, it has 423 pins and is called the PGA 423 package.
- ☐ *int-microPGA 603.* This package has 603 pins and is used by the Xeon processors. It uses a zero–insertion force (ZIF) socket.
- ☐ *FC-mPGA and FC-mPGA4.* This package has 604 pins and is used by the Xeon processors.
- ☐ *OOI or OLGA (Organic Land Grid Array).* Used by some Pentium 4s, this 423-pin package is similar to the PGA package but is designed to dissipate heat faster.
- ☐ *FC-PGA (Flip Chip Pin Grid Array).* This package looks like the PPGA package and uses 370 pins in Socket 370. It is called a flip chip package because the processor is turned upside down so that the CPU die itself is on top of the processor housing, making it possible to apply a thermal solution directly to the die. Pins on the bottom of the package are staggered. Some Pentium III and Celeron processors use this package.
- ☐ *FC-PGA2 (Flip Chip Pin Grid Array 2).* This package is similar to the FC-PGA package but has an integrated heat sink. When used by a Pentium III or Celeron processor, it has 370 pins. When used by the Pentium 4, it has 478 pins.
- ☐ *mPGA 478.* This package has 478 pins and is used by the Celeron and Pentium 4.
- ☐ *FC-LGA775 (Flip-Chip Land Grid Array), FC-LGA, or FC-LGA4.* This is the newest Pentium package used by the Pentiums and Celerons. It uses 775 lands rather than pins.

AMD has its own processor packages different from Intel. These flat and thin packages are listed next:

- ☐ *CPGA (Ceramic Pin Grid Array).* This is a flat package with pins on the underside used by several AMD processors, including the Duron, AMD-K6-2, and AMD-K6-III. Number of pins varies among processors.
- ☐ *OPGA (Organic Pin Grid Array).* This package is used by the AMD Athlon MP and Athlon XP and some models of the AMD Duron.
- ☐ *µPGA (Micro Pin Grid Array).* This package is used by the AMD 64-bit processors, including the AMD Opteron, Athlon 64 X2 Dual Core, Athlon 64, and Athlon 64 FX.

SLOTS AND SOCKETS

Table F-5 lists several of the types of sockets and slots used by CPUs.

Table F-5 Processor sockets and slots for desktop computers

Connector Name	Used by processor	Description
Socket 4	Classic Pentium 60/66	273 pins 21 × 21 PGA grid supplies 5 V
Socket 5	Classic Pentium 75/90/100/120/133	320 pins 37 × 37 SPGA grid supplies 3.3 V
Socket 7	Pentium MMX, Fast Classic Pentium, AMD K5, AMD K5, Cyrix M	321 pins 37 × 37 SPGA grid supplies 2.5 C to 3.3 V
Super Socket 7	AMD K5-2, AMD K5-III	321 pins 37 × 37 SPGA grid supplies 2.5 V to 3.3 V
Socket 8	Pentium Pro	387 pins 24 × 26 SPGA grid supplies 3.3 V
Socket 370 or PGA370 Socket	Pentium III FC-PGA, Celeron PPGA, Cyrix III	370 pins in a 37 × 37 grid supplies 1.5 V or 2 V
Slot 1 or SC242	Pentium II, Pentium III	242 pins in 2 rows, rectangular shape supplies 2.8 V and 3.3 V
Slot A	AMD Athlon	242 pins in 2 rows, rectangular shape supplies 1.3 V and 2.05 V
Socket A or Socket 462	AMD Athlon and Duron	462 pins, SPGA grid, rectangular shape supplies 1.5 V to 1.85 V
Slot 2 or SC330	Pentium II Xeon, Pentium III Xeon	330 pins in 2 rows, rectangular shape supplies 1.5 V to 3.5 V
Socket 423	Pentium 4	423 pins 39 × 39 SPGA grid supplies 1.7 V and 1.75 V
Socket 478	Pentium 4	478 pins in a dense micro PGA (mPGA) supplies 1.7 V and 1.75 V
Socket PAC418	Itanium	418 pins supplies 3.3 V
Socket PAC611	Itanium 2	611 pins supplies 3.3 V
Socket 603 and 604	Xeon, Xeon DP and Xeon MP	603 pins or 604 pins supply 1.5 and 1.7 V
Sockets 754, 939, and 940	Athlon 64, Sempron, Opteron, and Athlon 64 FX	754, 939, or 940 pins; Socket 754 is the most current socket
Socket LGA775	Core Duo, Pentium, and Celeron	775 lands, not pins, and supplies 1.5 to 1.6 Vs

INTEL CHIPSETS

Table F-6 lists Intel chipsets for desktop computers.

Table F-6 Intel chipsets for desktop computers

Common Name	Model Number	Processor Supported	System Bus Speed Supported	Memory Supported
i900 Express Series	975X	Pentium 4 with HT, Pentium D, Pentium 4 Extreme Edition with HT, Core 2 Duo, Core 2 Extreme	1066 or 800 MHz	Dual-Channel DDR2 up to 8 GB
	Q965, P965, G965, Q963*	Pentium D, Pentium 4 with HT, Core 2 Duo	1066, 800, or 533 MHz	Dual-Channel DDR2 up to 8 GB
	946GZ, 946PL	Core 2 Duo, Pentium D, Pentium 4 with HT and all other processors using the LGA775 socket	800 or 533 MHz	Dual-Channel DDR2 up to 4 GB
	955X	Pentium Extreme Edition, Pentium D, Pentium 4 Extreme Edition with HT, Pentium 4 with HT	1066 MHz or 800 MHz	Dual-Channel DDR2 up to 8 GB
	945GT	Core Duo	667 or 533 MHz	Dual-Channel DDR2 up to 4 GB
	945G, 945P, 945GZ, 945PL	Pentium D, Pentium 4 with HT, and all other System Bus Pentium processors	1066MHz, 800 MHz, or 533 MHz	Dual-Channel DDR2 up to 4 GB
	925XE	Pentium 4	1066 MHz or 800 MHz	Dual-Channel DDR2 533/400
	925X	Pentium 4, Pentium 4 Extreme Edition	800 MHz	Dual-Channel DDR2 533/400
	915P, 915G, 915GV	Pentium 4	800 MHz, 533 MHz	Dual-Channel DDR2 533/400, DDR 400/333
	915P, 915G, 915GV	Pentium 4	800 MHz, 533 MHz	Dual-Channel DDR2 533/400, DDR 400/333

(continued)

Table F-6 Intel chipsets for desktop computers (continued)

Com-mon Name	Model Number	Processor Supported	System Bus Speed Supported	Memory Supported
	915GL, 915PL	Pentium 4 or Celeron D	800 MHz or 533 MHz	Dual-Channel DDR 400/333,
	910GL	Pentium 4, Celeron, Celeron D	533 MHz	Dual-Channel DDR 400/333
i800 Series	875P	Pentium 4	800 MHz or 533 MHz	Dual-Channel DDR 400/ 333/266
	865G, 865PE, or 865GV, 865P, 848P	Pentium 4, Celeron, or Celeron D	800 MHz, 533 MHz, or 400 MHz	Dual-Channel DDR 400/333/266 or DDR 400/ 333/266
	860	Dual Xeon DP processors	400 MHz	PC800/600 RDRAM
	850E, 850	Pentium 4	533 MHz or 400 MHz	PC1066/800/600 RDRAM
	845, 845E, 845G, 845GL, 845PE, 845GE, 845GV PC133	Pentium 4 or Celeron	533 MHz or 400 MHz	DDR 333/266/ 200, SDRAM
	840	Dual Pentium III or Pentium III Xeon	133 MHz or 100 MHz	PC800/600 RDRAM
	820, 820E	Dual Pentium III or Pentium II	133 MHzor 100 MHz	PC800/700/600 RDRAM
	815, 815E, 815EP, or 815P, 815EG, 815G	Celeron or Pentium III	133 MHz, 100 MHz, or 66 MHz	PC133/100/66 SDRAM
	810E2, 810E, 810	Celeron or Pentium III	133 MHz, 100 MHz, or 66 MHz	PC100/66 SDRAM

* Intel Q965, P965, G965, and Q963 chipsets all support the LGA775 socket and SATA and eSATA (external SATA) storage.

Use Tables G-1 and G-2, which contain IRQ and I/O address assignments, to help solve resource conflicts in legacy systems. To find out what values are being used by your system, under DOS use MSD, and under Windows 9x and Windows 2000/XP use Device Manager.

Table G-1 IRQs and how they are commonly used

IRQ	Most Common Use	Other Uses
0	System timer	None; it's reserved for the system
1	Keyboard controller	None; it's reserved for the system
2	Cascade for IRQs 8–15	None; it's reserved for the system
3	COM2	COM4, sound card, modem, network card, tape accelerator card
4	COM1	COM3, sound card, modem, network card, tape accelerator card
5	LPT2 or sound card	COM3, COM4, modem, network card, tape accelerator card
6	Floppy disk controller	Tape accelerator cards that use the floppy drive controller
7	LPT1	COM3, COM4, modem, sound card, network card, tape accelerator card
8	Real-time clock	None; it's reserved for the system
9	None; it's considered available for peripherals	PCI device, sound card, network card, SCSI host adapter
10	None; it's considered available for peripherals	PCI devices, sound card, network card, SCSI host adapter
11	None; it's considered available for peripherals	PCI devices, sound card, network card, SCSI host adapter, video card
12	PS/2 mouse	PCI devices, sound card, network card, SCSI host adapter, video card
13	Math coprocessor	None; it's reserved for the system
14	Primary IDE channel	SCSI host adapters
15	Secondary IDE channel	Network card, SCSI host adapter

Table G-2 I/O addresses

I/O Address	Description
000–00F	DMA controller, channels 0, 1, 2, and 3
010–01F	System use
020–03F	Interrupt controller #1
040–05F	System timer
060–06F	Keyboard
060	PS/2 mouse
061	Speaker
070–07F	Real-time clock, nonmaskable interrupt and CMOS RAM
081–087	DMA page register (0, 1, 2, 3)
089–08F	DMA page register (4, 5, 6, 7)
090–09F	System use
0A0–0AF	Interrupt controller #2
0C0–0DF	DMA controller, channels 4, 5, 6, 7
0F0–0FF	Math coprocessor
130–15F	SCSI host adapter
170–17F	Secondary IDE controller, master drive
1F0–1FF	Primary IDE controller, master drive
200–20F	Joystick port
220–22F	SCSI host adapter or sound card
230–23F	SCSI host adapter
240–26F	Sound card or network card
270–27F	Plug and Play devices or LPT2 or LPT3
278–27F	LPT2 or LPT3
280–2BF	Network card
2E8–2EF	COM4
2F8–2FF	COM2
300–30F	Sound card (MIDI port) or network card
360–36F	Tape accelerator card
370–37F	Secondary IDE controller, slave drive
378–37F	LPT1
380–38F	Sound card (FM synthesizer)
3B0–3BF	VGA/monochrome video or LPT1
3C0–3CF	VGA/EGA video
3D0–3DF	Available
3F0–3F7	Floppy drive controller
3F6–3F7	Primary IDE controller, slave drive
3F8–3FF	COM1

Tables H-1 through H-11 list important URLs alphabetically by hardware and software components.

Table H-1 BIOS manufacturers and other sources for BIOS information and upgrades

Company	URL
Abit	www.abit-usa.com
Acer	www.acer.com
ALi	www.ali.com.tw
American Megatrends, Inc. (AMI)	www.megatrends.com or www.ami.com
Amptron	www.amptron.com
AOpen	www.aopen.com.tw
Asus	www.asus.com.tw
Bare-Bone	www.bare-bone.com
Biostar	www.biostar-usa.com
Compaq and Hewlett-Packard (HP)	www.thenew.hp.com or www.h18000.www1.hp.com
CTL	www.ctlcorp.com
Dell	www.support.dell.com
Driver Guide (a database of firmware, drivers, and documentation)	www.driverguide.com
Driverzone by Barry Fanion	www.driverzone.com
eSupport.com (BIOS upgrades)	www.esupport.com
Gateway	www.gateway.com
HP or Compaq	www.thenew.hp.com or www.h18000.www1.hp.com
IBM	www.ibm.com/support
Intel	www.intel.com
Lenovo (includes IBM ThinkPads)	www.pc.ibm.com/us and www.lenovo.com
Marco Volpe	www.mrdriver.com
Micron	www.micron.com
Micro-Star (MSI)	www.msicomputer.com
NEC	www.nec-computers.com
Packard Bell	www.packardbell.com
PCCHIPS	www.pcchips.com.tw
PCPartner	www.pcpartner.com
Phoenix	www.phoenix.com/pcuser

(continued)

Table H-1 BIOS manufacturers and other sources for BIOS information and upgrades (continued)

Company	URL
Phoenix Technologies (First BIOS, Phoenix, and Award)	www.phoenix.com
PINE Technology	www.pinegroup.com
Taipei Computer (Computex)	www.computex.com.tw
Taiwan Commate	www.tcommate.com.tw
The Driver Forum	www.driverforum.com/bios
Toshiba	www.toshiba.com
Unicore (BIOS upgrades)	www.unicore.com
VIA Technologies	www.viatech.com
Wim's BIOS	www.wimsbios.com

Table H-2 Motherboard manufacturers

Company	URL
Abit	www.abit.com.tw
American Megatrends, Inc. (AMI)	www.megatrends.com or www.ami.com
Amptron	www.amptron.com
Aopen	www.aopen.com
ASRock	www.asrockamerica.com
ASUS	www.asus.com
A-Trend	www.atrend.com
Azza	www.azzaboard.com
BCM	www.bcmcom.com
BIOSTAR Group	www.biostar.com.tw
Dell	www.dell.com
DFI	www.dfiweb.com
ECS	www.ecsusa.com
ECS Elitegroup	www.ecs.com.tw
EpoX	www.epox.com
Famous Tech	www.magic-pro.com/en
FongKai	www.fkusa.com
Ford Lian	www.fordlian.com
FreeTech	www.freetech.com
Gateway	www.gateway.com
Genoa	www.genoasys.com
Gigabyte Technology Co., Ltd.	www.gigabyte.com.tw
IBM	www.ibm.com/us
Intel Corporation	www.intel.com
Iwill Corporation	www.iwill.net
Lenovo (includes IBM ThinkPad notebooks)	www.lenovo.com

(continued)

Table H-2 Motherboard manufacturers (continued)

Company	URL
MicroStar International	www.msicomputer.com
Motherboards.com	www.motherboards.com
Motherboards.org	www.motherboards.org
NEC	www.nec.com
NVIDIA	www.nvidia.com
Octek	www.ocean-usa.com
PC Chips	www.pcchips.com.tw
PC Partner	www.pcpartner.com
QDI	www.qdigrp.com
Samsung	www.sosimple.com
SiS	www.sis.com
Soyo	www.soyo.com
Supermicro Computer, Inc.	www.supermicro.com
Tyan Computer Corporation	www.tyan.com
Vextrec	www.vextrec.com
Wyse (Thin client systems)	www.wyse.com

Table H-3 CPU and chipset manufacturers

Company	URL
Ali, Inc.	www.ali.com.tw
AMD	www.amd.com
VIA Technologies, Inc. (Cyrix)	www.via.com.tw
Intel Corporation	www.intel.com
PowerLeap (CPU adapters and upgrades)	www.powerleap.com
NVIDIA Corporation	www.nvidia.com
Silicon Integrated Systems Corp. (known as SiS)	www.sis.com
QuickLogic Corporation	www.quicklogic.com
Texas Instruments	www.ti.com

Table H-4 Hard drive manufacturers

Company	URL
Beyond Micro	www.beyondmicro.com
Fantom	www.fantomdrives.com
Fujitsu America, Inc.	www.fujitsu.com
Hitachi	www.hitachi.com
IBM PC Company	www.ibm.com
Imation (removable drives)	www.superdisk.com
Iomega (removable drives)	www.iomega.com

(continued)

Table H-4 Hard drive manufacturers (continued)

Company	URL
PowerQuest (Partition Magic software)	*www.symantec.com*
Samsung	*www.samsung.com*
Seagate Technology (Also Conner Peripherals and Maxtor Corporation)	*www.seagate.com*
Sony	*www.sony.com*
SyQuest Technology (removable drives)	*www.syquest.com*
Toshiba	*www.toshiba.com*
Western Digital	*www.wdc.com*

Table H-5 Technical information and troubleshooting about PCs

Company	Description	URL
Administrator's Pak by Winternals	Diagnostics, repair, and data recovery for hard drive, network, and more; includes ERD Commander to deal with corrupted Windows XP system	*www.winternals.com*
BYTE Magazine/ CMP Media, LLC	Technical information	*www.byte.com*
Certify City	A+ Prep	*www.cramsession.com*
CNET, Inc.	Technical information and product reviews	*www.cnet.com*
Comp Guys Techweb	Technical troubleshooting	*www.compguystechweb.com*
Computing.NET	Technical information	*www.computing.net*
CyberCollege	Multimedia technology	*www.cybercollege.com*
DISK/TREND, Inc.	Hard drives	*www.disktrend.com*
Ed Scope, LLC	Technical information and hardware reviews	*www.basichardware.com*
F-Secure Corp.	Data security and viruses	*www.f-secure.com*
GetDataBack by Runtime Software	Data-recovery software	*www.runtime.org*
Hardware Central by Jupitermedia	Technical information and hardware reviews	*www.hardwarecentral.com*
How Stuff Works	Explanations of how computer hardware and software work	*www.howstuffworks.com*
Inboost.com	Performance information	*www.inboost.com*
InfoHQ	Info on buying and using computers	*www.infohq.com*
Jupitermedia Corporation	Encyclopedia of PC terms and hardware reviews	*www.webopedia.com* *www.earthwebhardware .com/computers*

(continued)

Table H-5 Technical information and troubleshooting about PCs (continued)

Company	Description	URL
Kingston Technology	Information about memory	www.kingston.com
Microsoft Technical Resources	Windows support and Microsoft applications support	www.support.microsoft.com
MicroSystems Development Technology	POST diagnostic cards Port test software, loop-back plugs Floppy drive diagnostic tools	www.msdus.com
MK Data/Michael Karbo	Tons of technical information	www.karbosguide.com
Motherboards Superstore	Technical information, hardware reviews, and buyer's guide on mother-boards and more (An aggregate site)	www.motherboards.com
Motherboards.org	Technical information, hardware reviews, and buyer's guide on mother-boards and more (An aggregate site)	www.motherboards.org
Norton SystemWorks by Symantec	PC maintenance and troubleshooting software suite includes Norton Antivirus, Norton Utilities, Norton GoBack, CheckIt Diagnostics, and System Optimizer	www.symantec.com
PartitionMagic by Symantec	Manages a hard drive, including resizing and copying partitions	www.symantec.com
PC Guide	Technical information and troubleshooting	www.pcguide.com
PC Today Online	Technical information and buyer's guide	www.pc-today.com
PC World	Technical information and buyer's guide	www.pcworld.com
Sangoma Technologies, Inc.	Communications technology for PC	www.sangoma.com
SiSoftware Sandra	Benchmarking, diagnostic, and tune-up software	www.sisoftware.co.uk
SpinRite by Gibson Research	Data-recovery software	www.grc.com
Suggest A Fix	PC support forum	www.suggestafix.com
Sysinternals by Microsoft	Tons of technical information about Windows and utilities to download	www.microsoft.com/technet/sysinternals/default.mspx
System Optimization	POST diagnostic cards, drivers, technical data	www.sysopt.com

(continued)

Table H-5 Technical information and troubleshooting about PCs (continued)

Company	Description	URL
The Elder Geek	Solutions for Windows, hardware, network, Internet, and system problems; includes downloads	*www.theeldergeek.com*
Tom's Hardware Guide	In-depth technical information and hardware reviews	*www.tomshardware.com*
Uniblue	Utility software to solve Windows problems	*www.liutilities.com*
Unicore	POST diagnostic cards BIOS upgrades	*www.unicore.com*
Virtual Dr.	Forum for solving PC problems and driver downloads	*www.virtualdr.com*
Web Tech Geek	Technical information	*www.webtechgeek.com*
Webopedia by Jupitermedia	Encyclopedia of computing terms	*www.webopedia.com*
Windows Help	Technical information	*www.windowshelp.com*
ZD Net Help	Technical information and downloads; (Publishes several technical magazines)	*www.zdnet.com*
Zoom Telephonics, Inc.	Modems	*www.modems.com*

Table H-6 Virus detection, removal, and information

Product or Site	Description	URL
AVG Anti-Virus by Grisoft Command	Antivirus software	*www.grisoft.com*
Antivirus	Antivirus software	*www.authentium.com*
Dr. Solomon's Software	Antivirus software	*www.drsolomon.com*
Esafe by Aladdin Knowledge Systems, Ltd.	Antivirus software	*www.esafe.com*
F-Prot by FRISK Software International	Antivirus software available as shareware	*www.f-prot.com*
F-Secure Antivirus by F-Secure Corp.	Virus information	*www.f-secure.com*
McAfee VirusScan by McAfee Associates, Inc.	Antivirus software	*www.mcafee.com*
NeatSuite by Trend Micro (for networks)	Antivirus software for networks	*www.trendmicro.com*
Norman by Norman Data Defense Systems, Inc. and Norman Virus Control	Complicated to use, but highly effective and sophisticated antivirus software	*www.norman.com*
Norton AntiVirus by Symantec, Inc.	Antivirus software	*www.symantec.com*

(continued)

Table H-6 Virus detection, removal, and information (continued)

Product or Site	Description	URL
Patricia Hoffman's Virus Summary	Lists and describes viruses	*www.vsum.com*
PC-cillin by Trend Micro (for home use)	Antivirus software for home use	*www.trendmicro.com*
Virus Bulletin	Virus information	*www.virusbtn.com*

Table H-7 Help with Windows troubleshooting and Windows drivers

Company	URL
Ask Dr. Tech	*www.askdrtech.com*
Computing.NET	*www.computing.net*
Driver Headquarters	*www.drivershq.com*
DriverUpdate.com (drivers)	*www.driverupdate.com*
Driverzone by Barry Fanion	*www.driverzone.com*
HelpWithWindows.com	*www.helpwithwindows.com*
Hermanson, LLC (drivers)	*www.windrivers.com*
InfiniSource, Inc.	*www.windows-help.net*
Marco Volpe (drivers)	*www.mrdriver.com*
Microsoft Support	*www.support.microsoft.com/ support/search/c.asp*
Microsoft technical resources	*www.msdn.microsoft.com*
PC Pitstop	*www.pcpitstop.com*
Sysinternals	*www.sysinternals.com*
The Driver Guide (drivers)	*www.driverguide.com*
Windows IT Library	*www.windowsitlibrary.com*
Windows User Group Network	*www.wugnet.com*

Table H-8 Optical drive manufacturers

Company	URL
Addonics Technologies	*www.addonics.com*
Amacom	*www.amacom-tech.com*
AOpen	*www.usa.aopen.com*
Artec	*www.artecusa.com*
Aserton Group	*www.aserton.com*
ASUS	*www.asus.com*
Axonix	*www.axonix.com*
Behavior Tech Computer	*www.btc-corp.com*
BenQ	*www.benq.com*
Circo Technology	*www.circotech.com*
Creative Labs	*www.creativelabs.com*

(continued)

Table H-8 Optical drive manufacturers (continued)

Company	URL
Fantom	www.fantomdrives.com
Hewlett-Packard (HP)	www.products.hp-at-home.com
IBM	www.ibm.com
INOi	www.inio.com
Kanguru	www.kanguru.com
LITE-ON IT	www.us.liteonit.com
Memorex	www.memorex.com
NEC	www.nec.com
Panasonic	www.panasonic.com
Philips	www.philips.com
Pioneer	www.pioneerelectronics.com
Plextor	www.plextor.com
Primera	www.primera.com
Samsung	www.samsung.com
Sony Electronics	www.sonystyle.com
Targus	www.targus.com
TDK	www.tdk.com
Teac	www.teac.com
Toshiba	www.toshiba.com

Table H-9 Sound cards

Company	URL
AOpen America	www.usa.aopen.com
Aureal Semiconductor	www.aureal.com
Creative Labs	www.soundblaster.com
Dalco	www.dalco.com
Diamond Multimedia Systems	www.diamondmm.com
Guillemot Corporation (Hercules)	www.hercules.com
Inland Products	www.inland-products.com
PPA	www.ppa-usa.com
PPA International	www.ppa-usa.com
Razer USA	www.razerzone.com
Sabrent	www.sabrent.com
SIIG	www.siig.com
Turtle Beach Systems	www.turtlebeach.com

Table H-10 Video card manufacturers

Company	URL
3DFuzion (also BFG)	www.3dfuzion.com
AMD (ATI Technologies)	www.ati.amd.com
ASUSTeK Computer	www.asus.com
BFG Technologies	www.bfgtech.com
Biostar	www.biostar-usa.com
Chaintech	www.chaintechusa.com
Connect3D	www.connect3d.com
Creative Technologies	www.creative.com
Diablo Tek	www.diablotek.com
Diamond Multimedia	www.diamondmm.com
EVGA	www.evga.com
Gainward Co.	www.gainward.com
GeCube	www.gecube.com
Guillemot Corporation (Hercules)	www.hercules.com
Hightech Information Systems (HIS)	www.hisdigital.com
LeadTek	www.leadtek.com
Matrox Graphics	www.matrox.com
NVIDIA	www.nvidia.com
OCZ Technology	www.ocztechnology.com
PNY	www.pny.com
VisionTek	www.visiontek.com
xfx.com	www.xfx.com

Table H-11 Notebook computer manufacturers

Manufacturer	URL
Acer America	www.global.acer.com
Apple Computer	www.apple.com
Compaq and Hewlett–Packard	www.hp.com
Dell Computer	www.dell.com
Fujitsu/Fuji	www.fujitsu.com
Gateway	www.gateway.com
Lenovo (formally IBM ThinkPads)	www.lenovo.com
MPC Computers (also Micron Electronics)	www.mpccorp.com
NEC	www.nec.com
PC Notebook	www.pcnotebook.com
Sony (VAIO)	www.sonystyle.com
Toshiba America	www.csd.toshiba.com
WinBook	www.winbook.com

RECORDKEEPING

This appendix contains some suggested forms to use to track troubleshooting calls. Track these calls for the following reasons:

- [ ] To determine how you spend your time, what you work on the most, and what common problems you consistently see
- [ ] To solve future problems, because you have a record of what happened the last time you encountered a similar problem
- [ ] To determine where you need training or information
- [ ] To discover patterns that can help you identify what preventive maintenance or user training could be done to help prevent recurring problems

SERVICE CALL REPORT

The service call report form shown in Figure I-1 includes space to record the initial information about the request, the source of the problem, and its outcome. If you file these reports according to the problem description, you can use them later when trying to identify the source of a new problem.

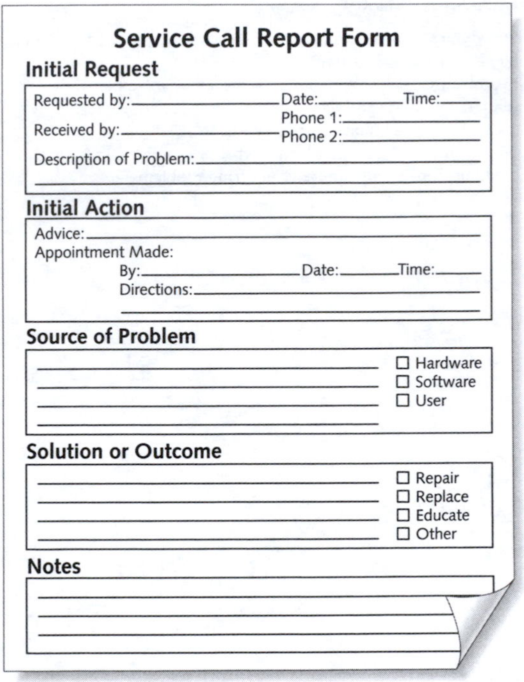

Service Call Report Form

Initial Request

Requested by:_____Date:_____Time:_____
Received by:_____Phone 1:_____
Phone 2:_____
Description of Problem:_____

Initial Action

Advice:_____
Appointment Made:
By:_____Date:_____Time:_____
Directions:_____

Source of Problem

_____ ☐ Hardware
_____ ☐ Software
_____ ☐ User

Solution or Outcome

_____ ☐ Repair
_____ ☐ Replace
_____ ☐ Educate
_____ ☐ Other

Notes

_____

Figure I-1 Service call report form

HELP DESK CALL REPORT

The help desk call report form shown in Figure I-2 will help keep the call on track if you use it as you talk with the customer. Later, it can serve as a reminder to make a follow-up call and can be a source of information for future calls.

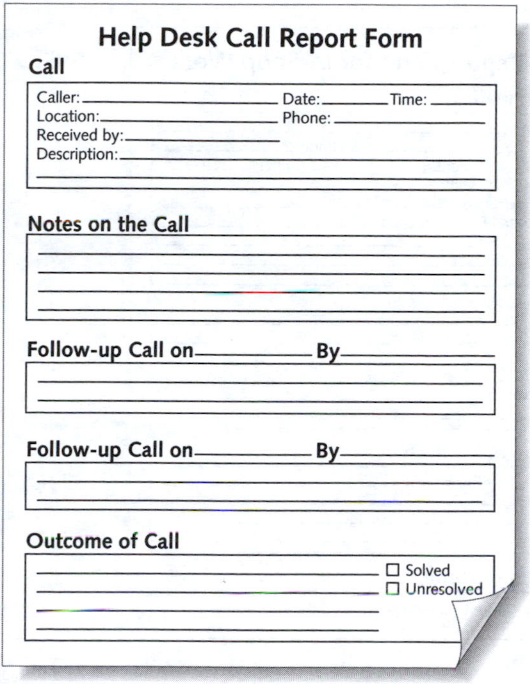

Help Desk Call Report Form

Call

Caller: _____ Date: _____ Time: _____
Location: _____ Phone: _____
Received by: _____
Description: _____

Notes on the Call

_____
_____
_____

Follow-up Call on_____ By_____

_____
_____

Follow-up Call on_____ By_____

_____
_____

Outcome of Call

_____ ☐ Solved
_____ ☐ Unresolved
_____

Figure I-2 Help desk call report form

INTAKE CALL REPORT

The form shown in Figure I-3 can help you track work from the time it enters the shop until the customer accepts the final results of your efforts. The sections of the form for analysis and description of work done can help in solving future problems.

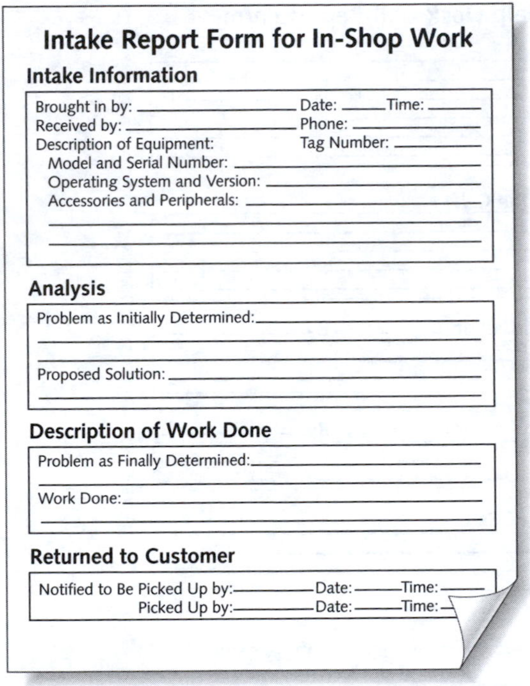

Intake Report Form for In-Shop Work

Intake Information

Brought in by: _____ Date: _____ Time: _____
Received by: _____ Phone: _____
Description of Equipment: Tag Number: _____
   Model and Serial Number: _____
   Operating System and Version: _____
   Accessories and Peripherals: _____

Analysis

Problem as Initially Determined: _____

Proposed Solution: _____

Description of Work Done

Problem as Finally Determined: _____

Work Done: _____

Returned to Customer

Notified to Be Picked Up by: _____ Date: _____ Time: _____
   Picked Up by: _____ Date: _____ Time: _____

Figure I-3 Intake report form for in-shop work

PC INFORMATION SHEET

The PC information sheet shown in Figure I-4 will help you keep track of what is on or is connected to the PC. It will help you know if the PC is up to date and, for a company with several PCs, it will help you locate the different peripheral devices such as printers, scanners, and video cameras.

PC Information Sheet

Location of unit: _____

Manufacturer: _____   Hard drive space: _____
Model #: _____   Amount of memory: _____
Serial #: _____   Type of memory: _____

Hardware:

Device	Manufacturer	Model #	Serial #
Monitor			
CPU			
Motherboard			
Hard drive			
Floppy drive			
CD/DVD			
SCSI card			
Printer			
Scanner			
Other			
Other			

Software:

Type	Name/Vendor	Version #	Service Pack #	Upgrade Level
Operating System				
Virus Protection				
E-mail				
Browser				
Firewall				
Other				
Other				
Other				
Other				

Figure I-4 PC information sheet

CALLING A VENDOR FOR HELP

You will need the following information available when you call a vendor for assistance:

- ☐ PC manufacturer
- ☐ PC model number
- ☐ Operating system
- ☐ Operating system service packet level
- ☐ The registered owner and owner's address
- ☐ Date of purchase
- ☐ The **exact** error message
- ☐ For a hardware problem, you will need the model number and serial number of the device

ENTRY POINTS FOR START-UP PROCESSES

This appendix contains a summary of the entry points that can affect Windows startup. Entry points are:

Programs and shortcuts to programs stored in these start-up folders:

- [ ] C:\Documents and Settings*username*\Start Menu\Programs\Startup
- [ ] C:\Documents and Settings\All Users\Start Menu\Programs\Startup
- [ ] C:\Windows\Profiles\All Users\Start Menu\Programs\Startup
- [ ] C:\Windows\Profiles*username*\Start Menu\Programs\Startup

Scripts used by Group Policy that can be stored in these folders:

- [ ] C:\WINDOWS\System32\GroupPolicy\Machine\Scripts\Startup
- [ ] C:\WINDOWS\System32\GroupPolicy\Machine\Scripts\Shutdown
- [ ] C:\WINDOWS\System32\GroupPolicy\User\Scripts\Logon
- [ ] C:\WINDOWS\System32\GroupPolicy\User\Scripts\Logoff

Scheduled tasks stored in this folder:

- [ ] C:\Windows\Tasks

Entries in these legacy initialization files:

- [ ] System.ini
- [ ] Win.ini.

Registry keys known to affect start up:

- [ ] HKCU\Software\Microsoft\Windows\CurrentVersion\RunOnce
- [ ] HKCU\Software\Microsoft\Windows\CurrentVersion\RunOnceEx
- [ ] HKLM\Software\Microsoft\Windows\CurrentVersion\RunOnce
- [ ] HKLM\Software\Microsoft\Windows\CurrentVersion\RunOnceEx
- [ ] HKCU\Software\Microsoft\Windows\CurrentVersion\Policies\Explorer\Run
- [ ] HKLM\Software\Microsoft\Windows\CurrentVersion\Policies\Explorer\Run
- [ ] HKLM\Software\Microsoft\Windows\CurrentVersion\ ShellServiceObjectDelayLoad
- [ ] HKLM\Software\Microsoft\Windows NT\CurrentVersion\ Winlogon\Userinit
- [ ] HKLM\Software\Microsoft\Windows NT\CurrentVersion\Winlogon\Shell
- [ ] HKCU\Software\Microsoft\Windows NT\CurrentVersion\Windows
- [ ] HKCU\Software\Microsoft\Windows NT\CurrentVersion\Windows\Run
- [ ] HKLM\Software\Microsoft\Windows\CurrentVersion\Run
- [ ] HKCU\Software\Microsoft\Windows\CurrentVersion\Run
- [ ] HKLM\System\CurrentControlSet\Control\Services
- [ ] HKLM\System\CurrentControlSet\Control\Session Manager
- [ ] HKCU\Software\Microsoft\Command

- □ HKCU\Software\Microsoft\Command Processor\AutoRun
- □ HKCU\Software\Microsoft\Windows\CurrentVersion\RunOnce\Setup\
- □ HKCU\Software\Microsoft\Windows NT\CurrentVersion\Windows\load
- □ HKLM\Software\Microsoft\Windows NT\CurrentVersion\Windows\
  AppInit_DLLs
- □ HKLM\Software\Microsoft\Windows NT\CurrentVersion\Winlogon\System
- □ HKLM\Software\Microsoft\Windows NT\CurrentVersion\Winlogon\Us
- □ HKEY_CLASSES_ROOT\batfile\shell\open\command\
- □ HKEY_CLASSES_ROOT\comfile\shell\open\command\
- □ HKEY_CLASSES_ROOT\exefile\shell\open\command\
- □ HKEY_CLASSES_ROOT\htafile\shell\open\command\
- □ HKEY_CLASSES_ROOT\piffile\shell\open\command\
- □ HKEY_CLASSES_ROOT\scrfile\shell\open\command\

Other ways processes can be launched at start up:

- □ Services can be set to launch at start up. To manage services, use the
  Services Console (services.msc).
- □ Device drivers are launched at startup. For a listing of installed devices, use
  Device Manager.

FILE EXTENSIONS AND FORMATS

The following table lists some well-known file extensions and the formats they represent.

Table K-1 File extensions and formats

File extension	File format
AIF	Adobe Illustrator File, similar to an EPS file
ANI	Animated cursor file for Windows
ANS	ANSI text file
APS	Microsoft Visual C++ file
ASC	ASCII text file
AVI	Audio Video Interleaved file; Microsoft video format for Windows
BAK	Backup file
BAS	Basic program file containing code
BAT	Batch file containing DOS-like commands
BIN	Binary file
BMP	Windows BitMaP file, a Microsoft image-format file
CAB	Microsoft cabinet file used for compressed software distribution
CAM	Casio digital camera file
CDA	CD audio track file
CLP	CliPboard file used to store various data when using the clip, cut, or paste features in Windows
COM	Command file; program file
CPL	Windows Control Panel applet
CRT	Certificate file
CUR	Cursor Resource file for Windows; contains image data for cursors
DAT	Data file
DBF	Database file used by dBASE
DCR	Shockwave file
DCX	3D version of a PCX image-format file
DER	Certificate file
DIB	Device Independent Bitmap file; similar to a BMP file
DIC	Text file
DLL	Dynamic Link Library file containing program modules
DOC	Word-processing document
DOT	Microsoft Word document template file
DRV	Driver file
EMF	Enhanced Metafile Format graphics file for Windows

(continued)

Table K-1 File extensions and formats (continued)

File extension	File format
EPS	Encapsulated PostScript image file used for desktop publishing on both MACs and PCs
EXE	Executable program file
G3	Group 3 Facsimile Apparatus format file used for faxing documents
GIF	Graphics Interchange Format file developed by CompuServe for Web publishing with low resolution and small file size
HLP	Help file
HTML/HTM	Hypertext document
ICA	Citrix file
ICO	Windows Icon file used to provide a graphic icon for desktop shortcuts
INF	Information file
INI	Initialization file (most likely a text file)
ISO	Lists the files on a CD
JPEG/JPG/JFF /JIF/JTF	Joint Photographic Experts Group fine-compression image file used for Web publishing
LIB	Library file
LOG	Log file
LWF	LuraWave Format file created to improve image quality over a JPEG file
MDB	Microsoft Access database file
MID/MIDI	Musical Instrument Digital Interface file to direct electronic musical instruments
MOV	Quick Time Movie format file by Apple Computer for movies and other streaming data flow
MP1	MPEG1 audio file
MP2	MPEG2 audio file
MP3	MPEG3 audio file
MPA/MPE/MPG	MPEG video clip
MPG/MPEG	Moving Picture Experts Group file for full-motion video and compressed audio
PBM	Portable Bitmap file format used for various bitmap images
PCX	Paintbrush file used by word-processing and desktop publishing programs
PDF	Adobe Acrobat document
PGM	Portable Greymap file format used by greymap images

(continued)

Table K-1 File extensions and formats (continued)

File extension	File format
PNG	Portable Network Graphics format combines the best features of GIF files and JPEG files and used for Web publishing
PPM	Portable Pixelmap format files used for color images
PPS	Microsoft PowerPoint slide show file
PPT	Microsoft PowerPoint presentation file
PSD	PhotoShop Software Development file used by Adobe Photoshop and similar software in development process
QBW	QuickBooks for Windows file
RAS/SUN	Sun Raster bitmap file used by Sun Microsystems
RLE	Run Length Encoded file format for raster images*
RTF	Rich text file
SCR	Executable screen saver file
SYS	Operating system file
TGA	Truevision Advanced Raster Graphics Adapter format file used for image capturing
TIF/TIFF	Tagged Image File Format used for raster images* used by MACs and PCs
TXT	Plain text file
VBS	VBScript file that is executable
WAV	Windows uncompressed audio file
WMF	Windows MetaFile format used for images, which uses smaller file sizes than BMP files
XLS	Microsoft Excel spreadsheet file
ZIP	Compressed or zipped file

* A raster file is an image file that stores data as mathematical coordinates.

APPENDIX

L

WHERE TO GO FOR MORE HELP:
HARDWARE RESOURCES

If you have exhausted the resources in this book and *A+ Guide to Managing and Maintaining Your PC*, *A+ Guide to Software*, or *A+ Guide to Hardware* and still have not solved the problem, try the following additional resources:

☐ Technical support on the Internet and manufacturers' help desks
☐ Hardware and software diagnostic tools
☐ Course Technology publishes a full range of networking, hardware, and software texts. Check our online catalog at *www.course.com* for additional resources.

 See Appendix M for a list of utility software products.

TECHNICAL SUPPORT ON THE INTERNET AND HELP DESKS

 Use Appendix H as your guide to search the Internet for additional help and information (page H-1).

☐ Begin with the manufacturer's Web site for the hardware product you believe to be the source of the problem. Search for FAQs about problems with the product, white papers, forums, and technical support pages.
☐ Try general technical Web sites listed in Appendix H (page H-4). Search on the product or the problem. Look for troubleshooting tips, steps to try, known problems with a product, and so on.
☐ Call technical support for the hardware product that you believe to be the source of the problem. When you call, have this information available:
  ▪ The model number and detailed description of the product
  ▪ Date of purchase of the hardware device (have receipt available, if possible)
  ▪ Manufacturer and model of your computer and the OS version installed
  ▪ Exact wording of the error message, if you've gotten one
  ▪ Description of the problem
  ▪ Hardware and software configuration for your system
  ▪ Paper and pen to take notes as you talk

HARDWARE DIAGNOSTIC TOOLS

Table L-1 lists and describes hardware diagnostic tools.

Table L-1 Hardware diagnostic tools

Tool	Description
Loopback port testers	Tests serial and parallel ports using software and a loopback plug that plugs into the port. Verifies that the port is working properly and helps resolve resource conflicts.
PortTest	By MSD, Inc. See *www.msdusa.com*.
PC-Technician	By Windsor Technologies, Inc. See *www.windsortech.com*. This diagnostic software tests much more than just ports. It comes with loopback plugs.
PCI/POST card	By Unicore Software, Inc. See *www.unicore.com*. This diagnostic POST card comes with self-booting diagnostic software, comprehensive manual, and set of three loopback plugs.
POST diagnostic cards	POST cards (also called checkpoint cards or diagnostic cards) are used to troubleshoot a "dead" motherboard: • Insert the card in a PCI expansion slot and turn on the PC. • A number is displayed on an LCD panel on the card. The number is a POST code that BIOS puts on the bus when an error is encountered during POST. • The BIOS precedes the POST code with an I/O address. The POST card must be "listening" for that I/O address to read the POST code, so you must use a POST card compatible with the BIOS. I/O addresses used by BIOS include 80h, 84h, 284h, and 280h. Most common is 80h. • Look up the POST code in a table to determine its meaning. For a partial listing of POST codes and their meanings, see Appendix A. For more comprehensive lists, see these sources: – Web site of the BIOS manufacturer – Documentation that comes with the POST card – *The BIOS Companion* by Phil Croucher (*www.electrocution.com*) has a fairly comprehensive list of POST codes (212 pages of POST codes)
Amber Debug Card	By Phoenix Technologies. See *www.phoenix.com*.
PCI/POST card	By Unicore Software, Inc. See *www.unicore.com*. Comes with self-booting diagnostic software, comprehensive manual, and set of three loopback plugs.

(continued)

Table L-1 Hardware diagnostic tools (continued)

Tool	Description
Post Code Master	By MSD, Inc. See *www.msdusa.com*. Versions of the card include Mini-PCI Type III card for notebooks, PCI card, PCI card with serial port, and ISA card.
	Reports POST codes for more than 80 BIOSes including those by these BIOS manufacturers: • AMI American Megatrends • AT&T • Award Software • Chips & Technologies • Compaq • Dell • Hewlett-Packard (HP) • IBM Corporation • Intel • Microid Research • Mylex Corporation • NCR • Philips • Phoenix Technologies • Quadtel Corporation
PCI Post Diagnostic Card	By StarTech. See *www.startech.com*.
DDR or DDR2 Memory Testing Card	By Taipei Computer Association. See *www.computex.com.tw*.

WHERE TO GO FOR MORE HELP: SOFTWARE RESOURCES

Table M-1 provides the sources of utility software that you can use to diagnose and solve problems. When evaluating a software product before buying it, consider these questions:

- What does the product claim to do?
- What platform (hardware and software) does the product run on?
- Is the documentation thorough and easy to understand?
- What technical support does the product offer? For example, look for a Web site with a question-and-answer forum and a searchable knowledge base, technical support chat session or help line, or e-mail address to a technical support help desk.
- Can you evaluate the software for a certain period at no cost?
- What kind of product reviews in trade magazines or on industry Web sites has the product earned?

Table M-1 lists and describes software diagnostic tools.

Table M-1 Software diagnostic tools

Tool	Description
General-purpose utility software	Use this type of software when you are isolating a problem with an unknown source, trying to identify the source of a problem with a sluggish system, or trying to solve a problem that the software specifically claims it can solve.
AMIDiag	By American Megatrends. See *www.ami.com*. • Runs under DOS to isolate hardware problems • Diagnoses memory problems including cache memory
CheckIt Diagnostic Suite	By SmithMicro Software. See *www.checkit.com*. • Runs from a single bootable floppy disk so that it checks hardware without being dependent on the installed OS • Includes some utilities to optimize a system • Includes loopback plugs
Norton Utilities	By Symantec. See *www.symantec.com*. • General-purpose utility software • Includes utilities to recover lost or damaged files and to optimize a system • Tests hardware and OS

(continued)

Table M-1   Software diagnostic tools (continued)

Tool	Description
PC-Technician	By Windsor Technologies, Inc. See *www.windsortech.com*. • Tests hardware, including all of memory • Works independently of an OS, so that hardware problems are not masked by OS problems • Includes 200 tests and functions • Comes with documentation and loopback plugs • Lets you download #1-TuffTEST-Pro
SiSoftware Sandra	By SiSoftware. See *www.sisoftware.co.uk*. • Benchmarking, diagnostic, and tune-up software that can be used to solve hardware and software problems
Disk utilities	Use one of these products when you suspect a problem with a hard drive (hardware or file system) or another secondary storage medium, for problems with Windows system files, or when you need to manage hard drives.
PartitionMagic	By Symantec. See *www.symantec.com*. • Converts among FAT16, FAT32, and NTFS partitions • Lets you merge, convert, and resize partitions • Includes Boot Magic to manage dual-booted systems
SpinRite	By Gibson Research. See *www.grc.com*. • Recovers corrupted or missing files and file systems • Works with NTFS, FAT, and Linux file systems • Includes a DOS version that runs from a floppy disk to be used when the system will not boot from the hard drive
System Commander	By V Communications, Inc. See *www.v-com.com*. • Manages multiple operating systems and partitions • Lets you create, resize, and move partitions • Useful when you have several OSs installed on a single machine
Administrator's Pak by Winternals	By Winternals, recently purchased by Microsoft. See *www.microsoft.com/systemcenter/winternals.mspx*. • Several utilities in this software suite can be used to boot a system from CD (has its own operating system on the CD) • Can be used to repair a dead OS, recover data, change forgotten passwords, repair system files, repair partition tables, and rewrite the MBR program
Spybot Search & Destroy	By PepiMK Software. See *www.safer-networking.org*. • Privacy protection software that searches out and removes installed programs that track Internet activity or display pop-up ads

(continued)

Table M-1   Software diagnostic tools (continued)

Tool	Description
Imaging software	Use these products to make an image of a hard drive partition and duplicate that image to another hard drive or recover from a hard drive crash.
Acronis True Image	By Acronis. See *www.acronis.com*. • Creates an exact image of the entire hard drive • View contents of image
Norton Ghost	By Symantec Corp. See *www.symantec.com*. • Creates, converts, clones, splits, and resizes partitions • Lets you move applications to another partition, restore files, and view contents of images • Restores corrupted or missing files or directories
CMOS save and restore utilities	Free utilities, including those to save, verify, and restore CMOS settings, can be found on these sites (search on CMOS): • TweakHomePC. *See* www.thpc.com. • Programmers Heaven. See *www.programmersheaven.com*.

(continued)

GLOSSARY

This glossary defines the terms related to managing and maintaining a personal computer.

100BaseT — An Ethernet standard that operates at 100 Mbps and uses STP cabling. Also called Fast Ethernet. Variations of 100BaseT are 100BaseTX and 100BaseFX.

10Base2 — An Ethernet standard that operates at 10 Mbps and uses small coaxial cable up to 200 meters long. Also called ThinNet.

10Base5 — An Ethernet standard that operates at 10 Mbps and uses thick coaxial cable up to 500 meters long. Also called ThickNet.

32-bit flat memory mode — A protected processing mode used by Windows NT/2000/XP to process programs written in 32-bit code early in the boot process.

3-D RAM — Special video RAM designed to improve 3-D graphics simulation.

80 conductor IDE cable — An IDE cable that has 40 pins but uses 80 wires, 40 of which are ground wires designed to reduce crosstalk on the cable. The cable is used by ATA/100 and ATA/133 IDE drives.

802.11a/b/g — *See* IEEE 802.11a/b/g.

A+ Certification — A certification awarded by CompTIA (The Computer Technology Industry Association) that measures a PC technician's knowledge and skills.

access point (AP) — A device connected to a LAN that provides wireless communication so that computers, printers, and other wireless devices can communicate with devices on the LAN.

ACPI (Advanced Configuration and Power Interface) — Specification developed by Intel, Compaq, Phoenix, Microsoft, and Toshiba to control power on notebooks and other devices. Windows 2000/XP and Windows 98 support ACPI.

active backplane — A type of backplane system in which there is some circuitry, including bus connectors, buffers, and driver circuits, on the backplane.

Active Directory — A Windows 2000 Server and Windows Server 2003 directory database and service that allows for a single point of administration for all shared resources on a network, including files, peripheral devices, databases, Web sites, users, and services.

active matrix — A type of video display that amplifies the signal at every intersection in the grid of electrodes, which enhances the pixel quality over that of a dual-scan passive matrix display.

active partition — The primary partition on the hard drive that boots the OS. Windows NT/2000/XP calls the active partition the system partition.

active terminator — A type of terminator for single-ended SCSI cables that includes voltage regulators in addition to the simple resistors used with passive termination.

adapter address — *See* MAC address.

adapter card — A small circuit board inserted in an expansion slot and used to communicate between the system bus and a peripheral device. Also called an interface card.

administrator account — In Windows NT/ 2000/XP, an account that grants to the administrator(s) rights and permissions to all hardware and software resources, such as the right to add, delete, and change accounts and to change hardware configurations.

Advanced Options menu — A Windows 2000/XP menu that appears when you press F8 when Windows starts. The menu can be used to troubleshoot problems when loading Windows 2000/XP.

Advanced SCSI Programming Interface (ASPI) — A popular device driver that enables operating systems to communicate with a SCSI host adapter. (The "A" originally stood for Adaptec.)

Advanced Transfer Cache (ATC) — A type of L2 cache contained within the Pentium processor housing that is embedded on the same core processor die as the CPU itself.

adware — Software installed on a computer that produces pop-up ads using your browser; the ads are often based on your browsing habits.

AirPort — The term Apple computers use to describe the IEEE 802.11b standard.

alternating current (AC) — Current that cycles back and forth rather than traveling in only one direction. In the United States, the AC voltage from a standard wall outlet is normally between 110 and 115 V. In Europe, the standard AC voltage from a wall outlet is 220 V.

ammeter — A meter that measures electrical current in amps.

ampere or amp (A) — A unit of measurement for electrical current. One volt across a resistance of one ohm will produce a flow of one amp.

amplifier repeater — A repeater that does not distinguish between noise and signal; it amplifies both.

ANSI (American National Standards Institute) — A nonprofit organization dedicated to creating trade and communications standards.

answer file — A text file that contains information that Windows NT/ 2000/XP requires in order to do an unattended installation.

antivirus (AV) software — Utility programs that prevent infection or scan a system to detect and remove viruses. McAfee Associates' VirusScan and Norton AntiVirus are two popular AV packages.

application program interface (API) call — A request from software to the OS to access hardware or other software using a previously defined procedure that both the software and the OS understand.

ARP (Address Resolution Protocol) — A protocol that TCP/IP uses to translate IP addresses into physical network addresses (MAC addresses).

ASCII (American Standard Code for Information Interchange) — A popular standard for writing letters and other characters in binary code. Originally, ASCII characters were seven bits, so there were 127 possible values. ASCII has been expanded to an 8-bit version, allowing 128 additional values.

asynchronous SRAM — Static RAM that does not work in step with the CPU clock and is, therefore, slower than synchronous SRAM.

AT — A form factor, generally no longer produced, in which the motherboard requires a full-size case. Because of their dimensions and configuration, AT systems are difficult to install, service, and upgrade. Also called full AT.

AT command set — A set of commands that a PC uses to control a modem and that a user can enter to troubleshoot the modem.

ATAPI (Advanced Technology Attachment Packet Interface) — An interface standard, part of the IDE/ATA standards, that allows tape drives, CD-ROM drives, and other drives to be treated like an IDE hard drive by the system.

attenuation — Signal degeneration over distance. Attenuation is solved on a network by adding repeaters to the network.

ATX — The most common form factor for PC systems presently in use, originally introduced by Intel in 1995. ATX motherboards and cases make better use of space and resources than did the AT form factor.

ATX12 V power supply — A power supply that provides a 12 V power cord with a 4-pin connector to be used by the auxiliary 4-pin power connector on motherboards used to provide extra power for processors.

audio/modem riser (AMR) — A specification for a small slot on a motherboard to accommodate an audio or modem riser card. A controller on the motherboard contains some of the logic for the audio or modem functionality.

authentication — The process of proving an individual is who they say they are before they are allowed access to a computer, file, folder, or network. The process might use a password, PIN, smart card, or biometric data.

authorization — Controlling what an individual can or cannot do with resources on a computer network. Using Windows, authorization is granted by the rights and permissions assigned to user accounts.

autodetection — A feature of system BIOS and hard drives that automatically identifies and configures a new drive in CMOS setup.

Autoexec.bat — A startup text file once used by DOS and used by Windows to provide backward-compatibility. It executes commands automatically during the boot process and is used to create a 16-bit environment.

Automated System Recovery (ASR) — The Windows XP process that allows you to restore an entire hard drive volume or logical drive to its state at the time the backup of the volume was made.

Automatic Private IP Address (APIPA) — An IP address in the address range 169.254.x.x, used by a computer when it cannot successfully lease an IP address from a DHCP server.

autorange meter — A multimeter that senses the quantity of input and sets the range accordingly.

Baby AT — An improved and more flexible version of the AT form factor. Baby AT was the industry standard from approximately 1993 to 1997 and can fit into some ATX cases.

back side bus — The bus between the CPU and the L2 cache inside the CPU housing.

backplane system — A form factor in which there is no true motherboard. Instead, motherboard components are included on an adapter card plugged into a slot on a board called the backplane.

backup — An extra copy of a file, used in the event that the original becomes damaged or destroyed.

Backup Operator — A Windows 2000/XP user account that can back up and restore any files on the system regardless of its having access to these files.

bandwidth — In relation to analog communication, the range of frequencies that a communications channel or cable can carry. In general use, the term refers to the volume of data that can travel on a bus or over a cable stated in bits per second (bps), kilobits per second (Kbps), or megabits per second (Mbps). Also called data throughput or line speed.

bank — An area on the motherboard that contains slots for memory modules (typically labeled bank 0, 1, 2, and 3).

baseline — The level of performance expected from a system, which can be compared to current measurements to determine what needs upgrading or tuning.

basic disk — A way to partition a hard drive, used by DOS and all versions of Windows, that stores information about the drive in a partition table at the beginning of the drive. Compare to dynamic disk.

batch file — A text file containing a series of OS commands. Autoexec.bat is a batch file.

baud rate — A measure of line speed between two devices such as a computer and a printer or a modem. This speed is measured in the number of times a signal changes in one second. *See also* bits per second (bps).

beam detect mirror — Detects the initial presence of a laser printer's laser beam by reflecting the beam to an optical fiber.

best–effort protocol — *See* connectionless protocol.

binary number system — The number system used by computers; it has only two numbers, 0 and 1, called binary digits, or bits.

binding — The process by which a protocol is associated with a network card or a modem card.

BIOS (basic input/output system) — Firmware that can control much of a computer's input/output functions, such as communication with the floppy drive and the monitor. Also called ROM BIOS.

bit (binary digit) — A 0 or 1 used by the binary number system.

bits per second (bps) — A measure of data transmission speed. For example, a common modem speed is 56,000 bps, or 56 Kbps.

block mode — A method of data transfer between hard drive and memory that allows multiple data transfers on a single software interrupt.

blue screen — A Windows NT/2000/XP error that displays against a blue screen and causes the system to halt. Also called a stop error.

Bluetooth — A standard for wireless communication and data synchronization between devices, developed by a group of electronics manufacturers and overseen by the Bluetooth Special Interest Group. Bluetooth uses the same frequency range as 802.11b, but does not have as wide a range.

BNC connector — A connector used with thin coaxial cable. Some BNC connectors are T-shaped and called T-connectors. One end of the T connects to the NIC, and the two other ends can connect to cables or end a bus formation with a terminator.

boot loader menu — A startup menu that gives the user the choice of which operating system to load such as Windows 98 or Windows XP which are both installed on the same system, creating a dual boot.

boot partition — The hard drive partition where the Windows NT/2000/XP OS is stored. The system partition and the boot partition may be different partitions.

boot record — The first sector of a floppy disk or logical drive in a partition; it contains information about the disk or logical drive. On a hard drive, if the boot record is in the active partition, then it is used to boot the OS. Also called boot sector.

boot sector — *See* boot record.

boot sector virus — An infectious program that can replace the boot program with a modified, infected version, often causing boot and data retrieval problems.

Boot.ini — A Windows NT/2000/XP hidden text file that contains information needed to start the boot and build the boot loader menu.

bootable disk — For DOS and Windows, a floppy disk that can upload the OS files necessary for computer startup. For DOS or Windows 9x/Me, it must contain the files Io.sys, Msdos.sys, and Command.com.

bootstrap loader — A small program at the end of the boot record that can be used to boot an OS from the disk or logical drive.

bridge — A device used to connect two or more network segments. It can make decisions about allowing a packet to pass based on the packet's destination MAC address.

bridging protocol — *See* line protocol.

Briefcase — A system folder in Windows 9x/Me that is used to synchronize files between two computers.

broadband — A transmission technique that carries more than one type of transmission on the same medium, such as cable modem or DSL.

broadcast — Process by which a message is sent from a single host to all hosts on the network, without regard to the kind of data being sent or the destination of the data.

brouter — A device that functions as both a bridge and a router. A brouter acts as a router when handling packets using routable protocols such as

TCP/IP and IPX/SPX. It acts as a bridge when handling packets using nonroutable protocols such as NetBEUI.

brownouts — Temporary reductions in voltage, which can sometimes cause data loss. Also called sags.

browser hijacker — A malicious program that infects your Web browser and can change your home page or browser settings. It can also redirect your browser to unwanted sites, produce pop-up ads, and set unwanted bookmarks. Also called a home page hijacker.

BTX (Balanced Technology Extended) — The latest form factor expected to replace ATX. It has higher quality fans, is designed for better air flow, and has improved structural support for the motherboard.

buffer — A temporary memory area where data is kept before being written to a hard drive or sent to a printer, thus reducing the number of writes to the devices.

built-in user account — An administrator account and a guest account that are set up when Windows NT/2000/XP is first installed.

burst EDO (BEDO) — A refined version of EDO memory that significantly improved access time over EDO. BEDO was not widely used because Intel chose not to support it. BEDO memory is stored on 168-pin DIMM modules.

burst SRAM — Memory that is more expensive and slightly faster than pipelined burst SRAM. Data is sent in a two-step process; the data address is sent, and then the data itself is sent without interruption.

bus — The paths, or lines, on the motherboard on which data, instructions, and electrical power move from component to component.

bus mouse — A mouse that plugs into a bus adapter card and has a round, 9-pin mini-DIN connector.

bus riser — *See* riser card.

bus speed — The speed, or frequency, at which the data on the motherboard is written and read.

bus topology — A LAN architecture in which all the devices are connected to a bus, or one communication line. Bus topology does not have a central connection point.

byte — A collection of eight bits that can represent a single character.

cabinet file — A file with a .cab extension that contains one or more compressed files and is often used to distribute software on disk. The Extract command is used to extract files from the cabinet file.

cable modem — A technology that uses cable TV lines for data transmission requiring a modem at each end. From the modem, a network cable connects to an NIC in the user's PC, or a USB cable connects to a USB port.

call tracking — A system that tracks the dates, times, and transactions of help-desk or on-site PC support calls, including the problem presented, the issues addressed, who did what, and when and how each call was resolved.

CAM (Common Access Method) — A standard adapter driver used by SCSI.

capacitor — An electronic device that can maintain an electrical charge for a period of time and is used to smooth out the flow of electrical current. Capacitors are often found in computer power supplies.

CardBus — A PCMCIA specification that improved on the earlier PC Card standards. It improves I/O speed, increases the bus width to 32 bits, and supports lower-voltage PC Cards, while maintaining backward compatibility with earlier standards.

cards — Adapter boards or interface cards placed into expansion slots to expand the functions of a computer, allowing it to communicate with external devices such as monitors or speakers.

carrier — A signal used to activate a phone line to confirm a continuous frequency; used to indicate that two computers are ready to receive or transmit data via modems.

CAS Latency (CL) — A feature of memory that reflects the number of clock cycles that pass while data is written to memory.

CAU (Controlled-Access Unit) — *See* MAU.

CCITT (Comité Consultatif International Télégraphique et Téléphonique) — An international organization that was responsible for developing standards for international communications. This organization has been incorporated into the ITU. *See also* ITU.

CD (change directory) command — A command given at the command prompt that changes the default directory, for example CD \Windows.

CDFS (Compact Disc File System) — The 32-bit file system for CD discs and some CD-R and CD-RW discs that replaced the older 16-bit mscdex file system used by DOS. *See also* Universal Disk Format (UDF).

CDMA (code-division multiple access) — A protocol standard used by cellular WANs and cell phones.

CD-R (CD-recordable) — A CD drive that can record or write data to a CD. The drive may or may not be multisession, but the data cannot be erased once it is written.

CD-RW (CD-rewritable) — A CD drive that can record or write data to a CD. The data can be erased and overwritten. The drive may or may not be multisession.

central processing unit (CPU) — Also called a micro-processor or processor. The heart and brain of the computer, which receives data input, processes information, and executes instructions.

chain — A group of clusters used to hold a single file.

CHAP (Challenge Handshake Authentication Protocol) — A protocol used to encrypt account names and passwords that are sent to a network controller for validation.

checksum — A method of checking transmitted data for errors, whereby the digits are added and their sum compared to an expected sum.

child directory — *See* subdirectory.

child, parent, grandparent backup method — A plan for backing up and reusing tapes or removable disks by rotating them each day (child), week (parent), and month (grandparent).

chip creep — A condition in which chips loosen because of thermal changes.

chipset — A group of chips on the motherboard that controls the timing and flow of data and instructions to and from the CPU.

CHS (cylinder, head, sector) mode — An outdated method by which BIOS reads from and writes to hard drives by addressing the correct cylinder, head, and sector. Also called normal mode.

circuit board — A computer component, such as the main motherboard or an adapter board, that has electronic circuits and chips.

CISC (complex instruction set computing) — Earlier CPU type of instruction set.

clamping voltage — The maximum voltage allowed through a surge suppressor, such as 175 or 330 volts.

clean install — Installing an OS on a new hard drive or on a hard drive that has a previous OS installed, but without carrying forward any settings kept by the old OS, including information about hardware, software, or user preferences. A fresh installation.

client/server — A computer concept whereby one computer (the client) requests information from another computer (the server).

client/server application — An application that has two components. The client software requests data from the server software on the same or another computer.

client-side caching — A technique used by browsers (clients) to speed up download times by caching Web pages previously requested in case they are requested again.

clock speed — The speed, or frequency, expressed in MHz, that controls activity on the motherboard and is generated by a crystal or oscillator located somewhere on the motherboard.

clone — A computer that is a no-name Intel- and Microsoft-compatible PC.

cluster — One or more sectors that constitute the smallest unit of space on a disk for storing data (also referred to as a file allocation unit). Files are written to a disk as groups of whole clusters.

CMOS (complementary metal-oxide semiconductor) — The technology used to manufacture microchips. CMOS chips require less electricity, hold data longer after the electricity is turned off, are slower, and produce less heat than earlier technologies. The configuration, or setup, chip is a CMOS chip.

CMOS configuration chip — A chip on the motherboard that contains a very small amount of memory, or RAM enough to hold configuration, or setup, information about the computer. The chip is powered by a battery when the PC is turned off. Also called CMOS setup chip or CMOS RAM chip.

CMOS setup — (1) The CMOS configuration chip. (2) The program in system BIOS that can change the values in CMOS RAM.

CMOS setup chip — *See* CMOS configuration chip.

COAST (cache on a stick) — Memory modules that hold memory used as a memory cache. *See* memory cache.

coaxial cable — Networking cable used with 10-Mbps Ethernet ThinNet or ThickNet.

cold boot — *See* hard boot.

combo card — An outdated Ethernet card that contains more than one transceiver, each with a different port on the back of the card, in order to accommodate different cabling media.

Command.com — Along with Msdos.sys and Io.sys, one of the three files that are the core components of the real-mode portion of Windows 9x/Me. Command.com provides a command prompt and interprets commands.

comment — A line or part of a line in a program that is intended as a remark or comment and is ignored when the program runs. A semicolon or an REM is often used to mark a line as a comment.

communication and networking riser (CNR) — A specification for a small expansion slot on a motherboard that accommodates a small audio, modem, or network riser card.

compact case — A type of case used in low-end desktop systems. Compact cases, also called low-profile or slimline cases, follow either the NLX, LPX, or Mini LPX form factor. They are likely to have fewer drive bays, but they generally still provide for some expansion.

Compact.exe — Windows 2000/XP command and program to compress or uncompress a volume, folder, or file.

Compatibility Mode utility — A Windows XP utility that provides an application with the older Microsoft OS environment it was designed to operate in.

compressed drive — A drive whose format has been reorganized in order to store more data. A Windows 9x compressed drive is really not a drive at all; it's actually a type of file, typically with a host drive called H.

compression — To store data in a file, folder, or logical drive using a coding format that reduces the size of files in order to save space on a drive or shorten transport time when sending a file over the Internet or network.

computer name — Character-based host name or NetBIOS name assigned to a computer.

Config.sys — A text file used by DOS and supported by Windows 9x/Me that lists device drivers to be loaded at startup. It can also set system variables to be used by DOS and Windows.

Configuration Manager — A component of Windows Plug and Play that controls the configuration process of all devices and communicates these configurations to the devices.

connectionless protocol — A protocol such as UDP that does not require a connection before sending a packet and does not guarantee delivery. An example of a UDP transmission is streaming video over the Web. Also called a best-effort protocol.

connection–oriented protocol — In networking, a protocol that confirms that a good connection has been made before transmitting data to the other end. An example of a connection-oriented protocol is TCP.

console — A window in which one or more Windows 2000/XP utility programs have been installed. The window is created using Microsoft Management Console, and installed utilities are called snap-ins.

constant angular velocity (CAV) — A technology used by hard drives and newer CD-ROM drives whereby the disk rotates at a constant speed.

constant linear velocity (CLV) — A CD-ROM format in which the spacing of data is consistent on the CD, but the speed of the disc varies depending on whether the data being read is near the center or the edge of the disc.

continuity — A continuous, unbroken path for the flow of electricity. A continuity test can determine whether or not internal wiring is still intact, or whether a fuse is good or bad.

control blade — A laser printer component that prevents too much toner from sticking to the cylinder surface.

conventional memory — DOS and Windows 9x/Me memory addresses between 0 and 640 K. Also called base memory.

cooler — A combination cooling fan and heat sink mounted on the top or side of a processor to keep it cool.

copyright — An individual's right to copy his/her own work. No one else, other than the copyright owner, is legally allowed to do so without permission.

CRC (cyclical redundancy check) — A process in which calculations are performed on bytes of data before and after they are transmitted to check for corruption during transmission.

credit card memory — A type of memory used on older notebooks that could upgrade existing memory by way of a specialized memory slot.

C-RIMM (Continuity RIMM) — A placeholder RIMM module that provides continuity so that every RIMM slot is filled.

cross-linked clusters — Errors caused when more than one file points to a cluster, and the files appear to share the same disk space, according to the file allocation table.

crossover cable — A cable used to connect two PCs into the simplest network possible. Also used to connect two hubs.

CVF (compressed volume file) — The Windows 9x/Me file on the host drive of a compressed drive that holds all compressed data.

data bus — The lines on the system bus that the CPU uses to send and receive data.

data cartridge — A type of tape medium typically used for backups. Full-sized data cartridges are $4 \times 6 \times 2\frac{5}{8}$ inches in size. A minicartridge is only $3\frac{1}{4} \times 2\frac{1}{2} \times 2\frac{5}{8}$ inches in size.

data line protector — A surge protector designed to work with the telephone line to a modem.

data migration — Moving data from one application to another application or from one storage media to another, and most often involves a change in the way the data is formatted.

data path — The number of bits transported into and out of the processor.

data path size — The number of lines on a bus that can hold data, for example, 8, 16, 32, and 64 lines, which can accommodate 8, 16, 32, and 64 bits at a time.

data throughput — *See* bandwidth.

datagram — *See* packet.

DC controller — A card inside a notebook that converts voltage to CPU voltage. Some notebook manufacturers consider the card to be an FRU.

DCE (Data Communications Equipment) — The hardware, usually a dial-up modem, that provides the connection between a data terminal and a communications line. *See also* DTE.

DDR SDRAM — *See* Double Data Rate SDRAM.

DDR2 SDRAM — A version of SDRAM that is faster than DDR and uses less power.

default gateway — The gateway a computer on a network will use to access another network unless it knows to specifically use another gateway for quicker access to that network.

default printer — The printer Windows prints to unless another printer is selected.

Defrag.exe — Windows program and command to defragment a logical drive.

defragment — To "optimize" or rewrite a file to a disk in one contiguous chain of clusters, thus speeding up data retrieval.

demodulation — The process by which digital data that has been converted to analog data is converted back to digital data. *See* modulation.

desktop — The initial screen that is displayed when an OS has a GUI interface loaded.

device driver — A program stored on the hard drive that tells the computer how to communicate with an input/output device such as a printer or modem.

DHCP (Dynamic Host Configuration Protocol) server — A service that assigns dynamic IP addresses to computers on a network when they first access the network.

diagnostic cards — Adapter cards designed to discover and report computer errors and conflicts at POST time (before the computer boots up), often by displaying a number on the card. Also called a POST diagnostic card or a checkpoint card.

diagnostic software — Utility programs that help troubleshoot computer systems. Some Windows diagnostic utilities are CHKDSK and SCANDISK. PC-Technician is an example of a third-party diagnostic program.

dialer — Malicious software installed on your PC that disconnects your phone line from your ISP and dials up an expensive pay-per-minute phone number without your knowledge.

dial-up networking — A Windows 9x/Me and Windows NT/2000/XP utility that uses a modem and telephone line to connect to a network.

differential backup — Backup method that backs up only files that have changed or have been created since the last full backup. When recovering data, only two backups are needed: the full backup and the last differential backup.

differential cable — A SCSI cable in which a signal is carried on two wires, each carrying voltage, and the signal is the difference between the two. Differential signaling provides for error checking and greater data integrity. Compare to single-ended cable.

digital certificate — A code used to authenticate the source of a file or document or to identify and authenticate a person or organization sending data over the Internet. The code is assigned by a certificate authority such as VeriSign and includes a public key for encryption. Also called *digital ID* or *digital signature*.

digital ID — *See* digital certificate.

digital signature — *See* digital certificate.

DIMM (dual inline memory module) — A miniature circuit board installed on a motherboard to hold memory. DIMMs can hold up to 2 GB of RAM on a single module.

diode — An electronic device that allows electricity to flow in only one direction. Used in a rectifier circuit.

DIP (dual inline package) switch — A switch on a circuit board or other device that can be set on or off to hold configuration or setup information.

direct current (DC) — Current that travels in only one direction (the type of electricity provided by batteries). Computer power supplies transform AC to low DC.

Direct Rambus DRAM — A memory technology by Rambus and Intel that uses a narrow network-type system bus. Memory is stored on a RIMM module. Also called RDRAM or Direct RDRAM.

Direct RDRAM — *See* Direct Rambus DRAM.

directory table — An OS table that contains file information such as the name, size, time and date of last modification, and cluster number of the file's beginning location.

discrete L2 cache — A type of L2 cache contained within the Pentium processor housing, but on a different die, with a cache bus between the processor and the cache.

disk cache — A method whereby recently retrieved data and adjacent data are read into memory in advance, anticipating the next CPU request.

disk cloning — *See* drive imaging.

disk compression — Compressing data on a hard drive to allow more data to be written to the drive.

disk imaging — *See* drive imaging.

Disk Management — A Windows 2000/XP utility used display, create, and format partitions on basic disks and volumes on dynamic disks.

disk quota — A limit placed on the amount of disk space that is available to users. Requires a Windows 2000/XP NTFS volume.

disk thrashing — A condition that results when the hard drive is excessively used for virtual memory because RAM is full. It dramatically slows down processing and can cause premature hard drive failure.

Display Power Management Signaling (DPMS) — Energy Star standard specifications that allow for the video card and monitor to go into sleep mode simultaneously. *See also* Energy Star.

distribution server — A file server holding Windows setup files used to install Windows on computers networked to the server.

DMA (direct memory access) channel — A number identifying a channel whereby a device can pass data to memory without involving the CPU. Think of a DMA channel as a shortcut for data moving to/from the device and memory.

DMA transfer mode — A transfer mode used by devices, including the hard drive, to transfer data to memory without involving the CPU.

DNS (domain name service or domain name system) — A distributed pool of information (called the name space) that keeps track of assigned domain names and their corresponding IP addresses, and the system that allows a host to locate information in the pool. Compare to WINS.

DNS server — A computer that can find an IP address for another computer when only the domain name is known.

docking station — A device that receives a notebook computer and provides additional secondary storage and easy connection to peripheral devices.

domain — In Windows NT/2000/XP, a logical group of networked computers, such as those on a college campus, that share a centralized directory database of user account information and security for the entire domain.

domain controller — A Windows NT/2000 or Windows Server 2003 computer which holds and controls a database of (1) user accounts, (2) group accounts, and (3) computer accounts used to manage access to the network.

domain name — A unique, text-based name that identifies a network.

DOS box — A command window.

Dosstart.bat — A type of Autoexec.bat file that is executed by Windows 9x/Me in two situations: when you select Restart the computer in MS-DOS mode from the shutdown menu or you run a program in MS-DOS mode.

dot pitch — The distance between the dots that the electronic beam hits on a monitor screen.

Double Data Rate SDRAM (DDR SDRAM) — A type of memory technology used on DIMMs that runs at twice the speed of the system clock.

doze time — The time before an Energy Star or "Green" system will reduce 80 percent of its activity.

Dr. Watson — A Windows utility that can record detailed information about the system, errors that occur, and the programs that caused them in a log file. Windows 9x/Me names the log file \Windows\Drwatson\WatsonXX.wlg, where XX is an incrementing number. Windows 2000 names the file \Documents and Settings\user\Documents\DrWatson\Drwtsn32.log. Windows XP calls the file Drwatson.log.

drive imaging — Making an exact image of a hard-drive, including partition information, boot sectors, operating system installation, and application software to replicate the hard drive on another system or recover from a hard drive crash. Also called *disk cloning* and *disk imaging*.

DriveSpace — A Windows 9x/Me utility that compresses files so that they take up less space on a disk drive, creating a single large file on the disk to hold all the compressed files.

drop height — The height from which a manufacturer states that its device, such as a hard drive, can be dropped without making the device unusable.

DSL (Digital Subscriber Line) — A telephone line that carries digital data from end to end, and can be leased from the telephone company for individual use. Some DSL lines are rated at 5 Mbps, about 50 times faster than regular telephone lines.

DTE (Data Terminal Equipment) — Both the computer and a remote terminal or other computer to which it is attached. *See also* DCE.

dual boot — The ability to boot using either of two different OSs, such as Windows 98 and Windows XP.

dual channel — A motherboard feature that improves memory performance by providing two 64-bit channels between memory and the chipset. DDR and DDR2 memory can use dual channels.

dual-core processing — Two processors contained in the same processor housing that share the interface with the chipset and memory.

dual-scan passive matrix — A type of video display that is less expensive than an active-matrix display and does not provide as high-quality an image. With dual-scan display, two columns of electrodes are activated at the same time.

dual-voltage CPU — A CPU that requires two different voltages, one for internal processing and the other for I/O processing.

dump file — A file that contains information captured from memory at the time a stop error occurred.

DVD (digital video disc or digital versatile disk) — A faster, larger CD format that can read older CDs, store over 8 GB of data, and hold full-length motion picture videos.

dye-sublimation printer — A type of printer with photo-lab-quality results that uses transparent dyed film. The film is heated, which causes the dye to vaporize onto glossy paper.

dynamic disk — A way to partition one or more hard drives, introduced with Windows 2000, in which information about the drive is stored in a database at the end of the drive. Compare to basic disk.

dynamic IP address — An assigned IP address that is used for the current session only. When the session is terminated, the IP address is returned to the list of available addresses.

dynamic RAM (DRAM) — The most common type of system memory, it requires refreshing every few milliseconds.

dynamic volume — A volume type used with dynamic disks for which you can change the size of the volume after you have created it.

dynamic VxD — A VxD that is loaded and unloaded from memory as needed.

ECC (error-correcting code) — A chipset feature on a motherboard that checks the integrity of data stored on DIMMs or RIMMs and can correct single-bit errors in a byte. More advanced ECC schemas can detect, but not correct, double-bit errors in a byte.

ECHS (extended CHS) mode — *See* large mode.

ECP (Extended Capabilities Port) — A bidirectional parallel port mode that uses a DMA channel to speed up data flow.

EDO (extended data out) — A type of outdated RAM that was faster than conventional RAM because it eliminated the delay before it issued the next memory address.

EEPROM (electrically erasable programmable ROM) — A type of chip in which higher voltage may be applied to one of the pins to erase its previous memory before a new instruction set is electronically written.

EIDE (Enhanced IDE) — A standard for managing the interface between secondary storage devices and a computer system. A system can support up to six serial ATA and parallel ATA IDE devices or up to four parallel ATA IDE devices such as hard drives, CD-ROM drives, and DVD drives.

electromagnetic interference (EMI) — A magnetic field produced as a side effect from the flow of electricity. EMI can cause corrupted data in data lines that are not properly shielded.

electrostatic discharge (ESD) — Another name for static electricity, which can damage chips and destroy motherboards, even though it might not be felt or seen with the naked eye.

Emergency Repair Disk (ERD) — A Windows NT record of critical information about your system that can be used to fix a problem with the OS. The ERD enables restoration of the Windows NT registry on your hard drive.

Emergency Repair Process — A Windows 2000 process that restores the OS to its state at the completion of a successful installation.

emergency startup disk (ESD) — *See* rescue disk.

Emm386.exe — A DOS and Windows 9x/Me utility that provides access to upper memory for 16-bit device drivers and other software.

Encrypted File System (EFS) — A way to use a key to encode a file or folder on an NTFS volume to protect sensitive data. Because it is an integrated system service, EFS is transparent to users and applications and is difficult to attack.

encrypting virus — A type of virus that transforms itself into a nonreplicating program in order to avoid detection. It transforms itself back into a replicating program in order to spread.

encryption — The process of putting readable data into an encoded form that can only be decoded (or decrypted) through use of a key.

Energy Star — "Green" systems that satisfy the EPA requirements to decrease the overall consumption of electricity. *See also* Green Standards.

enhanced BIOS — A system BIOS that has been written to accommodate large-capacity drives (over 504 MB, usually in the gigabyte range).

EPIC (explicitly parallel instruction computing) — The CPU architecture used by the Intel Itanium chip that bundles programming instructions with instructions on how to use multiprocessing abilities to do two instructions in parallel.

EPP (Enhanced Parallel Port) — A parallel port that allows data to flow in both directions (bidirectional port) and is faster than original parallel ports on PCs that allowed communication only in one direction.

EPROM (erasable programmable ROM) — A type of chip with a special window that allows the current memory contents to be erased with special ultraviolet light so that the chip can be reprogrammed.

error correction — The ability of a modem to identify transmission errors and then automatically request another transmission.

escalate — When a technician passes a customer's problem to higher organizational levels because he or she cannot solve the problem.

Ethernet — The most popular LAN architecture that can run at 10 Mbps (ThinNet or ThickNet), 100 Mbps (Fast Ethernet), or 1 Gbps (Gigabit Ethernet).

Execution Trace Cache — A type of Level 1 cache used by some CPUs to hold decoded operations waiting to be executed.

executive services — In Windows NT/2000/XP, a group of components running in kernel mode that interfaces between the subsystems in user mode and the HAL.

expansion bus — A bus that does not run in sync with the system clock.

expansion card — A circuit board inserted into a slot on the motherboard to enhance the capability of the computer.

expansion slot — A narrow slot on the motherboard where an expansion card can be inserted. Expansion slots connect to a bus on the motherboard.

expert systems — Software that uses a database of known facts and rules to simulate a human expert's reasoning and decision-making processes.

ExpressCard — The latest PCMCIA standard for notebook I/O cards that uses the PCI Express and USB 2.0 data transfer standards. Two types of Express-Cards are ExpressCard/34 (34 mm wide) and ExpressCard/54 (54 mm wide).

extended memory — Memory above 1024 K used in a DOS or Windows 9x/Me system.

extended partition — The only partition on a hard drive that can contain more than one logical drive.

extension magnet brush — A long-handled brush made of nylon fibers that are charged with static electricity to pick up stray toner inside a printer.

external cache — Static cache memory, stored on the motherboard or inside the CPU housing, that is not part of the CPU (also called L2 or L3 cache).

external command — Commands that have their own program files.

faceplate — A metal or plastic plate that comes with the computer case and fits over the empty drive bays or slots for expansion cards to create a well-fitted enclosure around them.

Fast Ethernet — *See* 100BaseT.

FAT (file allocation table) — A table on a hard drive or floppy disk that tracks the clusters used to contain a file.

FAT12 — The 12-bit wide, one-column file allocation table for a floppy disk, containing information about how each cluster or file allocation unit on the disk is currently used.

fault tolerance — The degree to which a system can tolerate failures. Adding redundant components, such as disk mirroring or disk duplexing, is a way to build in fault tolerance.

Fiber Distributed Data Interface (FDDI) — A ring-based network that does not require a centralized hub and can transfer data at a rate of 100 Mbps.

field replaceable unit (FRU) — A component in a computer or device that can be replaced with a new component without sending the computer or device back to the manufacturer. Examples: power supply, DIMM, motherboard, floppy disk drive.

file allocation unit — *See* cluster.

file extension — A three-character portion of the name of a file that is used to identify the file type. In command lines, the file extension follows the filename and is separated from it by a period. For example, Msd.exe, where exe is the file extension.

file system — The overall structure that an OS uses to name, store, and organize files on a disk. Examples of file systems are FAT32 and NTFS.

file virus — A virus that inserts virus code into an executable program file and can spread whenever that program is executed.

filename — The first part of the name assigned to a file. In DOS, the filename can be no more than eight characters long and is followed by the file extension. In Windows, a filename can be up to 255 characters.

firewall — Hardware or software that protects a computer or network from unauthorized access.

FireWire — *See* IEEE 1394.

firmware — Software that is permanently stored in a chip. The BIOS on a motherboard is an example of firmware.

flash ROM — ROM that can be reprogrammed or changed without replacing chips.

flat panel monitor — A desktop monitor that uses an LCD panel.

FlexATX — A version of the ATX form factor that allows for maximum flexibility in the size and shape of cases and motherboards. FlexATX is ideal for custom systems.

floppy disk drive (FDD) — A drive that can hold either a 5¼ inch or 3½ floppy disk.

flow control — When using modems, a method of controlling the flow of data to adjust for problems with data transmission. Xon/Xoff is an example of a flow control protocol.

folder — *See* subdirectory.

folder redirection — A Windows XP feature that allows a user to point to a folder that can be on the local PC or somewhere on the network, and its location can be transparent to the user.

forced perfect terminator (FPT) — A type of SCSI active terminator that includes a mechanism to force signal termination to the correct voltage, eliminating most signal echoes and interference.

forgotten password floppy disk — A Windows XP disk created to be used in the event the user forgets the user account password to the system.

form factor — A set of specifications on the size, shape, and configuration of a computer hardware component such as a case, power supply, or motherboard.

formatting — Preparing a hard drive volume or floppy disk for use by placing tracks and sectors on its surface to store information (for example, FORMAT A:).

FPM (fast page mode) — An outdated memory mode used before the introduction of EDO memory. FPM improved on earlier memory types by sending the row address just once for many accesses to memory near that row.

fragmentation — The distribution of data files on a hard drive or floppy disk such that they are stored in noncontiguous clusters.

fragmented file — A file that has been written to different portions of the disk so that it is not in contiguous clusters.

frame — The header and trailer information added to data to form a data packet to be sent over a network.

front-side bus (FSB) — *See* system bus.

FTP (File Transfer Protocol) — The protocol used to transfer files over a TCP/IP network such that the file does not need to be converted to ASCII format before transferring it.

full AT — *See* AT.

full backup — A complete backup, whereby all of the files on the hard drive are backed up each time the backup procedure is performed. It is the safest backup method, but it takes the most time.

full-duplex — Communication that happens in two directions at the same time.

fully qualified domain name (FQDN) — A host name and a domain name such as *jsmith.amazon.com*. Sometimes loosely referred to as a domain name.

gateway — A computer or other device that connects networks.

GDI (Graphics Device Interface) — A core Windows component responsible for building graphics data to display or print. A GDI printer relies on Windows to construct a page to print and then receives the constructed page as bitmap data.

General Packet Radio Service (GPRS) — A protocol standard that can be used by GSM or TDMA on a cellular WAN to send voice, text, or video data in packets similar to VoIP.

General Protection Fault (GPF) — A Windows error that occurs when a program attempts to access a memory address that is not available or is no longer assigned to it.

Gigabit Ethernet — The next generation of Ethernet. Gigabit Ethernet supports rates of data transfer up to 1 gigabit per second but is not yet widely used.

gigahertz (GHz) — One thousand MHz, or one billion cycles per second.

global user account — Sometimes called a domain user account, the account is used at the domain level, created by an administrator, and stored in the SAM (security accounts manager) database on a Windows 2000 or Windows 2003 domain controller.

graphics accelerator — A type of video card that has an on-board processor that can substantially increase speed and boost graphical and video performance.

graphics DDR (G-DDR), graphics DDR2, graphics DDR3 — Types of DDR, DDR2, and DDR3 memory specifically designed to be used in graphics cards.

grayware — A program that AV software recognizes to be potentially harmful or potentially unwanted.

Green Standards — A computer or device that conforms to these standards can go into sleep or doze mode when not in use, thus saving energy and helping the environment. Devices that carry the Green Star or Energy Star comply with these standards.

ground bracelet — A strap you wear around your wrist that is attached to the computer case, ground mat, or another ground so that ESD is discharged from your body before you touch sensitive components inside a computer. Also called static strap, ground strap, ESD bracelet.

group profile — A group of user profiles. All profiles in the group can be changed by changing the group profile.

GSM (Global System for Mobile communication) — An open standard for cellular WANs and cell phones that uses digital communication of data and is accepted and used worldwide.

guard tone — A tone that an answering modem sends when it first answers the phone, to tell the calling modem that a modem is on the other end of the line.

Guest user — A user who has limited permissions on a system and cannot make changes to it. Guest user accounts are intended for one-time or infrequent users of a workstation.

HAL (hardware abstraction layer) — The low-level part of Windows NT/2000/XP, written specifically for each CPU technology, so that only the HAL must change when platform components change.

half life — The time it takes for a medium storing data to weaken to half of its strength. Magnetic media, including traditional hard drives and floppy disks, have a half-life of five to seven years.

half-duplex — Communication between two devices whereby transmission takes place in only one direction at a time.

handshaking — When two modems begin to communicate, the initial agreement made as to how to send and receive data.

hard boot — Restart the computer by turning off the power or by pressing the Reset button. Also called a cold boot.

hard copy — Output from a printer to paper.

hard drive — The main secondary storage device of a PC, a small case that contains magnetic coated platters that rotate at high speed.

hard drive controller — The firmware that controls access to a hard drive contained on a circuit board mounted on or inside the hard drive housing. Older hard drives used firmware on a controller card that is connected to the drive by way of two cables, one for data and one for control.

hard drive standby time — The amount of time before a hard drive will shut down to conserve energy.

hard-disk loading — The illegal practice of installing unauthorized software on computers for sale. Hard-disk loading can typically be identified by the absence of original software disks in the original system's shipment.

hardware — The physical components that constitute the computer system, such as the monitor, the keyboard, the motherboard, and the printer.

hardware address — *See* MAC address.

hardware cache — A disk cache that is contained in RAM chips built right on the disk controller. Also called a buffer.

hardware interrupt — An event caused by a hardware device signaling the CPU that it requires service.

hardware profile — A set of hardware configuration information that Windows keeps in the registry. Windows can maintain more than one hardware profile for the same PC.

HCL (hardware compatibility list) — The list of all computers and peripheral devices that have been tested and are officially supported by Windows NT/2000/XP (see *www.microsoft.com/whdc/hcl/default.mspx*).

head — The top or bottom surface of one platter on a hard drive. Each platter has two heads.

heat sink — A piece of metal, with cooling fins, that can be attached to or mounted on an integrated chip (such as the CPU) to dissipate heat.

hertz (Hz) — Unit of measurement for frequency, calculated in terms of vibrations, or cycles per second. For example, for 16-bit stereo sound, a frequency of 44,000 Hz is used. *See also* megahertz.

hexadecimal notation (hex) — A numbering system that uses 16 digits, the numerals 0–9, and the letters A–F. Hexadecimal notation is often used to display memory addresses.

hibernation — A notebook OS feature that conserves power by using a small trickle of electricity. Before the notebook begins to hibernate, everything currently stored in memory is saved to the hard drive. When the notebook is brought out of hibernation, open applications and their data are returned to the state before hibernation.

hidden file — A file that is not displayed in a directory list. Whether to hide or display a file is one of the file's attributes kept by the OS.

high memory area (HMA) — In DOS or Windows 9x/Me, the first 64 K of extended memory.

High Voltage Differential (HVD) — A type of SCSI differential signaling requiring more expensive hardware to handle the higher voltage. HVD became obsolete with the introduction of SCSI-3.

high-level formatting — Formatting performed by means of the DOS or Windows Format program (for example, FORMAT C:/S creates the boot record, FAT, and root directory on drive C and makes the drive bootable). Also called OS formatting.

Himem.sys — The DOS and Windows 9x/Me memory manager extension that allowed access to memory addresses above 1 MB.

hive — Physical segment of the Windows NT/ 2000/XP registry that is stored in a file.

hop count — *See* time to live (TTL).

host — Any computer or other device on a network that has been assigned an IP address. Also called node.

host adapter — The circuit board that controls a SCSI bus supporting as many as seven or fifteen separate devices. The host adapter controls communication between the SCSI bus and the PC.

host bus — *See* memory bus or system bus.

host drive — Using Windows 9x, typically drive H on a compressed drive. *See* compressed drive.

host name — A name that identifies a computer, printer, or other device on a network.

hot-pluggable — *See* hot-swappable.

hot-swappable — A device that can be plugged into a computer while it is turned on and the computer will sense the device and configure it without rebooting, or the device can be removed without an OS error. Also called hot-pluggable.

HTML (HyperText Markup Language) — A markup language used for hypertext documents on the World Wide Web. This language uses tags to format the document, create hyperlinks, and mark locations for graphics.

HTTP (HyperText Transfer Protocol) — The communications protocol used by the World Wide Web.

HTTPS (HTTP secure) — A version of the HTTP protocol that includes data encryption for security.

hub — A network device or box that provides a central location to connect cables.

hypertext — Text that contains links to remote points in the document or to other files, documents, or graphics. Hypertext is created using HTML and is commonly distributed from Web sites.

i.Link — *See* IEEE 1394.

I/O addresses — Numbers that are used by devices and the CPU to manage communication between them. Also called ports or port addresses.

I/O controller card — An older card that can contain serial, parallel, and game ports and floppy drive and IDE connectors.

IBM Data Connector — *See* IDC.

IBM–compatible PC — A computer that uses an Intel (or compatible) processor and can run DOS and Windows.

ICMP (Internet Control Message Protocol) — Part of the IP layer that is used to transmit error messages and other control messages to hosts and routers.

IDC (IBM Data Connector) — A connector used with STP cable on a Token Ring network. Also called a *UDC (Universal Data Connector)*.

IDE (Integrated Drive Electronics or Integrated Device Electronics) — A hard drive whose disk controller is integrated into the drive, eliminating the need for a controller cable and thus increasing speed, as well as reducing price. *See also* EIDE.

IEEE 1284 — A standard for parallel ports and cables developed by the Institute for Electrical and Electronics Engineers and supported by many hardware manufacturers.

IEEE 1394 — Standards for an expansion bus that can also be configured to work as a local bus. It is expected to replace the SCSI bus, providing an easy method to install and configure fast I/O devices. Also called FireWire and i.Link.

IEEE 1394.3 — A standard, developed by the 1394 Trade Association, that is designed for peer-to-peer data transmission and allows imaging devices to send images and photos directly to printers without involving a computer.

IEEE 802.11a/b/g — IEEE specifications for wireless communication and data synchronization. Also known as Wi-Fi. Apple Computer's versions of 802.11b/g are called AirPort and AirPort Extreme.

IFS (Installable File System) — The Windows 9x/Me component that configures all devices and communicates these configurations to the device drivers.

IMAP4 (Internet Message Access Protocol version 4) — Version 4 of the IMAP protocol, which is an e-mail protocol that has more functionality than its predecessor, POP. IMAP can archive messages in folders on the e-mail server and can allow the user to choose not to download attachments to messages.

incremental backup — A time-saving backup method that only backs up files changed or newly created since the last full or incremental backup. Multiple incremental backups might be required when recovering lost data.

infestation — Any unwanted program that is transmitted to a computer without the user's knowledge and that is designed to do varying degrees of damage to data and software. There are a number of different types of infestations, including viruses, Trojan horses, worms, and logic bombs. *See* malicious software.

information (.inf) file — Text file with an .inf file extension, such as Msbatch.inf, that contains information about a hardware or software installation.

infrared transceiver — A wireless transceiver that uses infrared technology to support some wireless devices such as keyboards, mice, and printers. A motherboard might have an embedded infrared transceiver, or the transceiver might plug into a USB or serial port. The technology is defined by the Infrared Data Association (IrDA). Also called an *IrDA transceiver* or *infrared port*.

initialization files — Configuration information files for Windows. System.ini is one of the most important Windows 9x/Me initialization files.

inkjet printer — A type of ink dispersion printer that uses cartridges of ink. The ink is heated to a boiling point and then ejected onto the paper through tiny nozzles.

Institute of Electrical and Electronics Engineers (IEEE) — A nonprofit organization that develops standards for the computer and electronics industries.

instruction set — The set of instructions, on the CPU chip, that the computer can perform directly (such as ADD and MOVE).

intelligent UPS — A UPS connected to a computer by way of a USB or serial cable so that software on the computer can monitor and control the UPS. Also called *smart UPS*.

interlaced — A type of display in which the electronic beam of a monitor draws every other line with each pass, which lessens the overall effect of a lower refresh rate.

internal bus — The bus inside the CPU that is used for communication between the CPU's internal components.

internal cache — Memory cache that is faster than external cache, and is contained inside CPU chips (also referred to as primary, Level 1, or L1 cache).

internal command — Commands that are embedded in the Command.com file.

Internet Connection Firewall (ICF) — Windows XP software designed to protect a PC from unauthorized access from the Internet. Windows XP Service Pack 2 improved on ICF and renamed it Windows Firewall.

Internet Connection Sharing (ICS) — A Windows 98 and Windows XP utility that uses NAT and acts as a proxy server to manage two or more computers connected to the Internet.

Internet service provider (ISP) — A commercial group that provides Internet access for a monthly fee. AOL, Earthlink, and CompuServe are large ISPs.

intranet — A private network that uses the TCP/IP protocols.

Io.sys — Along with Msdos.sys and Command.com, one of the three files that are the core components of the real mode portion of Windows 9x/Me. It is the first program file of the OS.

IP (Internet Protocol) — The rules of communication in the TCP/IP stack that control segmenting data into packets, routing those packets across networks, and then reassembling the packets once they reach their destination.

IP address — A 32-bit address consisting of four numbers separated by periods, used to uniquely identify a device on a network that uses TCP/IP protocols. The first numbers identify the network; the last numbers identify a host. An example of an IP address is 206.96.103.114.

IPX/SPX (Internetwork Packet Exchange/Sequenced Packet Exchange) — A networking protocol suite first used by Novell NetWare, and which corresponds to the TCP/IP protocols.

IrDA transceiver — *See* infrared transceiver.

IRQ (interrupt request) line — A line on a bus that is assigned to a device and is used to signal the CPU for servicing. These lines are assigned a reference number (for example, the normal IRQ for a printer is IRQ 7).

ISA (Industry Standard Architecture) slot — An older slot on the motherboard used for slower I/O devices, which can support an 8-bit or a 16-bit data path. ISA slots are mostly replaced by PCI slots.

ISDN (Integrated Services Digital Network) — A digital telephone line that can carry data at about five times the speed of regular telephone lines. Two channels (telephone numbers) share a single pair of wires.

isochronous data transfer — A method used by IEEE 1394 to transfer data continuously without breaks.

ITU (International Telecommunications Union) — The international organization responsible for developing international standards of communication. Formerly CCITT.

joule — A measure of work or energy. One joule of energy produces one watt of power for one second.

JPEG (Joint Photographic Experts Group) — A graphical compression scheme that allows the user to control the amount of data that is averaged and sacrificed as file size is reduced. It is a common Internet file format. Most JPEG files have a .jpg extension.

jumper — Two wires that stick up side by side on the motherboard and are used to hold configuration information. The jumper is considered closed if a cover is over the wires, and open if the cover is missing.

Kerberos — A protocol used to encrypt account names and passwords that are sent to a network controller for validation. Kerberos is the default protocol used by Windows 2000/XP.

kernel — The portion of an OS that is responsible for interacting with the hardware.

kernel mode — A Windows NT/2000/XP "privileged" processing mode that has access to hardware components.

key — (1) In encryption, a secret number or code used to encode and decode data. (2) In Windows, a section name of the Windows registry.

key fob — A device, such as a type of smart card, that can fit conveniently on a key chain.

keyboard — A common input device through which data and instructions may be typed into computer memory.

keylogger — A type of spyware that tracks your keystrokes, including passwords, chat room sessions, e-mail messages, documents, online purchases, and anything else you type on your PC. Text is logged to a text file and transmitted over the Internet without your knowledge.

LAN (local area network) — A computer network that covers only a small area, usually within one building.

land grid array (LGA) — A feature of a CPU socket whereby pads, called lands, are used to make contact in uniform rows over the socket. *See also* pin grid array (PGA).

lands — Microscopic flat areas on the surface of a CD or DVD that separate pits. Lands and pits are used to represent data on the disk.

laptop computer — *See* notebook.

large mode — A mode of addressing information on hard drives that range from 504 MB to 8.4 GB, addressing information on a hard drive by translating cylinder, head, and sector information in order to break the 528-MB hard drive barrier. Also called ECHS mode.

large-capacity drive — A hard drive larger than 504 MB.

laser printer — A type of printer that uses a laser beam to control how toner is placed on the page and then uses heat to fuse the toner to the page.

Last Known Good configuration — In Windows NT/2000/XP, registry settings and device drivers that were in effect when the computer last booted successfully. These settings can be restored during the startup process to recover from errors during the last boot.

LBA (logical block addressing) mode — A mode of addressing information on hard drives in which the BIOS and operating system view the drive as one long linear list of LBAs or addressable sectors, permitting drives to be larger than 8.4 GB (LBA 0 is cylinder 0, head 0, and sector 1).

Level 1 (L1) cache — *See* internal cache.

Level 2 (L2) cache — *See* external cache.

Level 3 (L3) cache — *See* external cache.

license — Permission for an individual to use a product or service. A manufacturer's method of maintaining ownership, while granting permission for use to others.

Limited user — Windows XP user accounts known as Users in Windows NT/2000, which have read-write access only on their own folders, read-only access to most system folders, and no access to other users' data.

line conditioner — A device that regulates, or conditions, power, providing continuous voltage during brownouts and spikes.

line protocol — A protocol used to send data packets destined for a network over telephone lines. PPP and SLIP are examples of line protocols.

line speed — *See* bandwidth.

line-interactive UPS — A variation of a standby UPS that shortens switching time by always keeping the inverter that converts AC to DC working, so that there is no charge-up time for the inverter.

LMHosts — A text file located in the Windows folder that contains NetBIOS names and their associated IP addresses. This file is used for name resolution for a NetBEUI network.

local bus — A bus that operates at a speed synchronized with the CPU frequency. The system bus is a local bus.

local I/O bus — A local bus that provides I/O devices with fast access to the CPU. The PCI bus is a local I/O bus.

local printer — A printer connected to a computer by way of a port on the computer. Compare to network printer.

local profile — User profile that is stored on a local computer and cannot be accessed from another computer on the network.

local user account — A user account that applies only to a local computer and cannot be used to access resources from other computers on the network.

logic bomb — A type of malicious software that is dormant code added to software and triggered at a predetermined time or by a predetermined event.

logical drive — A portion or all of a hard drive partition that is treated by the operating system as though it were a physical drive. Each logical drive is assigned a drive letter, such as drive C, and contains a file system. Also called a volume.

logical geometry — The number of heads, tracks, and sectors that the BIOS on the hard drive controller presents to the system BIOS and the OS. The logical geometry does not consist of the same values as the physical geometry, although calculations of drive capacity yield the same results. The use of communicating logical geometry is outdated.

Logical Unit Number (LUN) — A number assigned to a logical device (such as a tray in a CD changer) that is part of a physical SCSI device, which is assigned a SCSI ID.

long mode — A CPU processing mode that processes 64 bits at a time. The AMD Athlon 64 and the Intel Itanium CPUs use this mode.

lost allocation units — *See* lost clusters.

lost clusters — File fragments that, according to the file allocation table, contain data that does not belong to any file. The command CHKDSK/F can free these fragments. Also called lost allocation units.

low insertion force (LIF) socket — A socket that requires the installer to manually apply an even force over the microchip when inserting the chip into the socket.

Low Voltage Differential (LVD) — A type of differential signaling that uses lower voltage than does HVD, is less expensive, and can be compatible with single-ended signaling on the same SCSI bus.

low-level formatting — A process (usually performed at the factory) that electronically creates the hard drive tracks and sectors and tests for bad spots on the disk surface.

low-profile case — *See* compact case.

LPX — A form factor in which expansion cards are mounted on a riser card that plugs into a motherboard. The expansion cards in LPX systems are mounted parallel to the motherboard, rather than perpendicular to it as in AT and ATX systems.

MAC (Media Access Control) address — A 48-bit hardware address unique to each NIC card and assigned by the manufacturer. The address is often printed on the adapter as hexadecimal numbers. An example is 00 00 0C 08 2F 35. Also called a physical address, an adapter address, or a hardware address.

macro — A small sequence of commands, contained within a document, that can be automatically executed when the document is loaded, or executed later by using a predetermined keystroke.

macro virus — A virus that can hide in the macros of a document file.

main board — *See* motherboard.

malicious software — Any unwanted program that is transmitted to a computer without the user's knowledge and that is designed to do varying degrees of damage to data and software. Types of infestations include viruses, Trojan horses, worms, adware, spyware, keyloggers, browser hijackers, dialers, and downloaders. Also called malware or an infestation.

malware — *See* malicious software.

mandatory user profile — A roaming user profile that applies to all users in a user group, and individual users cannot change that profile.

Master Boot Record (MBR) — The first sector on a hard drive, which contains the partition table and a program the BIOS uses to boot an OS from the drive.

master file table (MFT) — The database used by the NTFS file system to track the contents of a logical drive.

material safety data sheet (MSDS) — A document that explains how to properly handle substances such as chemical solvents; it includes information such as physical data, toxicity, health effects, first aid, storage, disposal, and spill procedures.

megahertz (MHz) — One million Hz, or one million cycles per second. *See* hertz (Hz).

memory — Physical microchips that can hold data and programming, located on the motherboard or expansion cards.

memory address — A number assigned to each byte in memory. The CPU can use memory addresses to track where information is stored in RAM. Memory addresses are usually displayed as hexa-decimal numbers in segment/offset form.

memory bus — *See* system bus.

memory cache — A small amount of faster RAM that stores recently retrieved data, in anticipation of what the CPU will request next, thus speeding up access. *See also* system bus.

memory dump — The contents of memory saved to a file at the time an event halted the system. Support technicians can analyze the dump file to help understand the source of the problem.

memory extender — For DOS and Windows 9x/Me, a device driver named Himem.sys that manages RAM, giving access to memory addresses above 1 MB.

memory paging — In Windows, swapping blocks of RAM memory to an area of the hard drive to serve as virtual memory when RAM is low.

memory-resident virus — A virus that can stay lurking in memory even after its host program is terminated.

microATX — A version of the ATX form factor. MicroATX addresses some new technologies that were developed after the original introduction of ATX.

microcode — A programming instruction that can be executed by a CPU without breaking the instruction down into simpler instructions. Typically, a single command line in a Visual Basic or C++ program must be broken down into numerous microcode commands.

MicroDIMM — A type of memory module used on sub-notebooks that has 144 pins and uses a 64-bit data path.

microprocessor — *See* central processing unit (CPU).

Microsoft Management Console (MMC) — A utility to build customized consoles. These consoles can be saved to a file with an .msc file extension.

Mini PCI — The PCI industry standard for desktop computer expansion cards, applied to a much smaller form factor for notebook expansion cards.

Mini-ATX — A smaller ATX board that can be used with regular ATX cases and power supplies.

minicartridge — A tape drive cartridge that is only $3\frac{1}{4} \times 2\frac{1}{2} \times \frac{3}{8}$ inches. It is small enough to allow two drives to fit into a standard 5½-inch drive bay of a PC case.

minifile system — In Windows NT/2000/XP, a simplified file system that is started so that Ntldr (NT Loader) can read files from any file system the OS supports.

Mini-LPX — A smaller version of the LPX motherboard.

mixed mode — A Windows 2000 mode for domain controllers used when there is at least one Windows NT domain controller on the network.

MMX (Multimedia Extensions) — Multimedia instructions built into Intel processors to add functionality such as better processing of multimedia, SIMD support, and increased cache.

modem — From MOdulate/DEModulate. A device that modulates digital data from a computer to an analog format that can be sent over telephone lines, then demodulates it back into digital form.

modem eliminator — *See* null modem cable.

modem riser card — A small modem card that uses an AMR or CNR slot. Part of the modem logic is contained in a controller on the motherboard.

modem speed — The speed at which a modem can transmit data along a phone line, measured in bits per second (bps). Also called line speed.

modulation — Converting binary or digital data into an analog signal that can be sent over standard telephone lines.

monitor — The most commonly used output device for displaying text and graphics on a computer.

motherboard — The main board in the computer, also called the system board. The CPU, ROM chips, SIMMs, DIMMs, RIMMs, and interface cards are plugged into the motherboard.

motherboard bus — *See* system bus.

motherboard mouse — *See* PS/2-compatible mouse.

mouse — A pointing and input device that allows the to move a cursor around a screen and select items with the click of a button.

MP3 — A method to compress audio files that uses MPEG level 1. It can reduce sound files as low as a 1:24 ratio without losing much sound quality.

MPEG (Moving Pictures Experts Group) — A processing-intensive standard for data compression for motion pictures that tracks movement from one frame to the next and only stores the data that has changed.

Msdos.sys — In Windows 9x/Me, a text file that contains settings used by Io.sys during booting. In DOS, the Msdos.sys file was a program file that contained part of the DOS core.

MultiBank DRAM (MDRAM) — A type of video memory that is faster than VRAM and WRAM, but can be more economical because it can be installed on a video card in smaller increments.

multicasting — A process in which a message is sent by one host to multiple hosts, such as when a video conference is broadcast to several hosts on the Internet.

multimeter — A device used to measure the various components of an electrical circuit. The most common measurements are voltage, current, and resistance.

multipartite virus — A combination of a boot sector virus and a file virus. It can hide in either type of program.

multiplier — The factor by which the bus speed or frequency is multiplied to get the CPU clock speed.

multi-processor platform — A system that contains more than one processor. The motherboard has more than one processor socket and the processors must be rated to work in this multi-processor environment.

multiscan monitor — A monitor that can work within a range of frequencies and thus can work with different standards and video cards. It offers a variety of refresh rates.

multisession — A feature that allows data to be read from or written to a CD during more than one session. This is important if the disk was only partially filled during the first write.

Multistation Access Unit (MSAU or MAU) — A centralized hub used in Token Ring networks to connect stations. Also called CAU.

multitasking — Doing more than one thing at a time. A true multitasking system requires two or more CPUs, each processing a different thread at the same time. Compare to cooperative multitasking and preemptive multitasking.

multithreading — The ability to pass more than one function (thread) to the OS kernel at the same time, such as when one thread is performing a print job while another reads a file.

name resolution — The process of associating a NetBIOS name or host name to an IP address.

narrow SCSI — One of the two main SCSI specifications. Narrow SCSI has an 8-bit data bus. The word "narrow" is not usually included in the names of narrow SCSI devices.

NAT (Network Address Translation) — A process that converts private IP addresses on a LAN to the proxy server's IP address before a data packet is sent over the Internet.

native mode — A Windows 2000 mode used by domain controllers when there are no Windows NT domain controllers present on the network.

NetBEUI (NetBIOS Extended User Interface) — A fast, proprietary Microsoft networking protocol used only by Windows-based systems, and limited to LANs because it does not support routing.

NetBIOS (Network Basic Input/Output System) — An API protocol used by some applications to communicate over a NetBEUI network. NetBIOS has largely been replaced by Windows Sockets over a TCP/IP network.

network adapter — *See* network interface card.

network drive map — Mounting a drive to a computer, such as drive E, that is actually hard drive space on another host computer on the network.

network interface card (NIC) — An expansion card that plugs into a computer's motherboard and provides a port on the back of the card to connect a PC to a network. Also called a network adapter.

network operating system (NOS) — An operating system that resides on the controlling computer in the network. The NOS controls what software, data, and devices a user on the network can access. Examples of an NOS are Novell Netware and Windows Server 2003.

network printer — A printer that any user on the network can access, through its own network card and connection to the network, through a connection to a standalone print server, or through a connection to a computer as a local printer, which is shared on the network.

NLX — A low-end form factor that is similar to LPX but provides greater support for current and emerging processor technologies. NLX was designed for flexibility and efficiency of space.

NNTP (Network News Transfer Protocol) — The protocol used by newsgroup server and client software.

node — *See* host.

noise — An extraneous, unwanted signal, often over an analog phone line, that can cause communication interference or transmission errors. Possible sources are fluorescent lighting, radios, TVs, lightning, or bad wiring.

noninterlaced — A type of display in which the electronic beam of a monitor draws every line on the screen with each pass.

non–memory-resident virus — A virus that is terminated when the host program is closed. Compare to memory-resident virus.

nonparity memory — Eight-bit memory without error checking. A SIMM part number with a 32 in it (4 × 8 bits) is nonparity.

nonvolatile — Refers to a kind of RAM that is stable and can hold data as long as electricity is powering the memory.

normal mode — *See* CHS mode.

North Bridge — That portion of the chipset hub that connects faster I/O buses (for example, AGP bus) to the system bus. Compare to South Bridge.

notebook — A portable computer that is designed for travel and mobility. Notebooks use the same technology as desktop PCs, with modifications for conserving voltage, taking up less space, and operating while on the move. Also called a laptop computer.

NTFS (NT file system) — The file system for the Windows NT/2000/XP operating systems. NTFS cannot be accessed by other operating systems such as DOS. It provides increased reliability and security in comparison to other methods of organizing and accessing files. There are several versions of NTFS that might or might not be compatible.

Ntldr (NT Loader) — In Windows NT/2000/XP, the OS loader used on Intel systems.

NTVDM (NT virtual DOS machine) — An emulated environment in which a 16-bit DOS application resides within Windows NT/2000/XP with its own memory space or WOW (Win16 on Win32).

null modem cable — A cable that allows two data terminal equipment (DTE) devices to communicate in which the transmit and receive wires are cross-connected and no modems are necessary.

NWLink — Microsoft's version of the IPX/SPX protocol suite used by Novell NetWare operating systems.

octet — Term for each of the four 8-bit numbers that make up an IP address. For example, the IP address 206.96.103.114 has four octets.

ohm (Ω) — The standard unit of measurement for electrical resistance. Resistors are rated in ohms.

on-board ports — Ports that are directly on the motherboard, such as a built-in keyboard port or on-board serial port.

operating system (OS) — Software that controls a computer. An OS controls how system resources are used and provides a user interface, a way of managing hardware and software, and ways to work with files.

operating system formatting — See high-level formatting.

overclocking — Running a processor at a higher frequency than is recommended by the manufacturer, which can result in an unstable system, but is a popular thing to do when a computer is used for gaming.

P1 connector — Power connection on an ATX or BTX motherboard.

P8 connector — One of two power connectors on an AT motherboard.

P9 connector — One of two power connectors on an AT motherboard.

packet — Segment of network data that also includes header, destination address, and trailer information that is sent as a unit. Also called data packet or datagram.

page fault — An OS interrupt that occurs when the OS is forced to access the hard drive to satisfy the demands for virtual memory.

page file — See swap file.

Pagefile.sys — The Windows NT/2000/XP swap file.

page-in — The process in which the memory manager goes to the hard drive to return the data from a swap file to RAM.

page-out — The process in which, when RAM is full, the memory manager takes a page and moves it to the swap file.

pages — 4-K segments in which Windows NT/2000/XP allocates memory.

parallel ATA (PATA) — An older IDE cabling method that uses a 40-pin flat data cable or an 80-conductor cable and a 40-pin IDE connector. See also serial ATA.

parallel port — A female 25-pin port on a computer that can transmit data in parallel, 8 bits at a time, and is usually used with a printer. The names for parallel ports are LPT1 and LPT2.

parity — An error-checking scheme in which a ninth, or "parity," bit is added. The value of the parity bit is set to either 0 or 1 to provide an even number of ones for even parity and an odd number of ones for odd parity.

parity error — An error that occurs when the number of 1s in the byte is not in agreement with the expected number.

parity memory — Nine-bit memory in which the ninth bit is used for error checking. A SIMM part number with a 36 in it (4 × 9 bits) is parity. Older PCs almost always use parity chips.

partition — A division of a hard drive that can be used to hold logical drives.

partition table — A table at the beginning of the hard drive that contains information about each partition on the drive. The partition table is contained in the Master Boot Record.

passive backplane — A type of backplane system in which the backplane contains no circuitry at all. All circuitry in a passive backplane system is contained on a mothercard plugged into a backplane.

passive terminator — A type of terminator for single-ended SCSI cables. Simple resistors are used to provide termination of a signal. Passive termination is not reliable over long distances and should only be used with narrow SCSI.

passphrase — A type of password that can contain a phrase where spaces are allowed. A passphrase is stronger than a one-word password.

patch — An update to software that corrects an error, adds a feature, or addresses security issues. Also called an update or service pack.

patch cable — A network cable that is used to connect a PC to a hub, switch, or router.

path — (1) A drive and list of directories pointing to a file such as C:\Windows\command. (2) The OS command to provide a list of paths to the system for finding program files to execute.

PC Card — A credit-card-sized adapter card that can be slid into a slot in the side of many notebook computers and is used by modems, network cards, and other devices. Also called a PCMCIA Card.

PC Card slot — An expansion slot on a notebook computer, into which a PC Card is inserted. Also called a PCMCIA Card slot.

PCI (Peripheral Component Interconnect) bus — A bus common on Pentium computers that runs at speeds of up to 33 MHz or 66 MHz, with a 32-bit-wide or 64-bit-wide data path. PCI-X, released in September 1999, enables PCI to run at 133 MHz. For some chipsets, it serves as the middle layer between the memory bus and expansion buses.

PCL (Printer Control Language) — A printer language developed by Hewlett-Packard that communicates to a printer how to print a page.

PCMCIA (Personal Computer Memory Card International Association) Card — *See* PC Card.

PCMCIA Card slot — *See* PC Card slot.

PDA (Personal Digital Assistant) — A small, handheld computer that has its own operating system and applications.

peer-to-peer network — A network of computers that are all equals, or peers. Each computer has the same amount of authority, and each can act as a server to the other computers.

peripheral devices — Devices that communicate with the CPU but are not located directly on the motherboard, such as the monitor, floppy drive, printer, and mouse.

phishing — (1) A type of identity theft where a person is baited into giving personal data to a Web site that appears to be the Web site of a reputable company with which the person has an account. (2) Sending an e-mail message with the intent of getting the user to reveal private information that can be used for identify theft.

physical address — *See* MAC address.

physical geometry — The actual layout of heads, tracks, and sectors on a hard drive. Compare to logical geometry.

PIF (program information file) — A file used by Windows to describe the environment for a DOS program to use.

pin grid array (PGA) — A feature of a CPU socket whereby the pins are aligned in uniform rows around the socket.

Ping (Packet Internet Groper) — A Windows and Unix command used to troubleshoot network connections. It verifies that the host can communicate with another host on the network.

pinout — A description of how each pin on a bus, connection, plug, slot, or socket is used.

PIO (Programmed I/O) transfer mode — A transfer mode that uses the CPU to transfer data from the hard drive to memory. PIO mode is slower than DMA mode.

pipelined burst SRAM — A less expensive SRAM that uses more clock cycles per transfer than non-pipelined burst but does not significantly slow down the process.

pits — Recessed areas on the surface of a CD or DVD, separating lands, or flat areas. Lands and pits are used to represent data on a disc.

pixel — A small spot on a fine horizontal scan line. Pixels are illuminated to create an image on the monitor.

PKI (public key infrastructure) — The standards used to encrypt, transport, and validate digital certificates over the Internet.

Plug and Play (PnP) — A standard designed to make the installation of new hardware devices easier by automatically configuring devices to eliminate system resource conflicts (such as IRQ or I/O address conflicts). PnP is supported by Windows 9x/Me, Windows 2000, and Windows XP.

polling — A process by which the CPU checks the status of connected devices to determine if they are ready to send or receive data.

polymorphic virus — A type of virus that changes its distinguishing characteristics as it replicates itself. Mutating in this way makes it more difficult for AV software to recognize the presence of the virus.

POP (Post Office Protocol) — The protocol that an e-mail server and client use when the client requests the downloading of e-mail messages. The most recent version is POP3. POP is being replaced by IMAP.

port — (1) As applied to services running on a computer, a number assigned to a process on a computer so that the process can be found by TCP/IP. Also called a port address or port number. (2) Another name for an I/O address. *See also* I/O address. (3) A physical connector, usually at the back of a computer, that allows a cable from a peripheral device, such as a printer, mouse, or modem, to be attached.

port address — *See* I/O address.

port forwarding — A technique that allows a computer on the Internet to reach a computer on a private network using a certain port when the private network is protected by a router using NAT as a proxy server. Port forwarding is also called tunneling.

port number — *See* port.

port replicator — A device designed to connect to a notebook computer in order to make it easy to connect the notebook to peripheral devices.

port settings — The configuration parameters of communications devices such as COM1, COM2, or LPT1, including IRQ settings.

port speed — The communication speed between a DTE (computer) and a DCE (modem). As a general rule, the port speed should be at least four times as fast as the modem speed.

POST (power-on self test) — A self-diagnostic program used to perform a simple test of the CPU, RAM, and various I/O devices. The POST is performed by startup BIOS when the computer is first turned on, and is stored in ROM-BIOS.

PostScript — A printer language developed by Adobe Systems which tells a printer how to print a page.

power conditioner — A line conditioner that regulates, or conditions, power, providing continuous voltage during brownouts.

power scheme — A feature of Windows XP support for notebooks that allows the user to create groups of power settings for specific sets of conditions.

power supply — A box inside the computer case that supplies power to the motherboard and other installed devices. Power supplies provide 3.3, 5, and 12 volts DC.

power-on password — A password that a computer uses to control access during the boot process.

PPP (Point-to-Point Protocol) — A protocol that governs the methods for communicating via modems and dial-up telephone lines. The Windows Dial-up Networking utility uses PPP.

PPPoE (Point-to-Point Protocol over Ethernet) — The protocol that describes how a PC is to interact with a broadband converter box, such as cable modem, when the two are connected by an Ethernet cable, connected to a NIC in a PC.

preemptive multitasking — A type of pseudo-multitasking whereby the CPU allows an application a specified period of time and then preempts the processing to give time to another application.

primary cache — *See* internal cache.

primary domain controller (PDC) — In a Windows NT network, the computer that controls the directory database of user accounts, group accounts, and computer accounts on a domain. *See also* backup domain controller.

primary partition — A hard disk partition that can contain only one logical drive.

primary storage — Temporary storage on the motherboard used by the CPU to process data and instructions. Memory is considered primary storage.

printer — A peripheral output device that produces printed output to paper. Different types include dot matrix, ink-jet, and laser printers.

printer maintenance kit — A kit purchased from a printer manufacturer that contains the parts, tools, and instructions needed to perform routine printer maintenance.

private IP address — An IP address that is used on a private TCP/IP network that is isolated from the Internet.

process — An executing instance of a program together with the program resources. There can be more than one process running for a program at the same time. One process for a program happens each time the program is loaded into memory or executed.

processor — *See* central processing unit (CPU).

processor speed — The speed, or frequency, at which the CPU operates. Usually expressed in GHz.

product activation — The process that Microsoft uses to prevent software piracy. For example, once Windows XP is activated for a particular computer, it cannot be legally installed on another computer.

program — A set of step-by-step instructions to a computer. Some are burned directly into chips, while others are stored as program files. Programs are written in languages such as BASIC and C++.

program file — A file that contains instructions designed to be executed by the CPU.

protected mode — An operating mode that supports preemptive multitasking, the OS manages memory and other hardware devices, and programs can use a 32-bit data path. Also called 32-bit mode.

protocol — A set of rules and standards that two entities use for communication.

Protocol.ini — A Windows initialization file that contains network configuration information.

proxy server — A server that acts as an intermediary between another computer and the Internet. The proxy server substitutes its own IP address for the IP address of the computer on the network making a request, so that all traffic over the Internet appears to be coming from only the IP address of the proxy server.

PS/2-compatible mouse — A mouse that plugs into a round mouse PS/2 port on the motherboard. Sometimes called a motherboard mouse.

public IP address — An IP address available to the Internet.

QIC (Quarter-Inch Committee or quarter-inch cartridge) — A name of a standardized method used to write data to tape. These backup files have a .qic extension.

Quality of Service (QoS) — A measure of the success of communication over the Internet. Communication is degraded on the Internet when packets are dropped, delayed, delivered out of order, or corrupted. VoIP requires a high QoS.

RAID (redundant array of inexpensive disks or redundant array of independent disks) — Several methods of configuring multiple hard drives to store data to increase logical volume size and improve performance, or to ensure that if one hard drive fails, the data is still available from another hard drive.

RAM (random access memory) — Memory modules on the mother-board containing microchips used to temporarily hold data and programs while the CPU processes both. Information in RAM is lost when the PC is turned off.

RAM drive — An area of memory that is treated as though it were a hard drive, but works much faster than a hard drive. The Windows 9x/Me startup disk uses a RAM drive. Compare to virtual memory.

RARP (Reverse Address Resolution Protocol) — A protocol used to translate the unique hardware NIC addresses (MAC addresses) into IP addresses (the reverse of ARP).

RDRAM — *See* Direct Rambus DRAM.

read/write head — A sealed, magnetic coil device that moves across the surface of a disk either reading data from or writing data to the disk.

real mode — A single-tasking operating mode whereby a program can use 1024 K of memory addresses, has direct access to RAM, and uses a 16-bit data path. Using a memory extender (Himem.sys) a program in real mode can access memory above 1024 K. Also called 16-bit mode.

Recovery Console — A Windows 2000/XP command interface utility and OS that can be used to solve problems when Windows cannot load from the hard drive.

rectifier — An electrical device that converts AC to DC. A PC power supply contains a rectifier.

refresh — The process of periodically rewriting data, such as on dynamic RAM.

refresh rate — As applied to monitors, the number of times in one second an electronic beam can fill the screen with lines from top to bottom. Also called vertical scan rate.

registry — A database that Windows uses to store hardware and software configuration information, user preferences, and setup information.

re-marked chips — Chips that have been used and returned to the factory, marked again, and resold. The surface of the chips may be dull or scratched.

Remote Assistance — A Windows XP feature that allows a support technician at a remote location to have full access to the Windows XP desktop.

repeater — A device that amplifies signals on a network so they can be transmitted further down the line.

rescue disk — A floppy disk that can be used to start up a computer when the hard drive fails to boot. Also called emergency startup disk (ESD) or startup disk.

resistance — The degree to which a device opposes or resists the flow of electricity. As the electrical resistance increases, the current decreases. *See* ohm and resistor.

resistor — An electronic device that resists or opposes the flow of electricity. A resistor can be used to reduce the amount of electricity being supplied to an electronic component.

resolution — The number of pixels on a monitor screen that are addressable by software (example: 1024 × 768 pixels).

restore point — A snapshot of the Windows Me/XP system state, usually made before installation of new hardware or applications.

REt (Resolution Enhancement technology) — The term used by Hewlett-Packard to describe the way a laser printer varies the size of the dots used to create an image. This technology partly accounts for the sharp, clear image created by a laser printer.

RIMM — A type of memory module developed by Rambus, Inc.

ring topology — A network topology in which the nodes in a network form a ring. Each node is connected only to two other nodes, and a centralized hub is not required.

RISC (Reduced Instruction Set Computing) chips — Chips that incorporate only the most frequently used instructions, so that the computer operates faster (for example, the PowerPC uses RISC chips).

riser card — A card that plugs into a motherboard and allows for expansion cards to be mounted parallel to the motherboard. Expansion cards are plugged into slots on the riser card.

RJ-11 — A phone line connection found on modems, telephones, and house phone outlets.

RJ-45 connector — A connector used with twisted-pair cable that connects the cable to the NIC.

roaming user profile — A user profile for a roaming user. Roaming user profiles are stored on a server so that the user can access the profile from anywhere on the network.

ROM (read-only memory) — Chips that contain programming code and cannot be erased.

ROM BIOS — *See* BIOS.

root directory — The main directory created when a hard drive or disk is first formatted. In Linux, it's indicated by a forward slash. In DOS and Windows, it's indicated by a backward slash.

rootkit — A type of malicious software that loads itself before the OS boot is complete and can hijack internal Windows components so that it masks information Windows provides to user-mode utilities such as Windows Explorer or Task Manager.

routable protocol — A protocol that can be routed to interconnected networks on the basis of a network address. TCP/IP is a routable protocol, but NetBEUI is not.

router — A device that connects networks and makes decisions as to the best routes to use when forwarding packets.

sags — *See* brownouts.

sampling rate — The rate of samples taken of an analog signal over a period of time, usually expressed as samples per second, or hertz.

SBAC (SCSI bus adapter chip) — The SCSI chip within a device housing that controls data transfer over the SCSI bus.

SCAM (SCSI Configuration AutoMatically) — A method of configuring SCSI device settings that follows the Plug and Play standard. SCAM makes installation of SCSI devices much easier, provided that the devices are SCAM-compliant.

scam e-mail — E-mail sent by a scam artist intended to lure you into a scheme.

scanner — A device that allows a computer to convert a picture, drawing, barcode, or other image into digital data that can be input into the computer.

scanning mirror — A component of a laser printer consisting of an octagonal mirror that can be directed in a sweeping motion to cover the entire length of a laser printer drum.

script virus — A type of virus that hides in a script which might execute when you click a link on a Web page or in an HTML e-mail message, or when you attempt to open an e-mail attachment.

SCSI (Small Computer System Interface) — A fast interface between a host adapter and the CPU that can daisy chain as many as 7 or 15 devices on a single bus.

SCSI ID — A number from 0 to 15 assigned to each SCSI device attached to the daisy chain.

SDRAM II — *See* Double Data Rate SDRAM (DDR SDRAM).

secondary storage — Storage that is remote to the CPU and permanently holds data, even when the PC is turned off, such as a hard drive.

sector — On a disk surface one segment of a track, which almost always contains 512 bytes of data.

security accounts manager (SAM) — A portion of the Windows NT/2000/XP registry that manages the account database that contains accounts, policies, and other pertinent information about local accounts.

sequential access — A method of data access used by tape drives, whereby data is written or read sequentially from the beginning to the end of the tape or until the desired data is found.

serial ATA (SATA) — An ATAPI cabling method that uses a narrower and more reliable cable than the 80-conductor cable. *See also* parallel ATA.

serial ATA cable — An IDE cable that is narrower and has fewer pins than the parallel IDE 80-conductor cable.

serial mouse — A mouse that uses a serial port and has a female 9-pin DB-9 connector.

serial port — A male 9-pin or 25-pin port on a computer system used by slower I/O devices such as a mouse or modem. Data travels serially, one bit at a time, through the port. Serial ports are sometimes configured as COM1, COM2, COM3, or COM4.

server-side caching — A technique used by servers on the Internet to speed up download times by caching Web pages previously requested in case they are requested again.

service — A program that runs in the background to support or serve Windows or an application.

service pack — *See* patch.

session — An established communication link between two software programs. On the Internet, a session is created by TCP.

SFC (System File Checker) — A Windows tool that checks to make sure Windows is using the correct versions of system files.

SGRAM (synchronous graphics RAM) — Memory designed especially for video card processing that can synchronize itself with the CPU bus clock.

shadow RAM or shadowing ROM — ROM programming code copied into RAM to speed up the system operation, because of the faster access speed of RAM.

shared memory — When the video system does not have dedicated video memory, but is using regular RAM instead. A system with shared memory generally costs less than having dedicated video memory. Also called *video sharing*.

shell — The portion of an OS that relates to the user and to applications.

shielded twisted-pair (STP) cable — A cable that is made of one or more twisted pairs of wires and is surrounded by a metal shield.

shortcut — An icon on the desktop that points to a program that can be executed or to a file or folder.

signal-regenerating repeater — A repeater that is able to distinguish between noise and signal. It reads the signal and retransmits it without the accompanying noise.

Sigverif.exe — A Windows 2000/XP utility that allows you to search for digital signatures.

SIMD (single instruction, multiple data) — A process that allows the CPU to execute a single instruction simultaneously on multiple pieces of data, rather than by repetitive looping.

SIMM (single inline memory module) — A miniature circuit board used in older computers to hold RAM. SIMMs hold 8, 16, 32, or 64 MB on a single module.

simple volume — A type of dynamic volume used on a single hard drive that corresponds to a primary partition on a basic disk.

single-ended (SE) cable — A type of SCSI cable in which two wires are used to carry a signal, one of which carries the signal itself; the other is a ground for the signal.

single-voltage CPU — A CPU that requires one voltage for both internal and I/O operations.

site license — A license that allows a company to install multiple copies of software, or to allow multiple employees to execute the software from a file server.

slack — Wasted space on a hard drive caused by not using all available space at the end of clusters.

sleep mode — A mode used in many "Green" systems that allows them to be configured through CMOS to suspend the monitor or even the drive, if the keyboard and/or CPU have been inactive for a set number of minutes. *See also* Green Standards.

slimline case — *See* compact case.

SLIP (Serial Line Internet Protocol) — A line protocol used by regular telephone lines that has largely been replaced by PPP.

smart card — Any small device that contains authentication information that can be keyed into a logon window or read by a reader to authenticate a user on a network.

smart card reader — A device that can read a smart card used to authenticate a person onto a network.

Smart Multistation Access Unit (SMAU) — *See* MAU.

smart UPS — *See* intelligent UPS.

SMARTDrive — A hard drive cache program that came with Windows 3.x and DOS and can be executed as a TSR from the Autoexec.bat file (for example, Device = Smartdrv.sys 2048).

SMTP (Simple Mail Transfer Protocol) — The protocol used by e-mail clients and servers to send e-mail messages over the Internet. *See* POP and IMAP.

SMTP AUTH (SMTP Authentication) — A protocol that is used to authenticate or prove that a client who attempts to use an email server to send email is authorized to use the server. The protocol is based on the Simple Authentication and Security Layer (SASL) protocol.

snap-ins — A Windows utility that can be installed in a console window by Microsoft Management Console.

SNMP (Simple Network Management Protocol) — A protocol used to monitor and manage network traffic on a workstation. SNMP works with TCP/IP and IPX/SPX networks.

social engineering — The practice of tricking people into giving out private information or allowing unsafe programs into the network or computer.

socket — *See* session.

SO-DIMM (small outline DIMM) — A type of memory module used in notebook computers that uses DIMM technology and can have either 72 pins or 144 pins.

soft boot — To restart a PC without turning off the power, for example, in Windows XP, by clicking Start, Turn Off Computer, and Restart. Also called warm boot.

soft power — *See* soft switch.

soft switch — A feature on an ATX or BTX system that allows an OS to power down the system and allows for activity such as a keystroke or network activity to power up the system. Also called soft power.

software — Computer programs, or instructions to perform a specific task. Software may be BIOS, OSs, or applications software such as a word-processing or spreadsheet program.

software cache — Cache controlled by software whereby the cache is stored in RAM.

solid ink printer — A type of printer that uses sticks or blocks of solid ink. The ink is melted and then jetted onto the paper as the paper passes by on a drum.

solid state device (SSD) — A storage device that uses memory chips to store data instead of spinning disks (such as those used by hard drives and CD drives). Examples of solid state devices are jump drives (also called key drives or thumb drives), flash memory cards, and solid state disks used as hard drives in notebook computers designed for the most rugged uses. Also called solid state disk (SSD).

solid state disk (SSD) — *See* solid state device.

SO-RIMM — (small outline RIMM) A 160-pin memory module used in notebooks that uses Rambus technology.

South Bridge — That portion of the chipset hub that connects slower I/O buses (for example, an ISA bus) to the system bus. Compare to North Bridge.

spacers — *See* standoffs.

spam — Junk e-mail you don't ask for, don't want, and that gets in your way.

spanned volume — A type of dynamic volume used on two or more hard drives that fills up the space allotted on one physical disk before moving to the next.

SPI (SCSI Parallel Interface) — The part of the SCSI-3 standard that specifies how SCSI devices are connected.

spikes — Temporary surges in voltage, which can damage electrical components. Also called swells.

spooling — Placing print jobs in a print queue so that an application can be released from the printing process before printing is completed. Spooling is an acronym for simultaneous peripheral operations online.

spyware — Malicious software that installs itself on your computer to spy on you. It collects personal information about you that it transmits over the Internet to Web-hosting sites that intend to use your personal data for harm.

SSE (Streaming SIMD Extension) — A technology used by the Intel Pentium III and later CPUs and designed to improve performance of multimedia software.

SSL (secure socket layer) — A secure protocol developed by Netscape that uses a digital certificate including a public key to encrypt and decrypt data.

staggered pin grid array (SPGA) — A feature of a CPU socket whereby the pins are staggered over the socket in order to squeeze more pins into a small space.

standby time — The time before a "Green" system will reduce 92 percent of its activity. *See also* Green Standards.

standoffs — Round plastic or metal pegs that separate the motherboard from the case, so that components on the back of the motherboard do not touch the case.

star bus topology — A LAN that uses a logical bus design, but with all devices connected to a central hub, making a physical star.

star ring topology — A topology that is physically arranged in a star formation but is logically a ring because of the way information travels on it. Token Ring is the primary example.

star topology — A LAN in which all the devices are connected to a central hub.

start bits — Bits that are used to signal the approach of data.

startup BIOS — Part of system BIOS that is responsible for controlling the PC when it is first turned on. Startup BIOS gives control over to the OS once it is loaded.

startup disk — *See* rescue disk.

startup password — *See* power-on password.

stateless — Term for a device or process that manages data or some activity without regard to all the details of the data or activity.

static electricity — *See* ESD.

static IP address — An IP address permanently assigned to a workstation.

static RAM (SRAM) — RAM chips that retain information without the need for refreshing, as long as the computer's power is on. They are more expensive than traditional DRAM.

static VxD — A VxD that is loaded into memory at startup and remains there for the entire OS session.

stealth virus — A virus that actively conceals itself by temporarily removing itself from an infected file that is about to be examined, and then hiding a copy of itself elsewhere on the drive.

stop error — An error severe enough to cause the operating system to stop all processes.

streaming audio — Downloading audio data from the Internet in a continuous stream of data without first downloading an entire audio file.

striped volume — A type of dynamic volume used for two or more hard drives that writes to the disks evenly rather than filling up allotted space on one and then moving on to the next. Compare to spanned volume.

subdirectory — A directory or folder contained in another directory or folder. Also called a child directory or folder.

subnet mask — A subnet mask is a group of four numbers (dotted decimal numbers) that tell TCP/IP if a remote computer is on the same or a different network.

subsystems — The different modules into which the Windows NT/2000/XP user mode is divided.

surge suppressor or surge protector — A device or power strip designed to protect electronic equipment from power surges and spikes.

Surround Sound — A sound compression standard that supports six separate sound channels using six speakers known as Front Left and Right, Front Center, Rear Left and Right, and Subwoofer. Surround Sound 7.1 supports two additional rear or side speakers. Also known as Dolby AC-3, Dolby Digital Surround, or Dolby Surround Sound.

suspend time — The time before a "Green" system will reduce 99 percent of its activity. After this time, the system needs a warm-up time so that the CPU, monitor, and hard drive can reach full activity.

swap file — A file on the hard drive that is used by the OS for virtual memory. Also called a page file.

swells — *See* spikes.

switch — A device used to segment a network. It can decide which network segment is to receive a packet, on the basis of the packet's destination MAC address.

synchronization — The process by which files and programs are transferred between PDAs and PCs.

synchronous DRAM (SDRAM) — A type of memory stored on DIMMs that runs in sync with the system clock, running at the same speed as the motherboard.

synchronous SRAM — SRAM that is faster and more expensive than asynchronous SRAM. It requires a clock signal to validate its control signals, enabling the cache to run in step with the CPU.

SyncLink DRAM (SLDRAM) — A type of DRAM developed by a consortium of 12 DRAM manufacturers. It improved on regular SDRAM but is now obsolete.

Sysedit — The Windows 9x/Me System Configuration Editor, a text editor generally used to edit system files.

system BIOS — BIOS located on the motherboard.

system board — *See* motherboard.

system bus — The bus between the CPU and memory on the motherboard. The bus frequency in documentation is called the system speed, such as 400 MHz. Also called the memory bus, frontside bus, local bus, or host bus.

system clock — A line on a bus that is dedicated to timing the activities of components connected to it. The system clock provides a continuous pulse that other devices use to time themselves.

system disk — Windows terminology for a bootable disk.

system partition — The active partition of the hard drive containing the boot record and the specific files required to load Windows NT/2000/XP.

system resource — A channel, line, or address on the motherboard that can be used by the CPU or a device for communication. The four system resources are IRQ, I/O address, DMA channel, and memory address.

System Restore — A Windows Me/XP utility, similar to the ScanReg tool in earlier versions of Windows, that is used to restore the system to a restore point. Unlike ScanReg, System Restore cannot be executed from a command prompt.

system state data — In Windows 2000/XP, files that are necessary for a successful load of the operating system.

System Tray — An area to the right of the taskbar that holds the icons for running services; these services include the volume control and network connectivity.

System.ini — A text configuration file used by Windows 3.x and supported by Windows 9x/Me for backward-compatibility.

TAPI (Telephony Application Programming Interface) — A standard developed by Intel and Microsoft that can be used by 32-bit Windows communications programs for communicating over phone lines.

taskbar — A bar normally located at the bottom of the Windows desktop, displaying information about open programs and providing quick access to others.

TCP (Transmission Control Protocol) — Part of the TCP/IP protocol suite. TCP guarantees delivery of data for application protocols and establishes a session before it begins transmitting data.

TCP/IP (Transmission Control Protocol/Internet Protocol) — The suite of protocols that supports communication on the Internet. TCP is responsible for error checking, and IP is responsible for routing.

TDMA (time-division multiple access) — A protocol standard used by cellular WANs and cell phones.

technical documentation — The technical reference manuals, included with software packages and peripherals, that provide directions for installation, usage, and troubleshooting. The information extends beyond that given in user manuals.

telephony — A term describing the technology of converting sound to signals that can travel over telephone lines.

terminating resistor — The resistor added at the end of a SCSI chain to dampen the voltage at the end of the chain.

termination — A process necessary to prevent an echo effect of power at the end of a SCSI chain, resulting in interference with the data transmission.

thermal printer — A type of line printer that uses wax-based ink, which is heated by heat pins that melt the ink onto paper.

ThickNet — *See* 10Base5 Ethernet.

ThinNet — *See* 10Base2 Ethernet.

thread — Each process that the CPU is aware of; a single task that is part of a longer task or program.

TIFF (Tagged Image File Format) — A bitmapped file format used to hold photographs, graphics, and screen captures. TIFF files can be rather large, and have a .tif file extension.

time to live (TTL) — Number of routers a network packet can pass through on its way to its destination before it is dropped. Also called hop count.

TLS (Transport Layer Security) — A protocol used to secure data sent over the Internet. It is an improved version of SSL.

token ring — An older LAN technology developed by IBM that transmits data at 4 Mbps or 16 Mbps.

top-level domain — The highest level of domain names, indicated by a suffix that tells something about the host. For example, .com is for commercial use and .edu is for educational institutions.

touch screen — An input device that uses a monitor or LCD panel as a backdrop for user options. Touch screens can be embedded in a monitor or LCD panel or installed as an add-on device.

tower case — The largest type of personal computer case. Tower cases stand vertically and can be as high as two feet tall. They have more drive bays and are a good choice for computer users who anticipate making significant upgrades.

trace — A wire on a circuit board that connects two components or devices.

track — One of many concentric circles on the surface of a hard drive or floppy disk.

training — *See* handshaking.

transceiver — The component on a NIC that is responsible for signal conversion. Combines the words transmitter and receiver.

transformer — A device that changes the ratio of current to voltage. A computer power supply is basically a transformer and a rectifier.

transistor — An electronic device that can regulate electricity and act as a logical gate or switch for an electrical signal.

translation — A technique used by system BIOS and hard drive controller BIOS to break the 504-MB hard drive barrier, whereby a different set of drive parameters are communicated to the OS and other software than that used by the hard drive controller BIOS.

Travan standards — A popular and improved group of standards for tape drives based on the QIC standards and developed by 3M.

triad — Three dots of color that make up one composite dot on a CRT screen.

Trojan horse — A type of infestation that hides or disguises itself as a useful program, yet is designed to cause damage when executed.

TSR (terminate-and-stay-resident) — A program that is loaded into memory and remains dormant until called on, such as a screen saver or a memory-resident antivirus program.

UART (universal asynchronous receiver-transmitter) chip — A chip that controls serial ports. It sets protocol and converts parallel data bits received from the system bus into serial bits.

UDC (Universal Data Connector) — *See* IDC (IBM Data Connector).

UDP (User Datagram Protocol) — A connectionless protocol that does not require a connection to send a packet and does not guarantee that the packet arrives at its destination. UDP is faster than TCP because TCP takes the time to make a connection and guarantee delivery.

unattended installation — A Windows NT/2000/XP installation that is done by storing the answers to installation questions in a text file or script that Windows NT/2000/XP calls an answer file so that the answers do not have to be typed in during the installation.

Universal Disk Format (UDF) file system — A file system for optical media used by all DVD discs and some CD-R and CD-RW discs.

unshielded twisted-pair (UTP) cable — A cable that is made of one or more twisted pairs of wires and is not surrounded by shielding.

upgrade install — The installation of an OS on a hard drive that already has an OS installed in such a way that settings kept by the old OS are carried forward into the upgrade, including information about hardware, software, and user preferences.

upper memory — In DOS and Windows 9x/Me, the memory addresses from 640 K up to 1024 K, originally reserved for BIOS, device drivers, and TSRs.

upper memory block (UMB) — In DOS and Windows 9x/Me, a group of consecutive memory addresses in RAM from 640 K to 1MB that can be used by 16-bit device drivers and TSRs.

UPS (uninterruptible power supply) — A device designed to provide a backup power supply during a power failure. Basically, a UPS is a battery backup system with an ultrafast sensing device.

URL (Uniform Resource Locator) — An address for a resource on the Internet. A URL can contain the protocol used by the resource, the name of the computer and its network, and the path and name of a file on the computer.

USB (universal serial bus) port — A type of port designed to make installation and configuration of I/O devices easy, providing room for as many as 127 devices daisy-chained together.

USB host controller — Manages the USB bus. If the motherboard contains on-board USB ports, the USB host controller is part of the chipset. The USB controller uses only a single set of resources for all devices on the bus.

user account — The information, stored in the SAM database, that defines a Windows NT/ 2000/XP user, including username, password, memberships, and rights.

user component — A Windows 9x/Me component that controls the mouse, keyboard, ports, and desktop.

user mode — In Windows NT/2000/XP, a mode that provides an interface between an application and the OS, and only has access to hardware resources through the code running in kernel mode.

user profile — A personal profile about a user that enables the user's desktop settings and other operating parameters to be retained from one session to another.

User State Migration Tool (USMT) — A Windows XP utility that helps you migrate user files and preferences from one computer to another in order to help a user make a smooth transition from one computer to another.

V.92 — The latest standard for data transmission over phone lines that can attain a speed of 56 Kbps.

value data — In Windows, the name and value of a setting in the registry.

VCACHE — A built-in Windows 9x/Me 32-bit software cache that doesn't take up conventional memory space or upper memory space as SMARTDrive did.

VESA (Video Electronics Standards Association) VL bus — An out-dated local bus used on 80486 computers for connecting 32-bit adapters directly to the local processor bus.

VFAT (virtual file allocation table) — A Windows 95 variation of the original DOS 16-bit FAT that allows for long filenames and 32-bit disk access.

video card — An interface card installed in the computer to control visual output on a monitor. Also called display adapter.

video sharing — *See* shared memory.

virtual device driver (VxD or VDD) — A Windows device driver that may or may not have direct access to a device. It might depend on a Windows component to communicate with the device itself.

virtual machine — One or more logical machines created within one phys-ical machine by Windows, allowing applications to make serious errors within one logical machine without disturbing other programs and parts of the system.

virtual memory — A method whereby the OS uses the hard drive as though it were RAM. Compare to RAM drive.

virtual real mode — An operating mode that works similarly to real mode and is provided by a 32-bit OS for a 16-bit program to work.

virus — A program that often has an incubation period, is infectious, and is intended to cause damage. A virus program might destroy data and pro-grams or damage a disk drive's boot sector.

virus hoax — E-mail that does damage by tempting you to forward it to everyone in your e-mail address book with the intent of clogging up e-mail systems or by persuading you to delete a critical Windows system file by convincing you the file is malicious.

virus signature — A set of distinguishing characteristics of a virus used by antivirus software to identify the virus.

VMM (Virtual Machine Manager) — A Windows 9x/Me program that controls virtual machines and the resources they use including memory. The VMM manages the page table used to access memory.

volatile — Refers to a kind of RAM that is temporary, cannot hold data very long, and must be frequently refreshed.

volt (V) — A measure of potential difference in an electrical circuit. A com-puter ATX power supply usually provides five separate voltages: +12 V, -12 V, +5 V, -5 V, and +3.3 V.

voltage — Electrical differential that causes current to flow, measured in volts. *See* volt.

voltage regulator module (VRM) — A device embedded or installed on the motherboard that regulates voltage to the processor.

voltmeter — A device for measuring electrical AC or DC voltage.

volume — *See* logical drive.

VRAM (video RAM) — RAM on video cards that holds the data that is being passed from the computer to the monitor and can be accessed by two devices simultaneously. Higher resolutions often require more video memory.

VxD — *See* virtual device driver.

wait state — A clock tick in which nothing happens, used to ensure that the microprocessor isn't getting ahead of slower components. A 0-wait state is preferable to a 1-wait state. Too many wait states can slow down a system.

WAN (wide area network) — A network or group of networks that span a large geographical area.

warm boot — *See* soft boot.

watt (W) — The unit used to measure power. A typical computer may use a power supply that provides 200 W.

wattage — Electrical power measured in watts.

WDM (Win32 Driver Model) — The only Windows 9x/Me Plug and Play component that is found in Windows 98 but not Windows 95. WDM is the component responsible for managing device drivers that work under a driver model new to Windows 98.

WEP (Wired Equivalent Privacy) — A data encryption method used on wireless networks that uses either 64-bit or 128-bit encryption keys that are static keys, meaning the key does not change while the wireless network is in use.

WFP (Windows File Protection) — A Windows 2000/XP tool that protects system files from modification.

wide SCSI — One of the two main SCSI specifications. Wide SCSI has a 16-bit data bus. *See also* narrow SCSI.

Wi-Fi — *See* IEEE 802.11b.

wildcard — A * or ? character used in a command line that represents a character or group of characters in a filename or extension.

Win.ini — The Windows initialization file that contains program configuration information needed for running the Windows operating environment. Its functions were replaced by the registry beginning with Windows 9x/Me, which still supports it for backward compatibility with Windows 3.x.

Win16 on Win32 (WOW) — A group of programs provided by Windows NT/2000/XP to create a virtual DOS environment that emulates a 16-bit Windows environment, protecting the rest of the OS from 16-bit applications.

Win386.swp — The name of the Windows 9x/Me swap file. Its default location is C:\Windows.

WINS (Windows Internet Naming Service) — A Microsoft resolution service with a distributed database that tracks relationships between NetBIOS names and IP addresses. Compare to DNS.

WinSock (Windows Sockets) — A part of the TCP/IP utility software that manages API calls from applications to other computers on a TCP/IP network.

wireless LAN (WLAN) — A type of LAN that does not use wires or cables to create connections, but instead transmits data over radio or infrared waves.

word size — The number of bits that can be processed by a CPU at one time.

workgroup — In Windows, a logical group of computers and users in which administration, resources, and security are distributed throughout the network, without centralized management or security.

worm — An infestation designed to copy itself repeatedly to memory, on drive space or on a network, until little memory or disk space remains.

WPA (WiFi Protected Access) — A data encryption method for wireless networks that use the TKIP (Temporal Key Integrity Protocol) encryption method and the encryption keys are changed at set intervals while the wireless LAN is in use.

WPA2 (WiFi Protected Access 2) — A data encryption standard compliant with the IEEE802.11i standard that uses the AES (Advanced Encryption Standard) protocol. WPA2 is currently the strongest wireless encryption standard.

WRAM (window RAM) — Dual ported video RAM that is faster and less expensive than VRAM. It has its own internal bus on the chip, with a data path that is 256 bits wide.

zero insertion force (ZIF) socket — A socket that uses a small lever to apply even force when you install the microchip into the socket.

zero-fill utility — A utility provided by a hard drive manufacturer that fills every sector on the drive with zeroes.

zone bit recording — A method of storing data on a hard drive whereby the drive can have more sectors per track near the outside of the platter.

INDEX